Probation
and the Community

A practice and policy reader

Edited by John Harding

Tavistock Publications
London and New York

First published in 1987 by
Tavistock Publications Ltd
11 New Fetter Lane, London EC4P 4EE

Published in the USA by
Tavistock Publications
in association with Methuen, Inc.
29 West 35th Street, New York, NY 10001

Typeset by Mayhew Typesetting, Bristol
Printed in Great Britain
by Richard Clay Ltd, Bungay

British Library Cataloguing in Publication Data
Probation and the community: a practice and
  policy reader.
  1. Probation — Great Britain
  I. Harding, John, 1940-
  364.6'3'0941   HV9345
ISBN 0-422-79580-1
ISBN 0-422-79590-9 Pbk

Library of Congress Cataloging in Publication Data
Probation and the community.
  (Social science paperbacks ; no. 352)
  Bibliography: p.
  Includes indexes.
  1. Probation — Great Britain. 2. Rehabilitation of
criminals — Great Britain. 3. Social work with
delinquents and criminals — Great Britain. I. Harding,
John. II. Series: Social science paperbacks ; 352.
HV9345.A5P75   1987   364.6'3'0941   86-14543
ISBN 0-422-79580-1
ISBN 0-422-79590-9 (pbk.)

Contents

List of contributors   vi
Acknowledgements   ix

Introduction   *John Harding*   1

PART I
Service development

1 The politics of probation   *Michael Day*   21
2 Probation practice in the criminal and civil courts
   Eric Cooper   35
3 Supervising offenders in the community: the team
   dimension   *Peter Lewis*   54
4 Probation and community service   *Michael Varah*   68
5 Removed from the community – prisoners and the
   Probation Service   *Tony Raban*   83
6 The changing face of probation in the USA
   Douglas R. Thomson   100

PART II
Issue and community-based practice

7 The residential, employment, and educational needs
   of offenders   *David Walton*   131
8 Responding to the drink/drug-using offender
   Robert Purser   152
9 Racism and the offender: a probation response
   Richard Green   180
10 Reparation: the background, rationale, and
   relevance to criminal justice   *John Harding*   194
11 Crime prevention – the inter-organizational approach
   Vivien Stern   209
12 Evaluating effectiveness   *John Hill*   226

Name index   241
Subject index   244

List of contributors

John Harding is the Chief Probation Officer for Hampshire. He formerly worked in the probation services of Nottinghamshire, Devon, and the West Midlands. His previous publications include *Victims and Offenders, Needs and Responsibilities*, Bedford Square Press (1982).

Michael Day is the Chief Probation Officer for the West Midlands and was formerly the Chief Probation Officer, Surrey.

Eric Cooper is an Assistant Chief Probation Officer in Merseyside, based in Liverpool, with particular interests in training and court work.

Peter Lewis is a Senior Probation Officer in Nottinghamshire, with experience in field teams, community service, and staff development.

Michael Varah is an Assistant Chief Probation Officer in the West Midlands, based in Birmingham. He was formerly the Senior Probation Officer for community service in Warwickshire.

Tony Raban is a Senior Probation Officer in Nottinghamshire with experience in prison and field teams.

Douglas R. Thomson is Associate Director of the Centre for Research in Law and Justice, University of Illinois at Chicago. Dr Thomson is a former probation volunteer whose research focus has been to examine the role and purpose of probation in the USA.

David Walton is an Assistant Chief Probation Officer in the West Midlands based in Birmingham. Prior to this appointment he was responsible for planning residential service provision for offenders in the county.

Robert Purser is the Director of the Alcohol Advisory Service for Coventry and Warwickshire. He has also worked as a probation officer in Coventry with special responsibility for homeless offenders.

Richard Green is a Senior Probation Officer in the West Midlands, based in Handsworth and Perry Barr, Birmingham.

Vivien Stern is the Director of the National Association for the Care and Resettlement of Offenders and is based in London.

John Hill is the Research and Information Officer for the West Midlands Probation Service.

My special thanks are due to the contributors in this volume for their help and support during the writing stages. I should also like to acknowledge the secretarial help from Corinne Creswell and Margaret James.

John Harding
Winchester, 1986

'It is a terrible business to mark a man out for the vengeance of men. But it is a thing to which a man can grow accustomed, as he can to other terrible things; he can even grow accustomed to the sun. And the horrible thing about all legal officials, even the best, about all judges, magistrates, barristers, detectives, and policemen, is not that they are wicked (some of them are good), not that they are stupid (several of them are quite intelligent), it is simply that they have got used to it. Strictly they do not see the prisoner in the dock; all they see is the usual man in the usual place. They do not see the awful court of judgment; they only see their own workshop.'

G.K. Chesterton, *Twelve Men*

'You to whom the answer is easy
Do not live in our time
You have not visited our city
You weep before you know who to pity
Here a good deed may be a crime
And a wrong be right
To you who go in darkness we say
It's not easy to know the light.'

Edward Bond, *Restoration*

'The rule of law is nothing without social justice. Social justice cannot be achieved without the rule of law.'

Lord Scarman (1985)

PART I

Service development

In Chapter 1, Michael Day discusses the political context in which the Probation Service operates. While the Service strives to maintain a humanitarian and compassionate response to the offender by means of programmes that are predictable, widely available, and properly accountable, it is also dependent upon the public and upon central and local government for continued funding. Day looks at the expectations of government for the Service in terms of efficiency, greater cost effectiveness, and more visible forms of social control, and the counter claims of some local authorities who might favour preventive strategies at the expense of statutory obligations. By contrast, he also examines internal service conflicts in which union interests can polarize probation practice to the point of abandoning the middle ground and compromise between competing tensions. Finally, Day warns that in an increasingly volatile political climate where the recession leads to a sharpened division between the haves and have-nots, it becomes increasingly hard for the Service to hold the balance between care and control, between social justice and the rule of the law.

Eric Cooper, in Chapter 2, starts and finishes his essay with the uncompromising assertion that probation practice in the courts should concentrate not on appeasing sentencers but on a clear concern for the offender. The task of court work is never easy for the probation officer balancing the highly formalized rituals of the courts against the unstructured world of the offender. Within this arena, Cooper finds subtle distinctions between the reception the probation officer receives from officials and sentencers in the criminal court, at times tense and adversarial, as opposed to the warm acknowledgement of the divorce court registrar and judge. In essence, Cooper's chapter takes us through the many cycles of probation change, particularly in post-war years, from the virtual abandonment of court work skills which followed expansionist duties and tasks in the mid-1960s and 1970s to a period of stocktaking in the last decade. The reassessment has been shaped by the demise of the treatment model, research into the social inquiry report, and the search for a new accountability which recognized that probation was moving in a different political and assurance in a climate of broad political agreement about its role and usefulness. Series of reports from central government have been fulsome in their praise and the occasional debates in either House, prompted by some extension of responsibility or perhaps some service grievance, as in 1983 on trainee salaries, have generated wide support. Successive Home Secretaries have publicly stressed the indispensable role of the Service and been careful to avoid open criticism, even at times when they have been discomforted by the Service's response to government proposals or involvement in some limited industrial action. All the signs are that in a changing political climate this consensus will be difficult to sustain.

The role of the probation officer turns on the exercise of discretion and the confidence vested in the Service by a range of people involved in the criminal justice process and the community. The capacity to mediate between different interests is dependent on that trust and has been strengthened by a reputation for professional integrity and independence. And the Service as a whole carries the hope of change by the individual in a setting where there is much defeat and despair. The Prison Service at one time shared in this hope, but the fading of this ideal is surely reflected in the disenchantment with the rehabilitative effects of residential training, the passing of approved schools, borstals, corrective training, and the introduction of something nearer a justice model, or 'just deserts'. The emphasis is on custody as a last resort for social protection. The elevation of non-custodial penalties locates hope more exclusively within community based provision in which the Probation Service has a lead role.

Yet there is risk involved in carrying that hope. This symbolic and more elusive dimension of probation's role has no weight in the measures of research and, in challenges to its cost effectiveness, it may have difficulty in proving its value. Extending responsibilities and expanding budgets bring it under closer scrutiny and it may be reviewed less benignly by the political paymasters. And then expectations change, not just in terms of value for money but in the emphasis they lay on the value of particular service responsibilities. The expression of this is not yet clear cut but, at the extremes of the political parties – and they are the ones who most often capture the headlines in the criminal justice debates – the indications are apparent.

The Conservative Government came into power in 1979 with a mandate to fight crime and uphold the rule of law. The first act of the then Home Secretary, now Lord Whitelaw, was to fulfil the election promise and implement in full the Edmund Davies recommendations on police pay. A commitment to speed up the prison building programme has followed. His successor in office, Leon Brittan, consistently expressed a tough approach to criminal justice policy, and the general direction of the Criminal Justice Act, 1982, the Green Paper on Intermittent Custody, and changes in parole release procedures have undeniably reflected a less liberal approach to crime control. Additional funding for the Probation Service has been justified by the relief that this might bring to other parts of an overloaded criminal justice system. Although the Service is theoretically split-funded 80/20 per cent between central and local government, taking into account training costs and those parts of the Probation Service operation like hostels and prison welfare which are 100 per cent supported, and the complicated formula for rate support grants, central government pays nearer 90 per cent of all probation expenditure. However, committees process budgets through the local authority which services them. Although its rights to control that budget are limited, in practice the local authority has power to hold it to a level consistent with its approach to other county council committees. Central government does declare a growth figure for the Service, but local politicians are little impressed. They object to a government extending a service's work and then requiring them to contribute to it, particularly when in turn they may be penalized financially for raising more revenue through the rates.

The main target of such penalties has been the metropolitan authorities, in every case Labour-controlled; the very authorities affected by the 1986 reorganization of local government. On the whole these administrations have been supportive of the Service's work, even if unhappy about central government's inclination to legislate for additional work and expect them to pay at least part of the bill. In some of these areas, the Probation Service has played a prominent part in Urban Aid funded programmes in the conviction that it is giving support to some of the socially most deprived and disadvantaged people in inner cities, particularly those unemployed and from the ethnic minorities. So we find different criteria influencing expenditure at central and local level. A Labour-controlled authority is more generally sympathetic to aspects of the Service's work which have a social welfare function. Through Urban Aid grants they have been prepared to support activity centres, employment schemes, arts programmes, and the like for offenders and those at risk, which in terms of its traditional and statutory responsibilities the Service might have found it hard to justify. These clear political priorities have certainly influenced the way in which probation committees have presented their budgets, and there is experience of a local authority refusing support to developments relating to statutory work – community service, parole, social inquiry work – but prepared to allow growth in preventive schemes.

So far that different stance has been of marginal relevance only in those cases with particular inner-city needs and with local administration politically distant from Whitehall. On the whole the Probation Service has been able to turn the shared financial responsibility for its work to advantage. It has achieved growth which may not have been possible if political control were exclusively with either central or local government. But there is no denying that the Service is susceptible to the influence of party political priorities and particular local needs and within limits that is entirely right. For elected representatives to feel that they had no say in the delivery of service would be a frustration which could easily lead to interference in budgeting matters that would be wholly unproductive. The danger lies in a more emphatic polarization between political philosophies which leaves the middle ground vacant and requires the Probation Service to give its allegiance to irreconcilable sets of priorities. If policies were shaped by local political control it would jeopardize the predictable service which an agency operating on a national system needs to maintain. But with central political control there would be little chance for a local committee to develop its service in response to the immediate environment.

For crucial to the role of the probation officer and the Probation Service is the reconciliation of the social welfare and 'policing' functions; holding the tension between care and control, using the professional skills of social work in helping people to cope with their circumstances and where intervention is possible effecting some change in factors which impede growth; exercising responsibility but also representing an authority which seeks to be just and accessible. That is a role not easy to sustain in a situation of political extremism, whether it be from right or left. The Probation Service as we know it depends upon a shared acknowledgement of the need for moderate policies, for reconciliation, for encouraging individual responsibility and freedom, but holding people to account for the consequence of their actions. It stands between the offender and the system but is also in reality part of that system, from which it derives its authority and obtains its finance. The role can be sustained only through a readiness to allow discretion and within the context of a liberal penal philosophy.

But, as I have suggested, strains come from two sources essentially political, which would emphasize one or other aspect of the probation role. The central position of the Service in managing a range of penalties gives it a more explicit controlling role and makes it an indispensable part of the machinery of criminal justice. A different emphasis would encourage the Service to involve itself in strategies directed at the relief of social disadvantage, and to see the role of probation officers as involving advocacy for those who are victims of a discriminatory and repressive system. At the extremes there is a clear-cut distinction between those who see the law and order system needing unqualified support to contain a potentially chaotic society, and those who view it as essentially oppressive, its officials as tools of the established order. The Probation Service is pressed to take sides, and they are political sides.

Two current issues point up this dilemma: race and the miners' strike. The deep and unresolved racial tensions in this country surfaced briefly and dramatically in the summer of 1981, and were repeated on a more horrifying scale four years later. Few believed that the response in the meantime had been adequate to the scale of the problem. Efforts are made at every level to create a better climate of understanding between white and black but even the willingness to enter the discussion is viewed by some influential black leaders as a betrayal of their cause. The sense of alienation is often such that there can be no dialogue. Police are regarded as the enemy, the army of oppression, who will resort to every kind of tactic and subterfuge to maintain the dependent status of black people. The answer of the alienated is separatism: develop resources and leadership from within the black community and trust only their own. If the services of the legal and penal system, lawyers or probation officers, are turned to, they should act as advocates for people who suffer discrimination and disadvantage and only those of similar race are to be relied upon to see things their way. And probation officers are regarded as part of the white man's justice. They would be expected to side with the police, the judges, the magistrates, because they are all involved in the same system. The magistrates' court is still a police court with all participants conspiring to suppress blacks and the truth. At the extreme there is this profound cynicism about the whole criminal justice system, and as social conditions for blacks become more intolerable that sense of alienation is likely to increase.

That may seem an exaggerated perception and those who seek to operate within the system with impartiality often feel affronted by the hostility shown to them and the excessively paranoid attitude it seems to convey. There is defensiveness and reaction against this apparent ingratitude and an understandable disinclination to persevere. But in those areas where there is a significant black population the Probation Service has somehow to pick its way and establish trust. That is not easily done where final loyalties are seen to lie, as they must, with the establishment which funds it. One way round this is to sponsor work through intermediary bodies which are not constrained in the same way as the Probation Service. They may employ black staff and can properly emphasize the advocacy role. The St Basil's Court workers in Birmingham Magistrates' Court who work with and prepare reports as necessary on young blacks who would resist contact with the Probation Service, and the Handsworth Alternatives Scheme developed with the National Association for the Care and Resettlement of Offenders (NACRO), providing educational, employment, and accommodation assistance to young blacks, are examples of such projects. But devices like this are not without their problems. The Probation Service has to keep its distance or its hand will show and jeopardize the trust which the black community is developing in these schemes. At the same time the Service may be seen as supporting individuals employed in these schemes who are outspoken critics of police or court, and encouraging bodies which are regarded as politically subversive.

But as well as sponsoring schemes like this the Service itself has to adapt and work in ways more relevant to black people. That too proves controversial as it moves out of the perceived isolation of office blocks and reaches closer to the black community. It may have radically to re-examine its ways of offering help to black offenders and concentrate on giving opportunities for creative talent in art, dance, and music rather than applying any social work methodology of individual or group counselling. But the risks of that are real – risk of losing control over work for which it is held accountable, risk of becoming identified with enterprises which may cause political controversy. A clear example of this hazard arose from the Cultural Centre, Handsworth, in Birmingham, a project developed by the West Midlands Probation Service. A responsibly organized and committee-approved trip was arranged to Ghana. It was intended to strengthen the links already made with the Dance Centre at Accra University and bring back to this country some of the dance heritage which influences many of the activities in the Centre. The trip was financed mainly through private charities and the young people themselves, but £2,000 underwriting money came from the county council. Banner headlines in the local press and the *Daily Telegraph* spoke of 'Rain-making on the rates', caricaturing the cultural origins of some of the dances learned. In December 1984, nearly two years later, this could still be quoted by the *Birmingham Post* as the kind of 'disreputable' sponsoring by metropolitan county councils which justified their abolition.

This experience points up the controversy that can be aroused by probation's involvement in community and race enterprises. For years the Service has talked rather romantically of the community dimension and preventive strategies, but if it is to progress beyond the stage of token projects, the recruitment of volunteers, and collaborative ventures with other agencies, it will have to address itself to some of the features of society that are associated with offending behaviour and social disadvantage. The way in which probation goes about this is constrained by the nature of its accountability as a public service. It is not as free as voluntary agencies, for instance, to act as an overt pressure group or to encourage activities which may openly challenge official policies. But it does have to look for ways of becoming more relevant to a community, helping it to respond constructively to the needs of offenders and those at risk, and using the authority of its own experience in dealing with crime and social deprivation to influence political decisions. Moves in that direction cause unease amongst probation committee members who are very conscious of their impartial role as magistrates.

There are parallels between the polarization of attitudes evident in race issues and the conflict created by the miners' strike. The hostility to the police, the cynical assumption that they were acting as direct agents of their political masters, the claims most stridently expressed by Tony Benn and those on the left of the Labour party, are reflected to some degree in large sections of the labour and trade union movements that the judiciary and the whole criminal justice machinery were used to buttress the policies of a Conservative administration. Defiance of the law was encouraged and justified. In such a situation the misgivings voiced in the Probation Service about its role in politically motivated offences seem tame. A resolution of the NAPO Annual General Meeting of 1975 highlighted this issue for the first time and met with predictable disapproval from the judiciary and the magistracy.

'This Association deplores the involvement of its members on a statutory basis, with those offenders whose actions are determined by motives of a patently political nature.
'Consequently we call upon the NEC to issue instructions to all members of the Association to refuse to conduct any social inquiry report on any such person charged under the conspiracy laws, and in Northern Ireland, those dealt with under the schedules of the Emergency Provisions Act, 1974, and further to refuse to carry out statutory supervision of any person convicted in similar circumstances.'

Here, it was claimed, was clear evidence that probation officers were allowing political considerations to colour their judgement and seeking to distinguish between those actions which were criminal proper and others which were prompted by political motives and only incidentally infringed the law of the land. The issue was largely prompted by events in Northern Ireland and terrorist acts in the UK, and was related to the obvious difficulty facing an officer in working at the inquiry or supervisory stage when there was no co-operation and possibly a refusal to accept the legitimacy and authority of the court.

The resolution reflected a genuine professional dilemma limited to particular circumstances, but more extensive industrial conflict which involves law breaking on a large scale, justified by prominent politicians and union leaders, poses an altogether greater problem for the Service. How does it then exercise an impartial professional responsibility?

There was similar disquiet over the NAPO policy urging staff not to complete social inquiries on defendants pleading not guilty, and there can be no doubt that the combination of these two resolutions undermined confidence in the impartiality of the probation officer. Although there were reputable professional arguments for these policies, they were interpreted as politically inspired by left-wing elements in the Service. Any discussion with the judiciary confirms that the misgivings remain. Yet a service which gives expression to a particular humanitarian attitude towards the offender and concerns itself with social justice and social policy is bound to be influenced by such matters of principle, although it has to be careful that in its work and in response to individual needs it does not allow wider political considerations to intrude, and so stand accused of putting causes before people. Officers have to separate out what is proper to the role of a professional association in influencing social or penal policy, and what is expected of them as officials in the system. It is not easy to achieve that kind of integrity.

As in any union, it is the more extreme and articulate who grab public attention and force issues, and the conference setting in which resolutions are debated encourages the rhetoric of extremism and over-simplification of complex matters. For the rest of the year people make the necessary adjustments of practice.

But with an annual conference having the authority to determine policy, and NAPO becoming better organized to press its opinions through local joint negotiating committees, its views become more influential on how the Service carries out its work. The political climate and industrial legislation of the late 1960s and early 1970s encouraged the involvement of staff representatives in policy and management issues. Much of this involvement has been entirely constructive but it can impose constraints. Union recognition agreements in area Services has brought the association more formally into consultation on professional developments, and uncertain management may let that slip into negotiation on matters over which it must retain control.

In fact, there is scant evidence to support any accusation of political subversion in the Probation Service. It would be entirely surprising if a professional group committed to caring for a disadvantaged section of the community, and composed of people with an academic training in sociology and social casework, did not have a strong radical element. Any service working as close to the formal system of social control as probation needs an internal reminder that it must not comply uncritically with demands made upon it. Resistance from NAPO has often represented a proper caution and resulted in constructive shifts in policy and practice. At times it appears resistant to change, with the conservatism of self-interest, protection of job skills and security, and too obvious a disinclination to enter into a compromise which might secure the best deal in a situation not of its making. But a proper distinction needs to be made between the stance of NAPO as a union and the attitude of the Service more generally. Organizations representing the concerns of employers and management, the Central Council of Probation Committees, and the Association of Chief Officers of Probation, are less free to distance themselves from Home Office policy, and their methods of exerting influence are less public. They must hold to the inner track of consultation and avoid public stances which would result in an unproductive dispute with their political masters. But they also have to retain the confidence of staff, and there are pressures coming from government interests on one hand and union on the other which can pull management and officers into opposing alignments, and undermine the very cohesion of the Service which remains its strength. There is an internal mirroring of the more obvious polarization in the world outside. There is even a breakaway association of senior probation officers (a kind of SDP) which claims to protect the old values and promote moderate policies, and in a number of ways we are beginning to see indications of external political argument showing through in the Service itself.

So some of the politics of probation are played out between the organizations of Service interests. With the Home Office being more explicit in determining a role for the Service consistent within the government's overall criminal justice and social welfare policies, the situation could become increasingly fraught and Service management has more consciously to take account of the political dimension in its development of practice. No longer can it be confident that it administers a predictable, widely appreciated service with general consensus, both inside and out, about its objectives and strategy. The Service has moved a long way towards becoming an integral part of the criminal justice system in managing a range of non-custodial penalties and exercising a significant role within the civil and criminal courts and penal institutions. But in a society which is experiencing the strains and deprivations of recession, which is becoming more competitive and divided between the haves and the have-nots, where the political debate becomes more polarized, a neutral position becomes less convincing. Like the established Church, the Probation Service may from the left be dismissed as part of the system and from the right as part of the problem.

I am conscious that in the space available to me I have touched on rather than fully explored a number of political considerations that affect the work of the Probation Service. I maintain that the way in which a society deals with its offenders and frames its penal code is essentially a political activity and therefore the Service is not operating in a professionally neutral area. The Probation Service has become a larger employer and been given more extensive responsibilities in managing the government's criminal justice programme. It is therefore caught up in its own internal industrial relations issues, with their attendant union and political implications, just like any other employer. At the same time it is an agent of government policy which may give greater emphasis to social control and cost effectiveness than to the considerations of social welfare and individual need that are central concerns of a social work profession. Probation holds within itself the tension of being a social control agency and a social work profession. The first conveys a conservatism, the second an essential radicalism. Given a climate of general consensus about criminal justice policy and the kind of activities in the welfare state which promote social equality and opportunity, the balance can be struck. But in a more volatile political situation, with less confidence in society's stability and a starker contrast in policies, it is less easy to arrive at the achievable compromise which is central to the Probation Service's approach.

© *1987 Michael Day*

2 Probation practice in the criminal and civil courts

Eric Cooper

The Probation Service was born, and has grown up in the courts, and has lived there for a hundred years. The police court missionary Thomas Holmes (1900: 35) recaptures the profound shock of his early years in the courts.

> 'I see them all; they are around me now. I breathe again the sickening whiff of stale debauch; I am faint with the unspeakable atmosphere; the chloride of lime is again in my throat and my nostrils tingle with it. But I see more; I see the matter-of-fact way in which all this was received. I see that no one wonders at it. I see that all this is looked upon as perfectly natural, for I see no look of wonder, no divine pity, no burning indignation – all, all received as a perfect matter of course, and all, all quite as it should be.'

On his first day in a London police court Holmes (1900: 42) confessed that he 'went into Kennington Park, sat down and cried like a child'. His account of his work and the gradual improvements that were brought about is studded with quotations from hymns and sacred literature. The explicit moral base of his work is paraded without self-consciousness or apology. Jarvis traces the early years of the London Police Court Mission and shows how 'the probation system' grew out of the English common law, aided by the American experience, based on 'a profound anxiety over the treatment of children in courts' (1972: 9). Gradually the appointment, pay, structure, and duties of probation officers were all incorporated into statutes, and eventually the 1948 Criminal Justice Act provided the framework on which the present-day Probation Service is based.

As recently as the early sixties a probation officer joining the Service could not fail to be acutely aware of its origins and special relationship with the courts. Having been interviewed and appointed on the spot by a large formal gathering of magistrates, his first and main task was quite simply to be present in court. In some places police court missionaries themselves were still in active service and the signs of their life and work were all around. He would still have taken all his work directly from the courts and be accountable to them for the progress of individual offenders through the case-committee of magistrates, who heard accounts of progress and offered advice. These tenuous links with the past are now being broken, but the origins of probation practice in the courts should not be lost or the difficulties and opportunities of a new era will lack their proper perspective. The 1960s' recruit was soon caught up in sweeping changes: 'The concept of saving the offender from socially unnecessary custody [was] sacrificed in the pursuit of "professional objectivity" and "effective sentencing" based on the principles of scientific treatment' (McWilliams 1981: 109).

Probation officers sometimes felt embarrassment and inner conflict about the religious fervour of their forebears as they became exposed to academic rigour and external scrutiny. Halmos (1965: 167) attempted to stem the ebbing tide of faith by commenting 'I suspect that human service is inevitably paradoxical when treated in terms of scientific objectivity. The counsellor need feel no shame about his single-minded and united self-division.'

Courts have always been uncomfortable places for probation officers, as they were for the early missionaries. Jarvis (1972: 3–8) provides sufficient evidence from their own records to indicate the varied responses they received from court officials and particularly the police, instancing some of the devices used to gain co-operation. Probation practice in the courts has changed little in this respect. The criminal courts are a structured world of legal definitions and detailed procedures in which all the main participants are supremely confident of their place and their correctness. The deviant behaviour which they are convened to consider arises out of the wilful, depressed, or chaotic lives of offenders out in the community. In court, however, it is distanced from its context, shaped into an acceptable legal mould, then scrutinized according to an elaborate set of rules and rituals which are thoroughly familiar to those whose place of work it is, but frequently alien to those who have to submit. Into this controlled and circumspect world comes the probation officer; of all the participants in the courtroom drama he is at the point of greatest tension. Clearly, if he leans too heavily towards one side he will run the risk of undermining his position in the eyes of the other. In a very real sense the greatest risk is in offending the court. If he gets the balance wrong to the detriment of the offender he will have another new opportunity to get it right with the next defendant, but if he gets it wrong in relation to the court he runs the risk of damaging his credibility in the eyes of the permanent court officials with whom he has to work regularly. Furthermore, the power available to offenders to influence the action of probation officers is very small indeed, but courts are relatively closed systems which cannot easily tolerate personal views or unpredicted behaviour unless they be refined and reduced by the procedures. There can hardly be a probation officer alive who has not experienced the power of courts to assert themselves to his disadvantage, either by means of a sharp public reprimand or through the many subtle means of influence which court officials use to structure their world and ensure conformity. The extreme danger for probation officers in courts is that in order to reduce the tension and uncertainty for themselves they will either become indistinguishable from other court officials or totally identified with the offender. The nature of the balancing act required from him in courts is even more complex than that however. He must manage the tension between the highly formalized rituals of the court and the unstructured world of the offender, but he most also seek to influence the sentencing practice of courts by the provision of appropriate information and collect other detailed facts to meet the administrative needs of his own organization.

In his research study Crolley (1981: 40–41) found officers' responses 'punctuated with references to personal beliefs and values'. He comments that they 'are religious, political, ideological and what may loosely be described as quasi-philosophical . . . these values not only affect their behaviour but more specifically the decisions they make . . .' about certain categories of work.

Furthermore 'The spirit of early court missionaries lives on. The Service still attracts and holds officers with religious beliefs. From the newest entrant to the most experienced Senior, expressions of religious motivation and loyalty to a specific Christian belief' emerged. He also found evidence of 'political ideology' and 'a mixture of old-fashioned morality and home-spun psychology'. The extent to which these values find opportunity for expression in the newly structured working environment seems to cause concern to a considerable number of staff.

Practice in civil courts has very recent origins in historical terms. Probation officers were well established in magistrates' domestic courts by the 1930s, but it was not until 1968 that divorce court welfare officers were required in every court (Bailey 1979: 115). Practice in civil courts is quite different from that in criminal matters and generally much more comfortable. When dealing with those child-centred issues which are the concern of welfare officers, civil courts make strenuous efforts to reduce the amount of formality involved. Many such hearings are held before registrars only and even when a judge is involved the matter will often be dealt with 'in chambers'.

The child himself will have done no wrong nor will the parents necessarily be in dispute with the court – only with each other! The police are not present. The independence of the welfare officer is made explicit and even when a civil court makes a supervision order it contains no conditions (Jarvis 1980: 103, 107). The duty of the welfare officer to promote the best interests of the child is the clearest possible statement of precisely those moral and humanitarian motives that underpin his career, and reflects backwards in time to the early concerns of the police court missionary. It is clear why probation officers should in many cases prefer to practise in civil courts, and the preoccupation of the Service with practice in criminal courts in recent years has paradoxically only served to enhance the warm and rewarding relationships which characterize civil court practice. It may be that some fundamental values have been cherished and protected there while adverse storms have raged elsewhere.

No generalized statements about probation practice in the courts can convey the complex strands of thought and action, challenge and response, that have so engrossed probation officers, academics, and others for the last two decades. To be faithful to the times it will be necessary to attempt to follow some of those strands.

The increasing strategic importance of the Probation Service

The first development that was profoundly to affect the probation officers' probation practice relationship with the courts was brought about by the advent of statutory after-care in the mid-1960s, which not only changed the title to include 'after-care' but much else besides. It had already been clearly suggested (Advisory Council 1963: 31) that this development would 'extend beyond its hitherto accepted role the relationship of probation officers to courts'. McWilliams (1981: 102) identifies the Home Office circular (1964) which by introducing the arrangements 'for the newly instituted compulsory after-care of detention centre trainees' effectively shifted power and decision making away from courts and individual probation officers to the executive. Further categories of compulsory after-care followed, each of them steadily increasing the proportion of the probation officer's workload which did not come direct from the courts. Furthermore the instructions stressed that reports to the Home Office were in future to be made by the Service through the principal probation officer and not directly by the individual supervising officer. The trend was consolidated by the introduction of parole in 1967, with its special emphasis on public accountability requiring clear procedures, effective controls, and executive decision making. But the process was only just beginning. In the early 1970s the newly formed social services departments assumed responsibility for juvenile offenders and the significance of this impending loss was immediately felt. Much debate and distress ensued. Some probation officers believed that this change would radically affect probation practice and move the Service even more firmly towards the 'heavy' end of the offender spectrum, and many of them moved to the new organization. In the event, the phased handover was not completed and a blurred boundary still exists between the two organizations in relation to juvenile offenders. The Service, however, did lose its primary position in juvenile courts which had for decades nourished the relationship between magistrates and probation officers, and provided a ready forum in which trust and understanding had been developed and constantly renewed. These movements towards the executive and away from the juvenile court seemed to presage a new outlook for probation practice and the words 'control' and 'surveillance' began to feature on Probation Service agendas, both formal and hidden.

In 1972 a new Criminal Justice Act introduced day training centres (on an experimental basis) and community service. The latter has probably been the most prominent single influence on the structure and function of the Service in modern times, but when required to bring it into being, the Probation Service was very reluctant to do so. Ten years later the Criminal Justice Act 1982 provided for an expanded range of conditions in probation orders based on day centres (which were now to be made generally available to courts) and participation in activities. In only twenty years the probation officer in court had moved from being a zealous friend of offenders at court to an organizer and provider of additional sentencing resources, and agent of the Home Office.

The medium by which the probation officer exercised his influence at court, the social inquiry report, continued to exist, but its development reflected all the dramatic shifts of the period and an increasing degree of direction about practice in courts. The Interdepartmental Committee on the Business of Criminal Courts (1961) had endorsed the practice of providing these reports and made the first formal suggestions as to their content. Home Office circulars (1971), (1977), and (1974) expanded on factors relating to their preparation and approved of 'experienced probation officers' making sentencing recommendations. Two further Home Office circulars (1983a) and (1983b) developed their strategic importance still further. The second of these refers encouragingly to the special contribution of the probation officer in that he 'may be the only person connected with the case

39

who has met the defendant in a comparatively informal setting' and 'is equipped to understand and interpret a defendant's attitude and disposition'.

A link is therefore acknowledged and reinforced between the present and the past. There can be no doubt that now 'the State intervenes in the relationship between practitioner and client in order to define needs and/or the manner in which such needs are catered for' (Johnson 1972: 77). The rapid expansion in the use of social inquiry reports is well documented but their increasing volume contributed to the weakening of links between individual officers and the local court, as the process became increasingly a matter of organizational efficiency, and as the circumstances in which reports would be requested and prepared became increasingly a matter of rule. Another comment by Johnson (1972: 79) captures the dominant feelings of those times: 'Elements of the bureaucratic role become interweaved with the occupational role in service organisations, the result being a general dilemma stemming from the problem of balancing administrative and consumer needs.'

In May 1984 the Home Secretary, drawing attention to the developments of the last twenty years, suggested an order of objectives and priorities for the Service to follow and promised yet another 'circular of guidance on social inquiry reports defining more clearly the role the Service plays in the court setting' (Home Office 1984: 20). It seems likely that probation practice will be even more closely regulated precisely where it used to enjoy most freedom, that is, in the courts.

Expansion and growth

Police court missionaries were originally the representatives of a religious mission devoted to temperance, and Thomas Holmes' Preface (1900) makes clear his gratitude to a private 'patron' who for many years helped to reduce his essential loneliness. The missionary could be whatever his magistrates and his conscience required him to be in relation to the pathetic individuals for whom he cared. This situation prevailed for almost half a century until the Criminal Justice Act of 1925 made 'provision . . . for larger units of administration by the formation of combined areas' (Jarvis 1980: 1). Even so, the position of officers practising in courts was not yet greatly affected, until the austerity of the post-war years began to give way to the greater sophistication of the early 1960s.

The advent of compulsory after-care had implications for structure and size as well as function, and the Home Office circular (1966) suggested the appointment of Assistant Principal Officers and an expansion in the number of senior officers. The creation of a management structure, though modest by comparison with other organizations, was nevertheless experienced as highly intrusive and incompatible with the traditional autonomy enjoyed by individual officers. Complex problems of responsibility arose (McWilliams 1981) and it is clear that at the very least, the old certainties that existed between courts and probation officers were being eroded. In numerical terms the expansion was dramatic. In 1961 the Probation Service had fewer than 2,000 staff of all grades but by 1979 over 5,000 staff were employed, and most significantly the increase in management grades of staff was greater in comparison with other grades every year until 1975 (*Probation and After-Care Statistics*). This steady growth itself became a norm apparently impervious to political and economic tides. Based as it was on new demands and responsibilities it created internal tensions and a subtly different view of the courts and the probation officers' responsibility towards them. It was simply impossible for the Service to continue as before and the 1970s were characterized by a rash of area 'experiments' which sought to reorder increasingly diverse duties and priorities (Millard 1979). A characteristic of these studies was that the courts were given a less prominent position in probation practice. The emphasis had switched to the community. Enthusiastic debates took place about the extent to which probation officers should still be regarded as officers of the court. Specialist court officers and ancillary staff became more prominent. James (1982: 109) commented:

> 'Given . . . that the National Activity Recording Survey . . . showed that officers spent 27% of their time in court just waiting, it is not surprising that ancillaries are increasingly used to undertake routine court work. The result of this is that whilst the Probation Service is still providing the same coverage and service to the courts, the probation officer is less in evidence in the courtroom.'

The quality of the probation officers' practice in courts was not only affected by internal developments. The courts too were expanding; benches were enlarged and the Clerk to the Justices was himself becoming increasingly the distant head of an expanding organization. Procedures agreed between chief probation officers and the Clerk to the Justices still depended in the final analysis on the quality of the relationship between the contributors to the daily drama of court proceedings, but the individual officer in court felt himself to be on the periphery and no longer at the centre. The ensuing tension is best described by Johnson (1972: 81): 'a client orientation is likely to be characteristic of practitioners close to the periphery whose relationships with their clients are more meaningful and immediate than those

effectively treat reluctant clients for their criminality.' In this era of severe introspection probation officers were also confronted with the possibility that even the treatment model of probation supervision had been quite simply a covert form of control. This was clearly very difficult for a group of people who viewed themselves as well intentioned, but vulnerable and misunderstood.

The effects of this prolonged process of attrition were felt most markedly perhaps in the courts themselves. Required to produce more and more social inquiry reports and supervising increasingly serious offenders in the community, probation officers found themselves deprived of the structure which had for so long housed their values and beliefs. The emperor was truly seen to have no clothes! The unrelieved criticism, occurring as it did in a climate of deepening recession, rising crime rates, and increasing emphasis on 'law and order' issues, came to be reflected in a loss of confidence in court practice. Political considerations also intruded unavoidably.

As Parsloe (1979: 23, 24, 26) pointed out:

'Sociologists, political theorists and those holding Marxist beliefs have . . . shattered this comfortable assumption that most, if not all, the laws probation officers upheld are widely and freely accepted in society. The idea that those in power are perhaps a minority who enforce their rules . . . now undermines the security of probation officers by redefining their acts as political rather than therapeutic.'

And added 'continuing doubts make them easy prey to attacks'. Political action in professional practice was urged by Walker and Beaumont (1981) but their exhortations are not yet likely to catch the imagination of most probation officers, whose values and inclinations tend to hinder the connection between organizational political action and 'the personal miseries of the lonely individual' (Halmos 1965: 23). Probation practice in the criminal courts had become unmanageable for many officers and it was not immediately evident where the route lay that would take them out of the morass and on to firmer ground.

The preoccupation of the service with its work in criminal courts tended to obscure the implications of an enormous expansion of its welfare report function in civil courts (James and Wilson 1983: 50). The work was absorbed with little management initiative or control, and little is known even now of its quality and content. As the climate of criminal courts became increasingly hostile to 'treatment' there appears to have been a growing application of therapeutic concepts to civil work which, fusing with elements of the 'rights' movement, produced an explosive interest in conciliation. The Service was compelled to face its civil work commitments and relate them to broader organizational issues. Questions began to arise about welfare reports (Murch 1980) and conciliation (Davis 1983), although the presence of probation officers in civil courts continued to receive warm tributes: 'I cannot tell you how immensely valuable from our point of view is the Divorce Court Welfare Service. We could not do our job . . . without it' (Sir John Arnold 1983).

Practice under the microscope

The newly dominant spirit of critical enquiring inevitably came to focus on the actual practice of probation officers in courts, to add to their discomfort.

Carlen and Powell (1979) proposed the existence of 'courtroom lore which enables the job at hand to be done with a minimum of inter-professional conflict' (p. 99). They show that officers resort to a variety of roles, amounting to gamesmanship, to cope with the strain of courtroom relationships and resolve the dilemma of 'control/treat-ment' (p. 101). The primary aim of probation officers in courts 'is to maintain credibility with the magistrates' (p. 105) and they discovered some of the common strategies used to achieve this. Competence consists of the ability to manipulate the rules of the courtroom. The social inquiry report is the 'major channel for probation officer/magistrate communication' (p. 114) which requires another set of strategies to ensure that the dialogue remains open and provides some satisfaction for each of the participants.

A study by Parker, Casburn, and Turnbull (1981) takes some of these issues a stage further by direct research observation of the performance of probation officers and social workers in two juvenile courts. They found the probation officers exhibited an air of 'belong-ing' (p. 143) in the court setting unlike their social work colleagues, but the cost of this seemed to be related to a higher level of passive inactivity and a distinct lack of enterprise in preparing offenders and their families for the formality of the court setting. He also found that probation officers 'subscribed to the necessity of game-playing' (p. 130), but there were indications that the comparative lack of action by probation officers in courts was a strategy which had been found by experience to produce the best results in that it was less chal-lenging to the courts and resulted in him being given the benefit of the doubt by the offender. 'The probation officers' desire to maintain their professional credibility and their general lack of overall strategy led them to acquiesce' (p. 137) before a punitive regime to which they were antipathetic. The social work in and around both court systems was markedly passive. 'During the hearing itself [probation officers] were either absent or marginal to proceedings . . . even . . . in preparing families for the court experience . . . probation officers showed little enterprise' (p. 143).

The price of professional credibility with the magistrates is seen to be a complete lack of influence and power in the court. Practice 'reflected the in-court regime rather than created or manipulated it' (p. 244). Parker goes further, however, in his study of offender perceptions of justice: 'Not only is the criminal process a mystification, a professional's game, but for many defendants those processes are but camouflage for a more sinister conspiracy' (1979: 148). His assertions suggest that probation officers would do well to enquire whether their practice in courts, their participation in this 'professional's game' contributes to the alienation that some offenders feel for the courts as the local apparatus of the State, and results in their own relegation to the side-lines.

Much less is known as yet about probation practice in civil courts but Murch (1980) in his analysis of the experience of divorcing parents has produced some pertinent findings. He deals with a small number of objections to welfare (probation) officers, which although 'unrepresentative of the majority . . . expose the risks involved in allowing welfare officers a large measure of unstructured discretion' (p. 110). In one case the officer's 'strong religious beliefs prejudiced his ability to make a balanced evaluation' (p. 110). In another the fact that 'the court was unlikely to go against the firm recommendation of the welfare report' as well as the personal insensitivity of the officer, highlighted the helplessness of a mother who felt the power of 'the social apparatus that labelled her . . .' (p. 112). He also draws attention to the danger of the 'unconscious imposition on litigants of the welfare officer's personal values . . . when many parents feel particularly vulnerable emotionally' (p. 177).

Competence in the civil work setting was judged by parents who participated in the study to consist of 'impartiality, family mindedness, avoidance of stigma, and openness' (p. 172). After tracing the decline of the Service's matrimonial work he details the 'development of the child-saving philosophy' (p. 190) that seems to have resulted in some areas in welfare officers 'becoming the initiating authority' (p. 196) and the practice of 'screening' all families with children, each of which require further thoughtful debate.

James and Wilson (1983) refer to the 'dramatic rise in the number of requests for reports' (p. 50) in custody and access cases. They studied the responses of probation officers in seven areas to questions about their civil work practice. Although united on the difficulty of the work and the need for more training, practitioners varied widely in most other respects, and, particularly important, the interviewing of children. They ask 'is it possible that some officers feel less competent than used to be the case to deal adequately with children, especially younger children?' The majority of officers nevertheless wish for even more extensive involvement 'even taking into account the Service's commitment to working with offenders' (p. 53). Referring to the growth of conciliation schemes they add that 'officers already have a substantial but covert involvement in conciliation during the process of report preparation' (p. 54). On a positive note 'the welfare officer is the only source of impartial and comprehensive information upon which the court can rely' (p. 53).

It is clear that much more needs to be known about probation practice in all courts. The importance of greater clarity about objectives and roles, and more training and support is evident from these studies. Bland assumptions are beginning to give way to detailed observation and enquiry but understanding is likely to be preceded by pain. In particular, further study is needed of the inter-relatedness of practice between criminal and civil courts.

The search for new meaning

When then was the response of probation officers to this threatening tide? The need for 'philosophical reconstruction' (Willis 1983: 340) was clear but while the theorists were constructing new models, probation officers developed their own coping strategies. One suggestion was that they controlled the volume of work referred to them by using their social inquiry report practice as a gatekeeping mechanism (Roberts and Roberts 1982). Furthermore, in an interesting survey of the experience of male offenders on probation, Willis (1983: 345) 'failed to find any support whatsoever for some fairly common views of probation . . . probation is mainly concerned with bringing relief and service to clients whose circumstances might have otherwise appeared to them as intolerable'. Willis added that this 'grass roots, practical response to the collapse of confidence in the treatment model' arose out of 'the pressing dynamics of need' and seemed to suggest a retreat to earlier, simpler activities in the face of a complicated and formal debate about the way forward. As Halmos noted in an earlier context 'strong convictions must be at work to sustain a perseverence not sustained by conclusive evidence' (1965: 159).

The discrepancy between what probation officers were doing and the language they felt it necessary to employ arose out of a largely unspoken fear that to admit the decline of the treatment ideal would be to deny the old values on which the Service was based. Weston (1978: 20) discredited this equation by pointing out

'probation is on a fairly deep foundation – that of unshakeable desire for and faith in the capacity of people to grow and improve in their personal and social functioning – and this managed to find expression before casework was thought of, and will continue when it is forgotten.'

Some writers offered a new respectability by proposing models for practice that promised to acknowledge the new realities. Bottoms and McWilliams described the position thus:

'We believe there is a need for a new paradigm of probation practice which is theoretically rigorous; which takes very seriously the exposed limitations of the treatment model; but which seeks to redirect the probation service's traditional aims and values in the new penal and social context. Such a paradigm must be realistic: it must take into account the present structural realities of the Service.'   (1979: 167)

Their proposals included the substitution of 'help' for 'treatment' based on an offer of unconditional help with problems identified by the offender which they believed made 'better conceptual sense' of existing practices and was consistent with similar movements in the wider social work field.

But how could 'traditional aims and values' be consistent with the formal requirements of the courts and an increasing clamour for overt social control? In an article entitled 'Sentenced to Social Work', Bryant and others also urged the formal acknowledgement that 'some offenders could benefit from social work help because of the people they are and the problems they face' (1978: 111), but went on to propose a view of the probation order that would bring together the needs of the offender and the social control requirements of the court. A 'primary contract' between the court and the offender would lay down in open court the conditions to which he would be subject and a 'subsidiary contract' would be on offer to the offender by the probation officer 'based on a joint assessment of his problems' (p. 111). In the courts, the helping role of the Service would in their view require a more active, high-profile presence.

It is important to note that these developments in the search for an appropriate new framework seemed to be validated by the restatement of the primary duty of the probation officer to 'advise, assist and befriend'. This relic of the 1907 Probation of Offenders Act and the very earliest days of the probation system in a quite different social order had seemed naïve during the sophisticated 1960s, but it reappeared in the Powers of the Criminal Courts Act 1973 (Schedule 3:8[i]). It once again seemed the most concise expression of those basic principles of practice which had been quietly nurtured during adverse times and which still bring mature men and women to work with offenders.

Probation practice in a changed climate

These tentative steps towards a new rationale were swiftly overshadowed by dramatic changes in the social and political realities surrounding them. The advent of a government publicly committed to direct action on law and order issues meant that the courts and the Probation Service were not to be left at leisure to determine their new relationship. Centralized direction accelerated the process already begun towards the definition of working objectives. At the same time, the social fabric has undergone an intense deterioration. Unemployment, poverty, and social need have all risen to levels unknown in living memory but reminiscent of the conditions that spawned the police court missionaries. Any doubt that the stratification of society itself was being reordered was dispelled by the riots of 1981 and the politically inspired alterations to social welfare provision and policy of the last few years. The ensuing dilemma for probation practice has been well expressed by Roberts (1984):

'It was not difficult to defend the values of the Service . . . when they were not under pressure. It is now, however, when those values are strongly under attack, that it becomes difficult to hold on to and defend them. . . . When a climate has been established which questions the cost of helping the vulnerable and less competent, which places a price on everything, it is not unnatural to wonder, ourselves, about the futility of constantly trying to reclaim the petty recidivist.'

Offenders are almost invariably located in the most deprived sections of an increasingly divided community and nowadays most are unemployed. The several strands of probation practice in courts should once again firmly espouse a moral purpose. Probation officers believe in, and attempt to raise, the dignity, worth, and competence of offenders. In the new social context they have to provide alternatives both to employment and to custody by means of the infinitely flexible probation order and a range of day centres, hostels, and other

49

programmes that support it. First, though, the probation officer has to persuade the court that an alternative to custody represents an adequate and accountable discharge of its wide public responsibilities. This demands that the primary channel of communication – the social inquiry report – should be responsible, informative, and unequivocal. The information and opinion it contains now need to reflect a sharper reality in which the links between social decline and offending are unavoidable. Courts are inevitably coming to feel the tensions of society more acutely but probation practice should grasp the nettle. Mathieson (1982: 661) asserted the necessity in clear terms: 'It is both proper and necessary for probation officers in their reports to give a prominent place to social comment relevant to the circumstances of the offender.' He was later supported by Sir Ralph Gibson (1983), President of the Central Council of Probation Committees, who said:

> 'The courts need such assistance more and more if they are to be able to make increased use of the non-custodial and supervisory measures which are made available by the probation service, especially when the offender faces (as many do) environmental conditions which are dauntingly adverse.'

There are, therefore, new tensions at work now in probation practice which inevitably affect its style and authority in courts. Required by government 'to undertake the supervision of a greater number of persistent and serious offenders who would otherwise face custodial sentences' (Home Office 1984 *Criminal Justice*: 21.10) the Probation Service must first gain the confidence of a largely unconvinced magistracy about its community facilities. It must achieve a responsible blend of planned, structured, and accountable supervision with sensitive and caring contact with individual offenders. There are likely to be even greater risks of conflict than in the past with courts under public pressure to deal effectively with serious crime. The temptation to avoid dispute and seek a compliant, unobtrusive role should be positively avoided in the view of one chief probation officer:

> 'We should bring all our professional skills to bear in bringing into view what this defendant's life is like . . . we bring into focus what no-one else would have bothered to look at. We present a piece of reality that would otherwise have been ignored.'   (Lacey 1984)

This uncomfortable and uncompromising vision of practice in the courts has the virtue of reminding us that ultimately the probation officer's concern is for the offender. When policies and procedures have run their course, practice consists of the human interaction between officer and offender. The danger is that this will once again become a subterranean activity if it cannot be reconciled with a penal philosophy that precludes human concern for the individual. We have already noted, with Parker's help, the stagnation and complacency following the games-playing that does not advise, assist, and befriend from the outset in court, because of the myths surrounding the probation officer's image and reputation. The best way for probation officers to preserve and enhance their status in courts is to operate consciously as a benign irritant, taking initiatives, speaking out courteously, acknowledging and accepting the risks and tension, 'that nothing may be left undone on the margin of the impossible' (Eliot 1939: 32).

The modern probation officer, however, is not entirely a free and self-motivating agent as the missionaries were. He belongs to 'the modern-day bureaucracies which probation services have become' (Bottoms and McWilliams 1979: 174) and which may tend to forget that they exist to provide services to offenders as well as to courts and governments. As we have noted previously, large organizations can diminish the importance of staff working on the periphery where the Service meets the offender. The provision of specialist staff in courts may contribute to fail-safe procedures, and provide critical information for both the Service and courts, but it will not necessarily enhance, and may ultimately undermine, the capacity of staff to identify with offenders and provide them with a humane service in courts. Any fragmentation of the Probation Service's duties in courts is more likely to lead to the cultivation of the powerful than of the powerless. As probation officers find themselves again after years of turmoil, chief officers would do well to invest adequate resources, status, and training in this most commonplace but profound activity – probation practice in the courts. After a hundred years of trying, it still demands personal conviction and delicate skill. Only the most able staff will meet its demands.

© *1987 Eric Cooper*

References

Advisory Council on the Treatment of Offenders (1963) *The Organization of After-Care*. London: HMSO.

Arnold, Sir J. (1983) Address to Central Council of Probation Committees. 24 May.

Bailey, R. (1979) *Pressures and Change in the Probation Service*. Cambridge Institute of Criminology.

Bean, P. (1976) *Rehabilitation and Deviance*. London: Routledge and Kegan Paul.

Bottoms, A.E. (1977) Reflections on the Renaissance of Dangerousness. *Howard Journal of Criminal Justice* 16(2).

Bottoms, A.E. and McWilliams, W. (1979) A Non-Treatment Paradigm for Probation Practice. *British Journal of Social Work* 9(2): 159–202.

Bryant, M., Coker, J., Estlea, B., Himmel, S., and Knapp, T. (1978) Sentenced to Social Work. *Probation Journal* 25: 110–14.

Carlen, P. and Powell, M. (1979) Professionals in the Magistrates' Courts. In H. Parker (ed.) *Social Work and the Courts*. London: Edward Arnold.

Crolley, T. (1981) *The Identification of Training Needs for Probation Officers*. Unpublished thesis, Cranfield Institute of Technology.

Davis, G. (1983) Conciliation and the Professions. *Family Law* 13(1): 6–13.

Eliot, T.S. (1939) *The Family Reunion*. London: Faber and Faber.

Gibson, Sir R. (1983) President's address to Central Council of Probation Committees. 24 May.

Halmos, P. (1965) *The Faith of the Counsellors*. London: Constable.

Holmes, T. (1900) *The London Police Courts*. London: Nelson.

Home Office (1962, 1972, 1976, 1980) *Probation and After-Care Statistics, England and Wales*. London: HMSO.

———— (1984) *Criminal Justice, A Working Paper* (L. Brittan). London: HMSO.

Home Office Circular 4/64 (1964) *Detention Centre After-Care*. (Section 13 Schedule 1 Criminal Justice Act 1961.) London: HMSO.

———— 225/66 (1966) *The Structure of the Probation and After-Care Service*. London: HMSO.

———— 59/71 (1971) *Reports to the Courts on Accused Persons*. London: HMSO.

———— 194/74 (1974) *Reports to the Courts on Accused Persons*. London: HMSO.

———— 118/77 (1977) *Social Inquiry Reports in Not Guilty Pleas*. London: HMSO.

———— 17/83 (1983a) *Social Inquiry Reports: General Guidance on Content*. London: HMSO.

———— 18/83 (1983b) *Social Inquiry Reports: Recommendations Relevant to Sentencing*. London: HMSO.

Interdepartmental Committee on the Business of the Criminal Courts (1961) (Streatfield Report). London: HMSO.

James, A.L. (1982) The Probation Officer at Court. *Howard Journal of Criminal Justice* 21(2): 105–17.

James, A.L. and Wilson, K. (1983) Divorce Court Welfare Work – Present and Future. *Probation Journal* 30(2): 50–5.

Jarvis, F.V. (1972) *Advise, Assist and Befriend.* London: National Association of Probation Officers.
—— (1980) *Probation Officer's Manual.* London: Butterworths.
Johnson, T. (1972) *Professions and Power.* London: Macmillan.
Jones, H. (1956) *Crime and the Penal System.* London: University Tutorial Press.
King, J.S. (1969) *The Probation and After-Care Service.* London: Butterworths.
Lacey, M. (1984) Address to Association of Chief Officers of Probation, Cardiff.
Mathieson, D.A. (1974) The Still Point in a Turning Court. *Probation Journal* 21(1): 4–8.
—— (1982) Social Comment – An Appropriate Role for the Probation Service. *Justice of the Peace* 146: 660–62.
McWilliams, W. (1981) The Probation Officer at Court: From Friend to Acquaintance. *Howard Journal of Criminal Justice* 20(2): 97–116.
Millard, D.A. (1979) *Pressures and Change in the Probation Service.* Cambridge Institute of Criminology.
Murch, M. (1980) *Justice and Welfare in Divorce.* London: Sweet and Maxwell.
Parker, H. (1979) Client/Defendant Perceptions of Juvenile and Criminal Justice. In H. Parker (ed.) *Social Work and the Courts.* London: Edward Arnold.
Parker, H., Casburn, M., and Turnbull, D. (1981) *Receiving Juvenile Justice.* Oxford: Basil Blackwell.
Parsloe, P. (1979) *Pressures and Change in the Probation Service.* Cambridge Institute of Criminology.
Perry, F.G. (1974) *Information for the Court – A New Look at Social Enquiry Reports.* Cambridge Institute of Criminology.
Principal Probation Officers' Conference (1968) *The Place of the Probation and After-Care Service in Judicial Administration.* Leicester: PPOC.
Roberts, J. and Roberts, C. (1982) Social Enquiry Reports and Sentencing. *Howard Journal of Criminal Justice* 21(2): 76–93.
Roberts, J. (1984) Address to the Annual Conference of the National Association of Probation Officers.
Walker, H. and Beaumont, B. (1981) *Probation Work. Critical Theory and Socialist Practice.* Oxford: Basil Blackwell.
Weston, W.R. (1978) Probation in Penal Philosophy: Evolutionary Perspectives. *Howard Journal of Criminal Justice* 17(1).
Willis, A. (1983) The Balance between Care and Control. *British Journal of Social Work* 13: 339–46.

3 Supervising offenders in the community: the team dimension

Peter Lewis

Introduction

In undertaking development work both locally and in the region, I am aware of contradictory tendencies in the Probation Service in relation to both team and community. I hear senior managers saying that the heyday of the team is over, teamwork is outdated, and attention must be given to 'area priorities and service tasks'. Yet I also see evidence that teamwork is required if staff are to provide the range of direct services needed. I encounter pressures on the Service to work with 'high-risk clients' or 'hard-end offenders' by offering closer personal supervision at an individual level, and those statements are accompanied by a denigration of interest in work with the community. Yet I cannot see how the community is to cope with those offenders in their midst without a change in community attitudes to offenders and the development of community-based resources for just those clients. It seems that the concepts of teamwork and work in the community are in danger of being dropped just when we might most need them. It will be a theme of this chapter that while there are dangers in a slavish devotion to either notion, some attention to team and to community is required if the service is to retain that sense of balance which has always been an important part of its style.

We shall be concerned here largely with field teamwork rather than with the many varied forms of specialist teams which have developed in recent years. Yet the growth of specialist units has also challenged thinking about organization and encouraged experimentation. This chapter is concerned with organizational issues rather than the social work methods with offenders covered in later chapters. The development and proliferation of methods has encouraged new forms of organization, and experiments in organization have gone hand in hand with attempts at new methods.

There is a great danger of myths on these topics. Nevertheless it is true that with the growth in the Service in the mid-1970s experimentation with teamwork did increase. Accounts of those developments were shared. Lewis (1978), Millard (1978), Harman (1978), and

54

Read and Millard (1978) are typical. The growth in the range of service activities and methods encouraged this but two other factors contributed. The increase in the senior grade led in many areas to earlier promotion for young officers who had been trained in ways which encouraged teamwork or who had themselves as main grade staff participated in such experiments. Second, a large number of younger officers had learnt about the unitary approach to social work and the injunction that such methods require team systems. (See Vickery (1974), Olsen (1975), and Evans (1978).) Another factor in these developments was the contribution of ancillary roles in the Service. The introduction of assistants into many teams, the later development of community service supervisor roles, a variety of project officers and accommodation scheme staff, all forced a rethink of traditional organization. If a newly appointed ancillary was not to sit and wait in vain for work to come his or her way, then a team had to think out consciously how it would use this shared resource. Another significant shared resource might be the office building itself, or space within it, especially as teams were increasingly decentralized in some services. This again encouraged a collective rethinking of roles and tasks in just the way that unitary theory suggested.

Team models

Every kind of team model can probably be found somewhere in the Service. There is no reason why that should not be so since different models suit different circumstances. Some teams may be so only in a formal sense: working with a common senior and shared back-up resources but little by way of shared approach to client work. Most teams, however, operate somewhere along a continuum from the formal linkage to processes of collaboration that require a greater degree of shared objectives, communication, and clarification of roles. In assisting with team development work I am persistently struck by the danger of assuming that teams have similar style or common understandings of such things as the senior's role or the function of team meetings.

Some of these issues can be illustrated by a brief account of my own field team experience as a senior. I have written elsewhere about the early development of that field team (Lewis 1978). Those early experiences led to a fairly stable period in which the roles of team members were defined by the service they offered to clients, largely in terms of work method. Thus one member of the team concentrated on family work, another on fairly routine monitoring of cases, a third on intensive short-term contact, and so on. This semi-specialization was possible because intake was largely undertaken by one officer writing most social inquiry reports. The intake and allocation process was both open and flexible, with a weekly team allocation meeting for decision-making and the communication of information. This relatively stable model of the mid-1970s was changed by four factors.

First, the continued turn-over of staff and the need to accommodate the new interests and developmental needs of staff meant that roles were swopped round and the pattern of operation was blurred. Second, the community context changed as the development of a large new estate posed a particular need for concentrated resources. Third, the pressure of new staff with an orientation to patch-based work led to questioning whether specialization should be by client method or by neighbourhoods. Fourth, the arrival of an extra officer and the appointment of the first assistant to work in the team raised the possibility of sub-groupings within the team and a redefinition of tasks. These developments led to the major restructuring of the team into two sub-groups, with each group having a responsibility for part of the team's patch and with some further specialization within sub-groups. The intake role of social inquiry writer was sacrificed at this point, but the separation of the intake role and the principle of re-allocation were retained. We thus had a team which had blended elements of method specialization with elements of patch-based work, while some specialist roles for the team as a whole were carried out by the senior and the assistant.

Since then the team has, under another senior, experienced further changes in the model. Apart from the change of senior, undoubtedly significant to any team's operation, two other factors need mentioning. First, there have continued to be major alterations in the community context. Community development on the large new estate occupied two staff for several years before resources were sufficiently developed to allow a change of focus on to another older estate with a lot of young offenders. This affected both the distribution of team resources and the shaping of individual roles. Second, the local Service as a whole underwent an exercise in defining objectives and in reorganizing task structures between teams. The team's relationship with other teams in the same city was seen as relevant to some broader social issues. To influence sentencing it also needed to work closely with other field teams serving the same court. All this led to collaborative work outside the team and roles have had to be redefined to allow for these functions too. It is a useful reminder that both the community context and the pattern of agency development profoundly affects the operation of individual teams. The team now has a layer of task responsibilities and external links on top of the existing team network of patch-based roles and semi-specialisms.

This account has been given not because there is something special about it, or even because it may be typical, but rather to illustrate issues about teamwork models in probation practice. Any group of officers who are co-ordinating their work, and adopting a common strategy to a patch will encounter some of the issues about roles which I have described. The degree of specialization is an obvious issue. Probation officers vary enormously as to how keen they are to specialize. Given the range of probation work, few can truly claim to be specialists. Yet the extent of specialization and of the combination of several functions in one role are issues to be resolved in team organization. There is also a constant dilemma about how far staff interests can dictate what they do. When I visit teams I am often told that 'staff do the type of work that interests them'. What happens if no one is interested in an important aspect of work or if too many people are interested in a minor part of the work? My own experience tells me that there has to be a process of give and take about how roles are assumed. Some staff will deliberately take on a difficult or unpopular role if they feel this will provide them with developmental challenges, or they will couple their preferred task with a less welcome one if that gets team dynamics unstuck. We should not underestimate the negotiations that go on about such issues. The senior particularly may have to ensure that tasks are allocated and resources distributed in a way that relates to actual client needs and to service policies.

This raises the difficult issue of the team culture and how it is developed. There will be variations in team investment in group co-ordination and trust. Undoubtedly, to develop a collaborative approach staff have to be willing to put time into communication, negotiation, and information exchange with colleagues. At particular times the demands for this may be considerable. Some staff will object that this is time taken away from face-to-face work with clients. Others will argue that it is only by a planned and co-ordinated approach that we can be sure we are not already wasting the time spent in client work. This communication needs to be more than shared feelings and perceptions: there needs to be hard data. How can decisions be made about the appropriate distribution of team resources without information about work-flow, client needs, and staff responsibilities? Many teams are realizing that hard data, facts about caseloads, trends, and the catchment area, are all needed if teams are to make better decisions. A number of teams are finding that wall graphs, punch-card systems, and even computers are assisting them in storing and assessing information.

The account of one field team given earlier in the chapter raises important points about the community context. The development of training in the unitary approach and patch-based work has encouraged staff to question the context of offending and wider community issues. Changes in the community context can precipitate the re-organization of a team model. Indeed, if there is an element of orientation to neighbourhood in the team model then it needs to be sensitive enough to pick up changes in population, housing policies, or patterns of offending. Initially the model will have to take account of the size, shape, and nature of the patches covered. Some teams make the mistake of saying that their clients appear to be rootless and therefore patch issues are irrelevant. This may be a case for developing neighbourhood resources to cope with apparently rootless people and is one of a range of factors that affects the model of teamwork adopted. Size and homogeneity of the team patch are other important features.

Two other factors remain to comment upon here. First, the location of the team's office will influence their model. A centralized court-based team is likely to face different issues from a team which is patch-based. Both will have to work at issues whose emphasis is affected by the advantages and disadvantages of the location. In a team which covers several patches the fact that the team office is in one patch rather than another will influence the model of work adopted. A second feature is the design and layout of the team office itself. Having had the good fortune to assist architects in planning two office conversions (and then having to live with the consequences), I am aware that the physical facilities can restrict or encourage the styles of client work. The accessibility and visibility of the premises can contribute to its use by clients and the broader community. This can alter the way officers perceive their role in the neighbourhood and with identified clients. Physical premises are a major resource which like staffing, client workload, and community context influence the appropriate model for teamworking.

Issues in teamwork

A key feature in any team model is intake and allocation. Where are decisions made about which clients are supervised and by whom? I have referred already to the importance in my own team of separating off the intake function with a specialist in social inquiry reports making consistent judgements across a range of new referrals, and also to the function of the allocation meeting in achieving an open system of work distribution. However, a number of teams have taken this much further, recognizing that intake is a discrete phase for the client as well as the officer: a phase in which assessment needs are shared with the client before he opts for a choice from the range of services available. Others have written in more detail about this concept of client induction (Brown and Seymour (1983), Stanley (1982)), and it is certainly becoming more common to provide this initial phase separately, either for individual clients or working as a team. All the workers seem agreed that such separate intake work requires a high degree of collective organization and is often the outcome of several years of sharing.

One reason for the development of intake functions has been the proliferation of services now offered to clients. During the 1970s a range of social work methods were tested out in the probation setting by newly qualified staff. The traditional 'chat with your probation officer' was replaced by a variety of more structured work methods. Individual work with offenders might take the form of task-centred casework, social skills training, behaviour modification, welfare rights advice, advocacy over accommodation, help with a job search, or any one of a range of methods. Increasingly clients could be worked with in their families or marital context in quite structured ways. There was a development of group work, moving away from traditional adolescent activity groups towards more adult groups with a social skills basis, alcohol education, mutual support, or community action as their focus.

Now the proliferation of methods is in itself a force for some semi-specialization and therefore role differentiation in teamworking. It encourages the notion that the team as a whole has a responsibility for all the clients on the patch and each officer contributes a range of services to be used by all clients. Second, these methods (particularly family and group work) often work better if two staff workers do it together. Shared work, like shared cases, is a powerful force for further collectivization and more confidence in team-sharing. Third, group work has a peculiar dynamic of its own. If staff experience for themselves in teamworking the supportive and uncomfortable features of group membership, they are both more likely to want to work with clients in groups, and better able to cope with any difficulties in those groups. The more they work with clients in groups the more powerful will group membership seem to them as a means of getting support and supervision in their group work. Fourth, these varied methods of working lead to clients being around the office in new capacities and larger numbers. The development of day rooms and drop-in facilities means that clients are present for longer periods of less formal inter-action. This has the effect of reminding the team of their responsibility for clients and encourages the development of a co-ordinated response to at least the more difficult and disruptive clients. It makes client–

officer interaction more public to clerical staff. Previously secretaries saw little of the clients whose records they typed, now there has been a growth in the opportunities for secretaries to witness officers in difficult interactions and to have extended informal contact with offenders. This has posed new problems of role and training for secretaries. It raises the questions: whose clients are these and are the secretaries a full part of the team itself? This gets resolved in a variety of ways – all too often dependent on the individual preferences of secretaries. I would certainly prefer teams to examine whether the secretaries are an integral part of the team and should be more clearly involved in team decision making.

As a trainer I am particularly conscious of the training needs that teamworking generates. I refer to the skills which staff must acquire if they are to play their new roles within a team. I have mentioned previously the changes in the senior role (Lewis 1978). The senior becomes much more of a group worker, co-ordinating individuals' actions and encouraging shared work. Amidst the varied activities of the team members it is important for someone to maintain an overview, a sense of direction, and the detachment to monitor activity. I have referred elsewhere to the senior's need to keep open a variety of communication lines and ensure parts of the network are well connected with each other (Lewis 1981). The analogy there was with a spider darting about to ensure that the web is in good order. The senior requires managerial and leadership skills to do that job effectively.

A feature of teamwork is that it requires skills in communication. Officers need to know how to keep colleagues in the picture both over their work in general and over specific clients. They must also be able to present an argument to their colleagues in a team meeting. The marshalling of evidence and the engagement of support for a course of action become keys to successful strategies. In that teamwork often involves more meetings, the skills to operate in meetings and to negotiate in groups are important. Indeed, since roles are not always allocated in grade terms, probation officers may well find themselves undertaking tasks previously associated with the senior. Thus an officer may chair a regular team or sub-group meeting, they may be called on to represent the Service externally at a community meeting, or they may be supervising an assistant or a volunteers' group on behalf of the team. Increasingly main grade staff are requiring training in skills previously thought to be the prerogative of seniors.

Some of these issues about teamworking can be illustrated by reference to another example. I referred earlier to the way that the physical circumstances and the community context affect teamworking. In the example I want to develop, two teams shared an office in a moderate-sized town and shared the same court. The joint work to the court became the focus for their acting together and gradually as they became more co-ordinated in their approach to court work, social inquiries, and magistrates' liaison they explored other ways of working together. A total of fourteen officers, several assistants, and two seniors seemed to be a set of resources that could be redistributed in new ways. In particular the flow of new cases for such a larger group of staff opened up the possibility of more client group work. Over a period of about two years the teams gradually moved towards a new model of teamwork which involved joint leadership of the whole unit operating together. This is now not as uncommon as it was and others are experiencing the advantages of such an operation.

The major advantage is the possibility of running a continuous client induction programme. Social inquiry reports are done by three specialists and if an order is made the case is immediately assigned to one of four monitoring officers. These officers have nominal responsibility for the case but effectively all work is shared out. The client is assigned within five weeks to an induction group lasting six weeks in which offending behaviour is examined and the clients encouraged to specify how they are to keep out of further trouble. This assessment is shared with the client, the social inquiry report writer, the induction group leader, and the monitoring officer. It should identify discrete work episodes and a contract for the duration of the order. Subsequently the case is reassessed by the monitor at regular intervals and if necessary referred back for allocation of further work episodes. Some of this work is done individually, some of it in regular client groups. Between them team members hope to deploy a range of skills and information, and to offer a variety of resources, both within the team and in joint activity in the community. A small sub-unit maintains close court liaison, another sub-group deals with youth custody referrals specializing by institution, and two staff workers undertake all the civil work on the patch. A development function in relation to the community and groups run by the team is held by another officer, freed up from cases for this purpose. The two seniors divide up the various sub-groups and team tasks between them and work closely together. The model is still evolving, but since other units are attempting similar work I should like to draw some issues from this illustration.

The connection between the variety of services to clients and the organization of the team is evident here. The apparent 'economies of scale', which allow for more client groups and for induction groups, are an advantage balanced by staff's membership of at least one smaller sub-group. The flow of new work allows for regular induction and consistent assessment of all new cases. The officers there see many advantages in this more open assessment of client need. They feel much more accountable to each other for decisions about recommending supervision and for undertaking work episodes in the promised way. Because assessments are usually shared in allocation meetings and are based on several officers' perceptions of the client, they are less likely to be biased by an individual officer's preferences. The degree of specialization in the team allows specialist expertise and knowledge to develop. The civil work officers, for instance, have worked out very sophisticated conciliation methods for dealing with custody issues. The court sub-group have engaged with clerks and magistrates to redefine service functions in court. The officers working with youth custody cases have run groups inside institutions to prepare clients for difficulties on release, and have developed effective relationships with key prison department staff.

A larger unit like this one needs to have good systems of monitoring. Here again the court sub-group have provided useful regular data about sentencing patterns, the impact of social inquiry reports, and the intake of clients. The induction groups help to identify collective client needs, and the officer undertaking development work in the community gathers statistics about community needs. The system of client records has changed considerably. The formal assessment documents form a significant part of the individual record and the details of daily contact are noted in handwriting on small T-cards in a visual display system. This system allows colour coding and movement of cards to demonstrate at a glance trends and changes in the team's work. The switch from typed records has allowed the secretaries to reassess how valuable secretarial resources are being used in the team. Secretaries themselves have been encouraged to look at the strength of their contribution and the semi-specialization of officers has meant some specialization by secretaries.

Other roles have changed too. The probation assistants all have more clearly defined roles than in many teams, and prefer this. The team culture of shared work, open discussion in allocation meetings, and the concept of work episodes means that assistants are more constructively used. The roles of the seniors are drastically altered. Not only do they have all the group leadership and overview functions I referred to, but also they have to look at how they work together. They acknowledge that they complement each other in terms of work style: one being seen as caring and nurturing, the other as active and decisive. By allocation of task functions and by close working together – including sharing the same room – they have managed to achieve the advantages of joint working without being split off from each other. The set-up relies very heavily on a variety of meetings. Not only does the team meet regularly for allocation and for review meetings but each sub-group meets fairly frequently. Officers have had to learn to operate in these group settings, to develop group skills in presentation, assertion, and negotiation, and to be prepared to represent colleagues to the rest of the team. The representational roles carried in the court, the community, and various custodial institutions also pose just the sort of skill problems I raised earlier.

Team relationships

Too often discussions of teamwork focus on the internal dynamics of the team rather than look at its relationship with the outside. Teams need to consider their relationships with the rest of the local Service, with other agencies locally, and with the wider community. Teams need links with other sections. The growth in specialist teams (in courts, community service, employment projects, day centres, etc.) requires careful linking with local field teams. Each team would do well to reassess regularly its links with such units and perhaps to locate responsibility for that link with one team member in particular. Many services now also have area-wide task groups to co-ordinate a particular activity (e.g. accommodation, social skills work, alcohol problems) and teams need to examine their contact with such groups. The most important links in the Service will probably be with headquarters staff and the senior needs to explore with the team how that link is to be managed. To what extent is the Assistant Chief Probation Officer kept in the picture or consulted, and by whom? Any team developing new methods needs to think very carefully about that. A team of experienced officers will soon find that some of its members are undertaking tasks on behalf of the wider Service and not just the team. Officers may be acting as student supervisors, leading training events, or running groups and projects for the wider Service. The team must take account of this external work.

The Probation Service will necessarily have a number of links with other agencies such as the courts, police, social services, and social security offices. The team would be well advised to survey those relationships from time to time and decide on a strategy for such work. Which agencies need to be cultivated? What is the best route into an unfamiliar agency? I have written elsewhere of the importance of checking on team boundaries with key agencies (Lewis 1982) and I would suggest that 'gatekeepers' can help the team to negotiate more effective transactions at such 'frontier points'.

The relationship of the team with the community requires slightly more attention and could in fact have been another chapter altogether. Justice can scarcely be done in this space but some issues do overlap with the notion of the team's relationships with others. For over a decade now ideas about work with the community have been challenging the Probation Service (Lewis 1971; Haxby 1978: Chapter 8). Unfortunately not all experiments have been well thought out and few have been properly written up. There is still a good deal of confusion as to why the Service should engage with the community. This has been fed by confusion about the purpose of the Service itself. Only recently have area services begun to prepare statements about their purposes and priorities, so that often officers have had no basis to start from in assessing community work. Questions about why officers are engaging with the community have quickly thrown up controversies about values and accountability. How far can the Service go in supporting conflict or is it committed to consensus and the status quo? To whom is an officer answerable for the time spent on community work and for decisions made? Traditionally officers have held themselves to be accountable to courts for individual client work, but with community work it was often apparent that magistrates support was not likely to be forthcoming for some of the more radical community activities officers wanted to follow. Support from colleagues or from the hierarchy seemed too uncertain to sustain long periods of community work, so that many projects have been time-limited and often reflections of officers' personal interests. With the debate about the purpose of the Service officers have been more willing to consider the objectives of community work.

In theory a full range of community work methods are possible from a Probation Service base, although it is doubtful if the more radical kinds of community action would fit easily into many services. At the other end of the spectrum most officers in their work with individual clients identify community resources they can mobilize to help an individual. A knowledge of these resources is crucial and, over time, a team is likely to acquire a good deal of information about needs and local facilities. They may identify gaps in provision and begin to make efforts to remedy these. Community organization arises where officers develop a network of communication between agencies in a neighbourhood, encouraging the exchange of information. Sometimes a group of agencies might then decide to exert collective pressure over an issue, or to direct resources to a specific neighbourhood. The Probation Service has experience of this through a wide range of neighbourhood forums or umbrella groups. Community development would be a stage beyond that where an officer worked with a group of residents to achieve a community objective, acting as a facilitator rather than a leader. These residents might or might not be offenders, but the objective should have some relevance to offending. If there were a lot of juvenile offending on an estate which was without a youth club, an officer could collaborate with other agencies to secure a youth club (community organization), or could assist a group of residents and parents to argue their case for a club (community development). It is in the definition of targets and priorities that the Service is most likely to remember its focus on offenders. The information available to a team in something like a caseload scan should help to pinpoint what action in the community is appropriate from an agency perspective, and which neighbourhoods are the ones on which to concentrate. The use of social survey and census data becomes important in reviewing these decisions.

The team may need to organize itself on lines which make it sensitive to community issues. Some degree of specialization by patch will help and the team may work in neighbourhood sub-groups in order to be alert to local problems. In some teams specialization may be taken a stage further by asking one officer to undertake some developmental work in the community. Teams need to think very carefully about their long-term commitment to the community. The timescale of the work is often quite long and there needs to be an agency commitment rather than just the interest of an individual officer.

The need for a framework

Many teams that are adopting a more collaborative approach have done so through a series of reviews in which team members have shared information, identified their skills and interests, and set collective targets. Good preparation and careful leadership are needed if this sort of review day exercise is to be valuable. It also needs to set a timescale for feedback and further review. Many teams find that this becomes a continuous process rather than just 'away days'. Engaging an outsider to chair the review can free the team senior to re-examine his or her own role. These reviews work best when information has been gathered in advance and presented in a simplified way. Monitoring needs to be a continuous process, built into the team's systems. Official statistics become more relevant and in the collection of information partnership with clerical staff is crucial.

Yet reviews can take place only within a framework. The team can build its own by a painful process of negotiation, target-setting, and further review but the process will work better within a service framework. Area services need to have clearer statements of objectives, tasks, and priorities. The failure to do this may well explain why some teams have gone in unpredictable directions. Given a framework, teams can develop mechanisms for connecting service objectives with team objectives. The service objectives further encourage the team to look at how they function within the context of the wider Service. Statements of tasks at team level can allow for some assessment of priorities at the local level and give the team a framework within which to allocate their scarce resources.

In turn the organization as a whole needs a process of review: a method by which teams and their members can engage with formulating service objectives and shape the area structures to achieve those. This organizational development is an important aspect of a healthy Service. Management style has to take account of the teamwork that has developed. Assistant Chief Officers will need to get out and about and meet with whole teams more often, not over-relying on seniors as the contact point. They must be prepared to communicate with team members in special roles and to support the senior in developing an appropriate leadership style. Training will become a team issue rather than an individual one. In reviewing its work the team must take account of the skills and information it needs collectively and may well want to formulate a collective training plan. Training managers who persist in individualizing training will confuse communication.

If we are to develop the range of client services needed to remain high up the tariff and keep offenders out of custody some form of role differentiation in teams is necessary. The confidence given by working in a collaborative way can often encourage officers to risk new ways of working. In order to provide a breadth of service we need to mobilize community resources and engage in partnerships with local groups. Work in the community and work in teams are key factors in consolidating the work of the Service as a whole. Timid management, or the myths and fantasies about teamwork, must not be allowed to impede the growth of teamwork in supervising offenders in the community.

© *1987 Peter Lewis*

References

Brown, A. and Seymour, B. (1983) *Intake Groups for Clients: A Probation Innovation*. Occasional paper no. 8, School for Advanced Urban Studies, University of Bristol.

Evans, R. (1978) Unitary Models of Practice and the Social Work Team. In M. Olsen (ed.) *The Unitary Model: Implications for Social Work Theory and Practice*. Birmingham: British Association of Social Workers.

Harman, J. (1978) A Teamwork Approach at IMPACT. *Social Work Today* 9(36).

Haxby, D. (1978) *Probation: A Changing Service*. London: Constable.

Lewis, P. (1971) Community Work: a Challenge to the Probation Service. *Social Work Today* 1(12).

——— (1978) An Approach to Teamwork. *Social Work Today* 9(36).

——— (1981) Spider's Stratagem. *Social Work Today* 13(5).

——— (1982) Frontier Posts. *Social Work Today* 13(25).

Millard, D. (1978) Prospects and Implications. *Social Work Today* 9(36).

Olsen, M. (1975) *Management in Social Services – The Team Leader Task*. Bangor: University College of North Wales.

Read, G. and Millard, D. (1978) *Teamwork in Probation*. Birmingham: Midland Regional Staff Development Office.

Stanley, A. (1982) A New Structure for Intake and Allocation in a Field Probation Unit. *British Journal of Social Work* 12(5).

Vickery, A. (1974) A Systems Approach to Social Work Intervention, Its Use for Work with Individuals and Families. *British Journal of Social Work*: 389.

4 Probation and community service

Michael Varah

This chapter explores the sentence of community service and reviews the key features of this rapidly developing scheme. It also assesses its impact on the Probation Service, the courts, the offenders, and the wider community.

Community service orders were introduced on an experimental basis early in 1973 as a direct result of the 1972 Criminal Justice Act. Following its successful introduction, by April 1979 every Petty Sessional Division in England and Wales was covered by a community service scheme. In Scotland, a community service scheme was also initiated in 1978 as a result of the Community Service by Offenders (Scotland) Act. In short, community service orders are a punishment conferred by the court whereby the offender, with his or her consent, surrenders available leisure time, to perform services to the community. The integration and acceptance of community service orders into the range of non-custodial sentences has been remarkable given that the idea was recommended by the Advisory Council on the Penal System only in 1970.

Since its inception, community service has received a positive reaction from the media, the public, and the courts. The reason for this lies partly in its intrinsic value as a sentence and partly in its versatility. Paradoxically, this very versatility allows it to be seen by some courts as an alternative to custody and others as a sentence in its own right.

In practice, the use of community service varies according to the attitudes of local sentencers and probation officers. Given the nature of legislation and the strong tradition of judicial freedom of action in sentencing, it is very difficult to maintain community service as a clear 'alternative to imprisonment'. The sole legal restriction placed upon its use was that it could be imposed only in cases which attracted a prison sentence. Nationwide, just over half of the probation areas in England and Wales see community service as a direct alternative to custody, the remainder as a sentence in its own right. In consequence it is estimated that only two out of five community service orders made on a national basis constitute a direct displacement of offenders from custody. If community service is to have a more significant impact

68

upon reducing the numbers sentenced to imprisonment, greater consistency and selectivity in its use for the more serious and persistent offender will have to be achieved.

The philosophy underpinning the practice of community service embraces the three concepts of punishment, rehabilitation, and reparation. To satisfy all these aims a common attitude towards the relative importance of these concepts needs to be attained by the Probation Service. The difference in area schemes reflects to some extent the confusion and uncertainty which exists as attempts are made to reconcile what may seem to be contradictory aims.

The main aspect of punishment stemming from this sentence is the deprivation of leisure time coupled with a firm approach to those who break their contract with the court. For those who 'breach' their order the consequences can be serious. Revocation of an order can, and often does, attract a more severe sentence, including a custodial sentence. Many areas use breach proceedings as a disciplinary measure whereby the court can use its powers to impose a fine on the offender and allow the order to continue. This can have a salutary effect upon an offender by reducing the temptation to flout the conditions of the order.

An essential aspect of the community service scheme is the opportunity it creates to promote a wide range of projects and personalized individual placements, through which offenders have the opportunity to enhance their feelings of worth and self-respect. Making full use of the offender's potential and skills, with visible positive results being achieved is the essence of rehabilitation. It would however be somewhat naïve to expect that as a direct consequence of being placed on an order (ranging between 40 and 240 hours) offenders would significantly reduce their future capacity to reoffend.

It must be stressed, however, that a community service order, however positive and constructive an experience, will usually be a drop in the ocean when set against the weight of negative experience, past and present, which the offender faces (NAPO 1977: 18).

The concept of reparation within community service has an essential appeal in that it aptly counterbalances the investment of unpaid work against the commission of an offence. While in principle community service may be a useful expiatory process, the reparative element indirectly helps many of the disadvantaged in our society. While this labour is 'paid' in hours awarded for satisfactory work completed, if costed out, the value of this work in financial terms would run into millions of pounds.

Although many would view community service as principally a punitive experience making a significant demand upon the offender's leisure time, this is balanced by making community service a creative and productive experience in such a way that the offender sometimes continues voluntarily after the order is completed.

Organization of community service

From the outset, the Probation Service was asked to administer community service despite the fact that it represented a totally new challenge to the Service and a considerable departure from its traditional work. The majority of probation areas manage community service with full-time specialist staff, both probation officers and community service supervisors, working either from a central office or area offices or a combination of both. The staff are directly responsible to the specialist senior probation officer/community service organizer although in some areas a probation officer divides his or her time between probation work and community service work. Whichever administrative model is adopted – centralized, decentralized, or partly decentralized – all schemes witness a marked departure from almost all other areas of probation work, in that the sheer number of full-time ancillaries/community service assistants and part-time sessional supervisors far exceeds the number of 'specialist' community service probation officers in each area. Therefore not only has community service, because of its high visible profile, become the 'shop window' of the Probation Service but, given the nature of the scheme, the Service has had to maintain this profile by absorbing a wide range of skilled but 'untrained' staff to manage the practical day-to-day work of the scheme in a way that enhances its development and credibility. In many respects the success of the national scheme is largely founded on the commitment and initiative of its staff who are coping with a rapid growth of offenders (1979 – 15,700 orders, 1983 – 35,100 orders, Home Office 1983) with only a limited increase in resources. The supervision of community service orders demonstrates the value of setting achievable targets and clear goals, of laying some emphasis on positive qualities rather than problems, and of involving clients in activity rather than conversation. A specialized and centralized structure may be more efficient but it is less able to make a positive contribution to the main-stream probation work by widening horizons and changing attitudes. The use of a decentralized structure but with a degree of centralized management may offer the best prospects for the future development of community service work. Many areas delegate a substantial degree of responsibility to ancillary staff and this has raised some important issues, not least of which relate to demands for better pay and for some form of career structure and appropriate training. The recruitment of a large number of ancillaries to supervise community service work has interjected a good deal of freshness and uncomplicated humanity into the Service (NAPO 1977: 13). If the Service is to retain its highly competent and committed ancillary staff, serious consideration must now be given to the central issues relating to pay and career structure. This could prevent ancillaries feeling exploited when they compare their rate of pay with that of probation officers and as a result are tempted to drift to alternative jobs with enhanced conditions of employment.

The nature of community service is significantly different from other probation work in that it is directly concerned with punishment, control, and authority. Its style of operation, its dependence upon the community to offer constructive practical work outlets, and its capacity to produce a high turnover of offenders and hours worked inevitably produces a degree of specialism or separatism not found on the same scale elsewhere in the Service. This has had a number of implications for the Service both in terms of additional resourcing for community service, and the attitudes of probation officers to this rapidly developing scheme. While initially some held doubts as to whether community service should be run by the Probation Service, there is now widespread acceptance by probation officers that the philosophy of community service is compatible with that of their own Service. However, at a time of economic standstill there is some concern that, because of the general acceptance and popularity of community service, additional resourcing, to cope with increased growth of orders, might be at the expense of other service developments. Although probation officers on current evidence have not appreciably altered their methods of working with clients, e.g. increasing their breach rate, it would be surprising if the development and success of this scheme did not have some positive messages for them. Indeed, they are increasingly seeking closer links within the community and more effective ways of working with the more persistent offenders.

Community service by offenders – a statistical view

The Home Office statistics for 1983 reveal that approximately 35,100 people commenced community service in 1983, 12 per cent more than in 1982. Only 5 per cent of this number were female and 48 per cent of the total were aged between seventeen and twenty. Of those commencing community service in 1983 10 per cent had been sentenced for offences of violence against the person, 41 per cent for theft and handling stolen goods, and 25 per cent were for burglary. The remaining 24 per cent were made subject to community service

71

orders for other offences including fraud and motoring offences. The number of community service orders made by magistrates' courts in 1983 was 27,000, while the crown court made 8,100 orders.

The previous criminal records of those commencing community service orders in the first half of 1983 indicated that 40 per cent had served a previous custodial sentence and only 11 per cent had no previous convictions. Of those commencing community service orders in the first half of 1983, 84 per cent were aged under twenty-one. In the same period about 20 per cent of orders were for fewer than 100 hours and about 17 per cent had 200 hours or more specified.

In 1983 over 5,500 persons were sentenced by the courts for breaching the requirements of a community service order, with over half this number receiving a fine and about a quarter receiving an immediate custodial sentence; however, at the crown court 63 per cent were returned to court and received an immediate custodial sentence. It is worth noting that research into breach proceedings in all areas (McWilliams 1980: 75) revealed 'relative consensus in some aspects of breach policy, but marked lack of consensus in others' and that 'differences in levels and strategies of breach orders constitute one of the main areas of debate between organizers and within the Probation Service more generally'.

For the last five years approximately 75 per cent of those receiving community service orders completed the specified number of hours. Just over 10 per cent of all orders were terminated for failure to comply with the requirements of the order and just under 10 per cent for conviction of another offence. The average time taken to complete an order varied according to the number of hours imposed, from just under six months for orders of fewer than 100 hours to nearly ten months for orders of 200 hours or more.

The nature of community service work

All community service areas would subscribe to the principle that imaginative and carefully thought-out work placements offer the best chance for the offender to contribute positively to the community. Fostering close links with members of the public also creates an opportunity to develop a greater understanding of offenders and to promote a sense of community responsibility for them. By this emphasis on what offenders can do, in a constructive sense, instead of a concentration on the negative aspects of their behaviour, the public perception of offenders is enhanced, and moves to develop non-custodial sentences may gain greater popular support as a result.

Most schemes try to offer a wide variety of work to their offenders thereby preserving the vital ingredient of any good scheme. The greater the range of personalized, group, or individual placements, the more offenders are likely to succeed in completing their orders. For by matching offenders to tasks in a way that enables them to use their particular skills both they and the recipients gain recognition and support in different ways.

Manual tasks such as gardening, painting and decorating houses for the elderly, renovating community halls or churches, or engaging in building work are common to most schemes. Indeed such tasks as building community centres, adventure playgrounds, canal restoration, and nature conservation have been successfully undertaken since the scheme began. Similarly practical work in old people's homes, centres for the handicapped, or with single-parent families enables offenders to contribute their skills in a more personalized way. Some schemes run workshops and use such facilities to carry out furniture repairs, vehicle maintenance, making or repairing toys. The range of tasks undertaken nationally is enormous and these are but a few examples.

The real value of any placement is not so much the nature of the work carried out, although this can be very important, but the offender's perception of the relevance of the task and the feelings of self-worth this generates. Skilled supervisors invariably ensure that tasks are completed satisfactorily, and within personalized placements the quality of supervision, often supplied by the recipient organization, enables schemes to maintain their credibility within the community and generate work for future offenders.

While the work undertaken is only that which would normally not be done by paid labour there is a danger that, with increasing government cutbacks in the public sector, jobs which were traditionally done by local authorities might be taken on by community service, especially if a perceived need, e.g. in hospitals or day centres, is not being met. Care also needs to be taken to ensure that government-sponsored job creation schemes do not conflict with the areas of work undertaken by community service. Many community service schemes cannot begin to match the resources made available to unemployed youngsters by some Manpower Services schemes; these offer identical work schemes to community service and can appear more attractive to those people who might, in their absence, have used their local community service scheme.

Females on community service orders

It is significant that over the last ten years the number of female offenders on community service has been approximately 5 per cent of the national total of people on orders. There may be a variety of reasons to explain this low number – few of which are entirely satisfactory. Clearly the number of females considered appropriate by the courts to do community service is very small set against the larger number of males who commit imprisonable offences. There may be a natural assumption on the part of probation officers, and indeed by many courts, that the practical nature of community service is more suited to males than females. Those schemes that reserve community service as a direct alternative to custody accept that relatively few females appear before the courts who are in immediate danger of losing their liberty, and this will inevitably result in a limited number of referrals for community service. Set against this, however, is the fact that females in some areas tend to attract prison sentences somewhat more readily than their male counterparts and community service may not be an option which has been sufficiently well explored in their case prior to a custodial sentence being imposed.

What is important as far as selection of tasks is concerned is whether the task allocated is appropriate for the particular community service worker, irrespective of gender. Female offenders do not always wish to be allocated tasks helping with a crèche, family centres, or working with elderly or handicapped people. Painting and decorating is a task which can be undertaken by females, and project work such as nature conservation or workshop activities might provide a welcome relief from the tasks assumed to be appropriate for the stereotype female. There is no doubt that some females require special consideration in task allocation, if their domestic circumstances and responsibilities restrict the hours they can make available to their community service work, or if the support they might require is not always available on the project of their choice. While these and other reasons exist to explain the low numbers of females placed on community service orders, there is little doubt that this particular aspect of the community service scheme deserves closer examination in the future.

Juveniles on community service

The Criminal Justice Act 1982 extended the power of the courts to make community service orders on sixteen-year-olds. Since no clear statement of financial provision accompanied this legislation, some areas therefore could not immediately find resources for this extension to their existing schemes, principally for financial reasons. As a consequence only thirty-six areas introduced a scheme for juveniles in the financial year 1983/84. However, a review of community service for juveniles (Adair 1984: 1) found that by June 1984 forty-six areas out of fifty-five, i.e. 83.6 per cent, were running schemes for sixteen-year-olds. Over a six-month period (January to June 1984) a national total of 989 orders were made on juveniles. Of these, approximately 50–55 were on females, which appears a similar proportion to community service in general. This would produce a national total of approximately 2,000 orders on juveniles per annum assuming the same rate of growth.

This survey also found that 78.3 per cent of the forty-six schemes accepting juveniles were integrated within existing adult schemes, 13 per cent were separate schemes, and 8.7 per cent were a mixture of methods. The average length of an order was approximately 91.5 hours, which seems high within the available range of 40 to 120 hours, unless taking into consideration that nearly all areas indicate that this sentencing option was reserved for those juveniles at risk of losing their liberty.

From a practitioner's viewpoint, it has been found that many juveniles have a greater potential for disruption, and offer in the main a lack of sound practical skills or the ability to apply themselves to any task for a substantial period. As a result, many areas have discovered a need to provide closer supervision and more opportunities to switch juveniles from one task to another. Particularly careful assessments of each individual are necessary in order that a suitable initial placement can be found. However, the early fears expressed by many of mixing juveniles with adults on community service have in the main proved unfounded. There are signs that running separate schemes is more costly and problematic than those schemes which integrate offenders of all ages.

Despite the extension of this popular sentence to sixteen-year-olds, coupled with a range of intensive intermediate schemes, the take-up rate by courts has not been quite as great as had been anticipated. Around 165 new orders per month are currently being made nationally, with the highest rate of orders for juveniles being made in the West Midlands. While the numbers made subject to youth custody orders continues to rise, it is becoming increasingly important to stress to the courts that this alternative to custody ought to be considered seriously before a custodial sentence is imposed upon a sixteen-year-old. It may be that more effective links need to be established in some areas with social services departments, to ensure that opportunities to recommend community service for juveniles are not missed – which would perhaps be due to a lack of knowledge about

75

the potential this scheme offers for the more persistent juvenile offender.

Community service for fine defaulters

Section 49 of the 1972 Criminal Justice Act would, if implemented, enable a magistrates' court to make a community service order in any case where it has power to issue a warrant of commitment for default in paying a fine. There is a growing debate that this provision should be implemented; but although in theory it appears a most attractive arrangement, the actual execution of it is beset with practical difficulties. In 1978 the Home Office noted that after wide-ranging consultations there exist some 'serious reservations' about putting into effect this particular measure. Their reservations were centred 'on the suitability of fine defaulters for community service, on the provision which would enable defaulters to cut short their services by payment of the sum outstanding, and on the effectiveness of such a measure in diverting defaulters from prison'. Before any probation department could consider responding positively to this provision – notwithstanding these reservations – the question of additional resourcing to cope with a significant potential increase in orders would need to be resolved. The added difficulties of devising an appropriate scale of hours to be worked, set against the amount of outstanding fine, given the wide variations which exist, and the need perhaps to create 'second class' community service work for this group, coupled with the problem of the offenders' motivation, all pose insuperable problems for organizers. As West (1978: 427) points out 'enforceability is really the crux of the problem'. It is, therefore, likely that this provision will simply remain on the statute books until these problems have been resolved.

Reconviction rates of offenders who have completed a community service order

Limited information exists to determine whether as a result of being made subject to a community service order offenders are deterred from committing further offences. Evidence exists (Pease 1977: 18) that 44.2 per cent of all those sentenced to community service during the experimental period were reconvicted within a year of the sentence. While few conclusions can be drawn from this given the limited data, interestingly a similar study (Leibrich, Galaway, and Underhill 1984: 12) found that 38 per cent of those made subject to community service orders were reconvicted within one year of receiving the sentence. However, this study concluded that 'reconviction rates are unlikely to provide a sensitive measure of a sentence's effectiveness'. Irrespective of reconviction rates there is no disputing the low cost of this sentence compared with that of keeping an offender in prison. A survey of offenders' opinions (Varah 1979: 122) indicated that 86 of 100 offenders who completed their orders felt they had positively gained from their community service order, and 76 indicated they would be prepared to continue their community service work on a voluntary basis. Community service is not designed primarily to prevent offenders re-offending and for many, simply to complete satisfactorily the number of hours ordered by the court is an achievement in itself.

The future of community service

There is now widespread acceptance that community service is a major instrument among the non-custodial alternatives and its rapid growth has far reaching implications for the Probation Service. Its credibility is in part dependent upon acquiring sufficient resources to match increased growth. There is already evidence that some Services are placing intermittent restrictions upon local courts wishing to make further community service orders when existing numbers exceed containable proportions. This 'stop-go' practice can disrupt a scheme, frustrate the courts, and may result in some offenders receiving a custodial sentence who might otherwise have been considered suitable for community service. If schemes continue to grow and are to be provided with additional resources at the expense of other service developments, an already difficult resource situation will be further exacerbated. On the other hand, it may be that many probation committees, encouraged by the perceived value of community service, would readily endorse plans for increased growth in this aspect of the Service's work. Indeed part of the appeal of community service for many magistrates it that it resurrects aspects relating to the traditional concept of punishment, which in recent years have tended to be superseded by the 'treatment-casework' model.

In some respects the tensions which exist between community service and the main-stream work of the Probation Service have been contained. However, with the annual numbers of community service orders now beginning to equal those of probation orders there exists some anxiety within the Service that future growth of community service will occur at the expense of other probationary work and consequently make it harder to justify its taking more resources, despite the perceived practical benefits it offers. While some additional government funding has been made available in the past to cater for the expansion of community service schemes, there is no guarantee that future funding will be forthcoming. Indeed, the 1983 Home Office 'Statement of National Aims and Objectives of the Probation Service' clearly indicates that future expansion of any aspect of the Service's work may well occur only through a reallocation of existing resources. In blunt terms this seems to be saying that the Probation Service must get its own house in order, determine what its priorities ought to be, and cut its cloth accordingly. The Service has traditionally been seen by some as the Cinderella of the criminal justice system in that the demands placed upon it through increased legislation have seldom been matched by commensurate financial provisions, to enable the Service to cater properly for a wide range of offenders within the community.

The danger of quantitative growth of community service is that it may lose out in a qualitative sense. Two fundamental questions need to be asked (Richards and Maull 1983: 103): first, 'What is the purpose of community service for offenders?' and second, 'How is this purpose to be realized in practice?' In the interests of efficiency, expediency, and economy of resources, it would be relatively easy to process large numbers of offenders through large-scale work parties, where the purely pragmatic intention was control, with the hours being worked through as quickly as possible. As Richards and Maull note this would force offenders to 'sweat their way to redemption through the punishing self-mortification of hard work'. Such a scenario is not only unattractive but would be seen as a retrograde step, not dissimilar from the days when convicts spent all day in the quarry breaking up boulders. If, however, community service is to embrace the treatment model, with individual offenders being carefully matched to projects in a sensitive and caring way, some schemes, already overloaded with offenders, would simply be unable to cope despite strenuous efforts to do so.

The future direction of community service is exposed to four potential scenarios – probationization, penalization, bureaucratization, and standardization (Pease and McWilliams 1980). If schemes embrace a decentralized model in a functional sense, community service will be under greater pressure from the probation service ethic to deal with all community service orders on 'treatment' lines and hence to probationize schemes. Given the reluctance of many probation officers to 'breach' clients, this might bring about a concomitant disinclination to maintain tight discipline for non-attendance or unsatisfactory work on schemes. This inevitably would reduce the morale of experienced community service staff whose attempts to maintain credibility and order could be undermined. The courts might either become disinclined to make orders on those in greatest danger of losing their liberty or opt to make orders on those offenders convicted of less serious offences.

The danger of schemes becoming 'penalized' is that they would subscribe to the notion of 'service to all in need' but in reality would become mechanized and impersonal; superficial efficiency would become the order of the day. Offenders who are to be punished for wrong doing might be additionally penalized with orders of excessive length simply because they are unemployed and 'have time on their hands'. With a work force noted for its lack of motivation due to the impersonal nature of the tasks it has to perform, greater enforcement problems would arise, resulting in increasing numbers being returned to court for non-compliance. The flow of recommendations from probation officers would diminish; community service as a popular sentence would decline, and morale amongst community service staff suffer, causing the rapid departure of committed staff who would then be replaced by new personnel with limited skills except for their ability to enforce discipline.

Any expanding scheme inevitably becomes seduced by the notion that all efficient systems are dependent upon a bureaucracy which displays characteristic tendencies of caution, regimentation, inflexibility, and an excessive attention to detail that diminishes initiative and imaginative response from those in the field. A move away from bureaucratic control might result in schemes separating from the Probation Service and becoming attracted by the advantages of amalgamation with a cluster of voluntary agencies. Local authorities already involved financially or administratively with some voluntary agencies would become more involved, either in the provision of work or by supplementing their diminishing work force with community service labour. The necessity to consider a probation officer's report prior to the making of an order might then lapse or be scrapped through amended legislation.

If schemes are alerted to these scenarios it is possible that efforts will be made to promote a standardization of community service which attempts to develop the most favourable circumstances in which an offender could undertake an order. Unfortunately during the first few years of the scheme's development no opportunity existed to consider nationally how area schemes should establish some degree of consistent practice. As a result 'this led to a range of well-entrenched variations in practice, not all of them reflecting the local circumstances and together amounting to unnecessary injustice' (Pease 1981: 48). Between April 1979 and April 1981, three national community service seminars took place and some lost ground was made up, but considerable variations in practice still exist. Standardization of schemes would promote greater consistency of practice, so that offenders transferring from one scheme to another are less likely to experience radically different 'ground rules' and can recognize similar important component parts from one scheme to another.

A paper given to the national seminar (Seymour 1980) attempted to lay some foundations towards establishing consistency between schemes. It recognized that local and regional variations are inevitable but that common threads could be woven between them all concerning fundamental aspects of community service. Courts should be clear about the place of community service on the tariff and sentencers ought to understand what community service is and what it can offer. All those connected with the scheme should be afforded opportunities to discuss issues of principle and practice. Objectives concerning staffing, resourcing, selection of projects, and criteria for breaching are some of the issues which require attention on a regional and then national scale. Seymour concluded:

> 'Community service should seriously consider the development and application of standards of good practice on the grounds of equity, developing the best service to the courts and clients and good management, but this should only happen on the basis of a careful analysis of situations using standards derived from experience and as a means of development as well as control.'

Clearly, the future success of community service rests on our ability to develop a consistent and reasonable framework within which to use this sanction.

The extent to which probation officers are prepared to rethink traditional views and practices may to some extent depend on their ability to acquire greater knowledge and insight as to the impact this sentence has upon the offenders and their community. Clients who 'appear to have failed' on probation orders and yet 'succeeded' on a community service work placement, in the author's experience, often wish their probation officers could witness what in some cases may be the first positive contribution they have made to their local community. There is still widespread reluctance for probation officers to demonstrate a practical interest in community service by visiting a local project, or discussing on site with an offender the relevance or value of the work carried out. It is clear that community service is here to stay and probation officers will find it increasingly difficult to plead overwork as an excuse not to visit local schemes. For those who do it is often a rewarding experience and one that boosts the morale of offenders and community service staff alike.

In 1984 the Home Secretary stated, 'There remains a feeling that justice would be better done if some way could have been found to require the offender to make some positive recompense to the victim or the community as a whole' (Brittan 1984). Throughout its development, community service offenders have responded to specific needs in the community – a form of indirect reparation. In future, community service schemes may become involved in reparation projects associated, in some instances, with the National Association of Victim Support Schemes. Some pilot schemes already exist using community service offenders to perform indirect reparation work to victims of crime. If these prove effective a more extensive programme might develop in a sensitive and constructive way, which would help offenders to understand more clearly the impact of crime on individuals in our society.

It is perhaps inevitable that the Probation Service should find itself at a critical point in terms of the future development of community service. Its rate of growth has exceeded all expectations, for within ten years of operation on a national scale, community service orders have matched probation orders as the most popular non-custodial options the Probation Service has to offer for the persistent offender. To maintain the credibility of schemes and keep pace with the growth of orders, issues concerning its tariff position, resourcing, and standardization will need to be addressed. Issues relating to proper rates of pay for community service staff, the need for a career structure and training to retain committed staff, and clearly thought-out job descriptions cannot be left to chance. Problems continue to exist relating to health and safety and insurance – a veritable minefield for many organizers – which are ignored at our peril. The temptation to use community service as a panacea for all offenders must be resisted, not because first-time offenders could not benefit from a community service order, but because the primary duty of the Probation Service is to maintain credible alternatives to custody, and actively to encourage their use. It is important, therefore, that the Probation Service develops a more consistent philosophy and practice in relation to community service, so that decisions about its future direction ensure its place in the criminal justice system in a way that upholds the finest traditions of the Service.

© *1987 Michael Varah*

References

Adair, H.S. (1984) *Follow-up Survey of Community Service for 16 Year Olds*. Community Service Committee, Association of Chief Officers of Probation (October): 1.

Brittan, L. Victim Support Schemes. Speech given by Home Secretary to Holborn Law Society, 14 March, 1984.

Home Office (1978) *Response to Expenditure Sub-Committee – Community Service for Fine Defaulters*. London: HMSO.

—— (1983) *Probation Statistics*. London: HMSO.

Leibrich, J., Galaway, B., and Underhill, Y. (1984) *Community Service Orders in New Zealand Summary*. Planning and Development Division, Department of Justice, New Zealand (March): 12.

McWilliams, B. (1980) Community Service Orders: Discretion and the Prosecution of Breach Proceedings – An Interim Report of Research. University of Manchester, Department of Social Administration.

NAPO (1977) *Report of a Working Group of the Professional Committee*. Community Service Orders – Practice and Philosophy: 18. London: National Association of Probation Officers.

Pease, K. (1977) *Community Service Assessed in 1976* – Home Office Research Study no. 39 (March): 18. London: HMSO.

—— (1981) Community Service Orders – A First Decade of Promise. Howard League for Penal Reform.

Pease, K. and McWilliams, W. (1980) The Future of Community Service. In K. Pease and W. McWilliams (eds) *Community Service by Order*. Edinburgh: Scottish Academic Press.

Richards, N. and Maull, G. (1983) Making Community Service into Service for the Community. *Probation Journal* (September): 103.

Seymour, B. Standards in Community Service Practice. A paper given at the National Community Service Seminar, August 1980, Keele University.

Varah, M. (1979) What about the Workers. *Probation Journal* (March): 122.

West, J. (1978) Community Service for Fine Defaulters. *Justice of the Peace* (July): 427.

5 Removed from the community – prisoners and the Probation Service

Tony Raban

The Probation Service is strangely ambivalent about through-care. Although there is a genuine desire among many probation officers to offer help to prisoners and their families, there is an unmistakable tension between the Service's main task of providing alternatives to custody and holding offenders in the community wherever possible. Prison remands and sentences demand that probation officers engage with the very system they are motivated to avoid. This has led to wide variations in commitment and practice, and may also explain why such a high proportion of the work is managed through specialisms. Looking at the place of through-care in the Service's overall priorities, one has to ask whether we too have sometimes contributed to the process of 'moral apartheid' described by Martin Davies (Davies 1974: ix).

The history of the Service's work with prisoners demonstrates how objectives have changed in the last twenty years. Up to 1966 prisoners' after-care was generally provided through voluntary organizations, in particular the Discharged Prisoners' Aid Societies, which were gathered into a national body, NADPAS, in 1937. The Maxwell Report (Home Office 1953) recommended the appointment of welfare officers in prisons, to help prisoners during their sentence, and to identify those likely to benefit from after-care. The Advisory Council on the Treatment of Offenders (Home Office 1963) took up these ideas and proposed that qualified social workers should be appointed by the Home Office, but this suggestion was rejected, and the work was allocated instead to the Probation Service in 1966.

A year later the task was defined in the following terms: 'The prison welfare officer should have a four-fold rule within the prison: as a social case worker, as the focal point of social work, as the normal channel of communication with the outside, and as the planner of after-care' (Home Office 1967: 1). In a list of twenty-one tasks, half appeared to be directed more to the running of the prison than to prisoners' needs, as Priestley and others observed (Priestley 1972). The result was a drift away from work focused on release, and an

83

assimilation into the administrative structure of the institution. The process was accelerated by the enthusiasm of probation officers in prisons, as outside, to demonstrate the potential of 'treatment' through the embryonic skills of casework, so that many came to see themselves as members of a team working to achieve the rehabilitation of the prisoner. Less attention was given to release, the work became increasingly reactive and bureaucratic (Othen 1975) and prison staff with an interest in inmates' welfare felt squeezed out by the 'experts' (Thomas 1977). In an attempt to rectify this the National Association of Probation Officers and the Prison Officers' Association now share a long-term goal which would transfer much of the work of prison probation officers to prison staff.

Meanwhile the Probation Service in the field has also undergone change. The idea of after-care (post release) has been extended to one of through-care (post sentence), building on some of the principles contained in the ACTO Report. But the involvement of a statutory agency also provided a convenient facility for the extension of statutory supervision after release. Parole, first introduced in 1967, was further extended by the 1982 Criminal Justice Act. The same Act also rationalized the provisions for young offenders, all of whom are now subject to at least three months' supervision if they are released before they reach the age of twenty-two. Furthermore, the number of life sentence prisoners has risen to about two thousand, resulting in a steady flow of men and women released on life licences. This predominance of statutory supervision raises questions about voluntary after-care; in particular, its place in the Service's present priorities, and the effect on prisoners' perceptions of the probation officer.

Changes in the product have been matched by changes in the packaging. In 1977 prison welfare officers were redesignated prison probation officers. 'The Probation Service' became 'The Probation and After-Care Service' in the 1967 Criminal Justice Act, and in 1982 the words 'and After-Care' were dropped again from the title, for reasons that were not made clear at the time and may yet emerge.

In the midst of these changes it is all too easy to lose sight of the people most directly affected, the prisoners themselves. But a greater danger is to assume that we and other 'professionals' can ever have more than a limited grasp of what imprisonment entails. The experience is unique. As one prisoner explains: 'I don't think you could say being in prison is like anything, because being in prison you're in the middle of a big nothing, and that's not "like" anything' (Parker 1973: 20). And Hanus Hermann, who was a political prisoner for six years, observes: 'Nothing short of actual incarceration, however, can communicate the total impact of life in prison. Prison visits are deceptive. . . . Only after having spent many years in prison did I realize how false was the picture of prison life and conditions formed as a visitor' (Hermann 1974: 209). It is important, therefore, to start by listening to what prisoners themselves have to say, and to relate this to our knowledge of institutions, in order that we can at least move towards a partial understanding of their experience.

The experience of imprisonment

Although prisons are invariably seen as an entity in themselves, they have more in common with other total institutions than is usually recognized. Like all such organizations, they have powerful encompassing tendencies, and are protected by extremely effective physical and psychological barriers, which prevent social intercourse with the outside community. Moreover, they contain elements from each of the five types of institution described by Goffman:

(i) catering for the incapable and harmless
(ii) providing for people who are incapable but pose some threat to the community
(iii) protecting the community against those who would cause some deliberate harm
(iv) the pursuit of some worklike task
(v) the provision of a retreat from the world. (Goffman 1970: 16)

Prisons appear to fall within the third category, but there are many in custody who pose no significant threat to society and are incarcerated for deterrent or punitive reasons. Others are held because of their nuisance value, or because there are inadequate resources elsewhere (particularly in the field of mental health). Where there are facilities for work, as in training prisons, the impartial observer might well conclude that these form an end in themselves, given the nature of the activities and the emphasis on efficiency and continuity of labour. For many recidivists, prison has indeed become a retreat, and even those less dependent on the institution are likely to become introspective and ruminative, as is evident in many letters, poems, and paintings. Prisons, therefore, share much with other total institutions, and their character is likely to be defined as much by complex informal processes as by penal policy.

How then is this world experienced by those sentenced to imprisonment?

'I read somewhere in a book sometime, about it was like you were a man trying to crawl to safety up the tilting deck of a ship as it was slowly sinking on its side into the water, and I think that's the nearest I can say to it. Only there was more to it, that he didn't put – that the ship never finally sinks and it never comes upright again either, so you don't drown but you don't survive. It's more like you're perpetually in between the two, living a completely sideways life.'   (Parker 1973: 91)

The process of entering prison will shake the individual's perception of himself and society. In addition to the obvious impact of the court hearing, pronouncement of sentence, and loss of family and friends, offenders undergo the 'stripping' process which divests them of much of their identity, reinforces the sense of loss, and underlines their powerlessness. The prisoner 'begins a series of abasements, degradations, humiliations, and profanations of self. His self is systematically, if often unintentionally, mortified' (Goffman 1970: 24). As the doors of the prison close, the barrier is sealed between the inmate and the outside world. He undergoes the 'first curtailment of self'. Important roles, relationships, and possessions are no longer available, and although some may eventually be re-established, others will be lost irretrievably. From this moment on, the person's sense of identity is under siege.

'It's as though it'd all been very carefully thought out as a deliberate way to humiliate you. First they write down all the details of you, then they take your personal possessions and seal them up in a packet, then they take your clothes off you and put them in a numbered box, and finally you end up standing there with just a towel round your waist. What they're doing is reducing your identity stage by stage, slowly wiping you out as a person until you're only one more piece of flesh with a name and a number. It's frightening to have it done to you, to realize how easily it can be done, how completely powerless you are to prevent them taking away your individuality.'   (Parker 1973: 26)

In this way the prisoner is 'shaped and coded into an object that can be fed into the administrative machinery of the establishment, to be worked on smoothly by routine operations' (Goffman 1970: 26), a process which is not necessarily made easier because it has been experienced before. It takes place very quickly, providing little opportunity for the person to prepare or adjust. 'Whatever the circumstances, however, the transition is always effected in a very brief space of time: a few words are spoken, and before their sound dies the prisoner's entire perspective of life, of society, of himself has changed' (Hermann 1974: 209).

Once inside, the prisoner's life is characterized by a sense of powerlessness and purposelessness. Where work is available it is likely to be monotonous. Life rotates around fixed routines which dominate staff as much as inmates and it is difficult, if not impossible, to avoid some level of dependency – a dependency which is aggravated by the limited scope for meaningful communication with people from the world beyond the walls. Letters are often cherished: 'I don't get many letters but if I do get one I read it every day for weeks till I've learned it and then I repeat it to myself in bed at night' (Parker 1973: 71). But even in letters, as in all prison life, there is no guarantee of privacy. Most are read by prison censors, and prisoners themselves may take advantage of others to whom a letter is of special importance (Catchpole 1974: 38–9). For many inmates, writing is an unfamiliar medium, and for some it is impossible. For those who can express themselves there is another danger. Things are read into letters that will cause misunderstandings and rifts that cannot be mended easily. It is one thing to verbalize feelings of exasperation or dejection, perhaps with some tacit acknowledgement that nothing is being asked for except that someone listens. It is another matter to commit them to paper, knowing that they will arrive days later, and that the recipient is almost powerless to offer help – at least, not of any spontaneous kind. Inevitably, many letters become trivialized. 'I never know what to put in letters, sometimes I just want to send out nothing but a list of questions, not because I want to know the answers but because I can't think of anything to say' (Parker 1973: 66).

Visits pose similar problems for prisoners and their families. Again, they take on a major significance as a vital link with the world outside. 'Apart from the date of your release the only thing you live for is your visits. You have a half-hour visit once a month, and you live from month to month because that's the only time you see someone who's connected with you and not with anyone else' (Parker 1973: 84). Many prisoners and their families see visits as particularly difficult if things are going badly for one or both parties, and this has not been shared. Attempts are made to present a cheerful face, to avoid upsetting the other person who is usually in no position to help, and to avoid opening a Pandora's box of feelings which may be impossible to close during the brief span of the visit. The artificiality of the setting in most prisons makes meaningful communication difficult, with the constraints of visits being conducted within the sight, and often within the hearing, of prison staff. And, inevitably, visits from friends and family provide a powerful reminder of the prisoner's predicament. Finally, it should not be forgotten that there are a significant number of prisoners who receive no visits or letters – sometimes over many years.

Other aspects of the prisoner's world, including food, work, accommodation, education, and training, are described by Davies (Davies 1974: 21–7) and recent reports on the prison system contain graphic information about the poor physical environment (e.g. May Report 1979, Parliamentary All-Party Report 1980, Home Office 1983a). All these features conspire to create a situation where the prisoner is made to feel like an object rather than a person. He does not experience opportunities to help him prepare for a responsible life in the community, but has to survive a purposeless existence in a distorted world, and there are only limited ways of achieving this.

Goffman lists four methods of adaptation (Goffman 1970: 61–4). *Situational withdrawal*, in which the inmate withdraws attention from everything except events which relate to him immediately, paying little attention to the perspectives of others around him, like the prisoner who recorded 'I write things down on scraps of paper in the night in the dark. I've had a lot of practice at it. Words, phrases, fragments, ideas for poems perhaps. Little bits of me that nobody knows about and I keep hidden' (Parker 1973: 90). The second method is the *intransigent line*, where the prisoner challenges the institutional norms and offers little if any co-operation. In *colonization* the inmate adopts the opposite stance, accepting the institutional world and seeking to gain maximum satisfaction within it. The fourth possibility, *conversion*, is where everything possible is done to live up to the official view of the model prisoner. Few inmates pursue any of these strategies to their extreme, but may use each of them at different stages. In most cases, prisoners will content themselves with 'playing it cool', selecting the right time and place to adopt any one of the above roles, thereby making the most of the limited opportunities, and reducing the damaging effects of the institution. In their study of the effects of long-term imprisonment, Cohen and Taylor also note that prisoners often have to make a conscious decision about how to relate to the institution if they are to survive a long sentence intact – whether to fight the system or conform (Cohen and Taylor 1972: 54). Most prisoners, however, display superficial conformity, while seeking to protect themselves from the dangers of 'colonization' or 'conversion', a process described by Roy Catchpole:

> 'It was three weeks before I knuckled under. I saw it was easier that way. A prison is no way to try to put the world to rights. The mark of a regular con is that he can do his time without any undue shocks. He comes into prison, gets friendly with the screws, makes a few influential mates, gets a decent job in the laundry or cook house, and before he's had time to think about his position in relation to

the world outside he's due for release. . . . I've yet to hear of the man who'll stick his hand into a blazing fire. I've yet to hear of a prisoner who refuses to take the easy way out. It's part of the art of living and surviving.' (Catchpole 1974: 74–5)

As the prisoner's release date draws near, new pressures emerge, and the process of release itself is often accompanied by rituals which mirror those experienced at the start of the sentence. The process of returning to the community is not simply a welcome release from the privations of imprisonment. Although many will face practical difficulties, there are often major social and emotional adjustments to be made, which can come as a great shock to prisoners and those close to them. There may well be mixed feelings of elation and anxiety before and at the point of release; of *stigmatization*, sometimes a purely subjective experience, but more often a reality for ex-prisoners; and of *disculturation*, the loss of social skills necessary to relate to other members of the community (Goffman 1970: 71). The prisoner, having painfully won certain privileges on the inside, now has to move from the top of a small world to the bottom of a large one. For some the prospect can seem overwhelming: 'There were so many problems to be faced, so many fears to be brought out into the open that I almost wished I had never been given my freedom' (Davies 1974: 131).

Although the pressures surrounding release are usually most acute for socially isolated offenders (Corden, Kuipers, and Wilson 1978), those who have families face some unexpected problems, resulting from what Hermann describes as the Shangri-La effect of prison.

'The length of time is not measured by the passage of the moon or by the revolutions of the earth. It is measured by the number of events that have happened. Looking back, the prisoner sees a series of identical days and identical weeks, so that a year that passed seems to be a week, but the year to come seems an eternity.'

The full impact of this may only be experienced when the prisoner is reunited with his family. 'The prisoner returns, he thinks that he is back, the family thinks he has come back. In fact all that has happened is that they are all again in the same place, but they do not live in the same time' (Hermann 1974: 219).

Certain groups within our prisons face particular difficulties. It used to be assumed that courts were more lenient with female offenders, but it now seems clear that this is not the case (Farrington and Morris 1983) and there is some suggestion that they may be penalized more heavily – possibly because they disturb a comfortable stereotype of the woman's role (Worrall 1981). Women's prisons contain a higher proportion of untried, unsentenced, and civil prisoners, and of those convicted two-thirds are serving short-term sentences (Home Office 1983a). The number of women going into prison is rising steadily (a 5 per cent increase was recorded in the 1983 Home Office report), suggesting that the problems faced by this group are likely to become more acute. There are fewer establishments for women than for men and although these are usually smaller and more informal, the prisoners are often located out of reach of their families. Of necessity, there is little segregation of the age groups, which is supported as a matter of policy on the basis that 'it is generally considered to be positively beneficial for younger women to share facilities with suitable adults' (Home Office 1980: 9). The psychiatric facilities for women have been subject to much criticism, both in terms of the conditions and the reliance on medication, and a recent report on Holloway Prison described the treatment of disturbed women as 'morally and ethically unjustifiable' (MIND and NCCL 1985). It has been argued that imprisonment is experienced differently by men and women, and that the latter are less prepared emotionally and socially for living in regimented single-sex institutions – that they are more accustomed to seeking support from a close friend or a small group. This is put forward as a reason for the intensity of relationships in women's prisons (Heidensohn 1975) although similar, if less overt, patterns can be found in all-male institutions. Finally, women serving long sentences may have to face the additional loss of knowing that they will no longer be able to bear children.

For the members of ethnic minorities the experience of imprisonment will be particularly bewildering, and they may have to face a series of cultural shocks in addition to the range of deprivations resulting from imprisonment itself. There is a disproportionately high number of young black offenders in custody, which appears to mirror social disadvantage in the community (Home Office 1983a) and although the Prison Department has taken some steps to promote a policy of racial equality there is clearly a long way to go. In addition to the problems of culture and religion, there may be basic difficulties of language, which are not necessarily overcome by the use of an interpreter who may come from a very different culture – particularly within the Asian sub-groups. This has obvious implications for those offering help or making assessments that have a direct bearing on release dates.

People serving indeterminate sentences face unique problems. Sapsford's study of life-sentence prisoners (Sapsford 1978) refers to the reduction in future time-perspective (which echoes some of Hermann's observations above), to the preoccupation with the past rather than the future, a noticeable increase in introversion, and to the growing dependence on the institution. He also records that life-sentence prisoners who have been inside for several years tend to receive fewer visits and letters than those serving determinate sentences. One man told Parker, 'I've never had a visit from no-one for over ten years now, no not a letter or a Christmas card or a birthday card or anything. I don't know no-one you see, that's why' (Parker 1973: 85). Once again the theme of loss is prominent, but the experience is made far more difficult because there is uncertainty about the outcome. People can often handle extreme pain when the reality is clear, but may find it impossible to adjust to potential loss, as when a child is abducted, or a soldier is reported missing. For life-sentence prisoners this experience is an integral part of their sentence, and invariably means that the prison is seen as having absolute power over the individual. In an unpublished survey of life-sentence prisoners at Nottingham Prison, several men described how they had submitted themselves to some form of self-imposed isolation during the first part of their sentence. One man referred to three and a half years' self-imposed 'solitary' and another to a 'four-year cut-off'. They also spoke of the importance of knowing what plans were being made on their behalf, preferring to be kept informed even if the news was bad, and to the value of maintaining contact with outsiders who had no particular brief within the prison. This gave them a reflection of themselves outside the norms of the institution, and also enabled some of them to begin to break down the 'monster' image which is so often imposed on those who have committed murder or other grave offences.

If this is how prison is experienced from the inside, how then is it seen by those involved in penal policy?

The context

'Crime is not a sickness, although some who perpetrate it are undoubtedly sick, and there is no cure – no cure at all – to be found in imprisonment' (Lord Windlesham 1984). This comment by the Chairman of the Parole Board reflects a major change in penal thinking over the last hundred years. The penitentiary movement of the mid-nineteenth century saw the convict as the victim of a society which had failed to provide the necessary protection against the vices of drink, gambling, and prostitution, and believed the cure lay in the provision of a well-ordered institution whose ideals would be instilled in the inmate, to the benefit of all. 'Indeed should society change places with the prisoners, so far as habits are concerned, taking to itself the regularity, and temperance, and sobriety of a good prison

. . . then . . . shall we see the triumph of peace, of right, and of Christianity' (Revd James B. Finley, Chaplain of Ohio Penitentiary, 1851, published in Howard League for Penal Reform (1979: 3). The reforming principle underlying the penitentiary was adopted in this country and its pervasive influence is with us still. The May Committee, for example, appeared to reject the idea of rehabilitation, only to reintroduce it in the guise of 'positive custody' (Home Office 1979: 72-3). The Home Secretary recently announced an extension of the 'short, sharp, shock' regime in detention centres, despite a research team's evidence that it had no impact on reconviction figures (Home Office 1984a). And there is evidence in social inquiry reports that social workers and probation officers are still prepared to recommend custody on correctional grounds (Thomas 1982).

In the field of child care there has been a growing recognition that any benefits which may be derived from an institution have to be set against the disadvantages of placing young people in an unnatural environment, exposing them to possible new risks, and disrupting their ties with the community. As a result, restrictions have been placed on the care order and establishments are being closed (e.g. Thorpe 1983 and Giller 1983). Regrettably, there is no immediate prospect of a similar response in the penal system, even though it is acknowledged that imprisonment is an ineffective method of reforming offenders, that it too has damaging effects on prisoners and their families, and lessens the individual's ability to survive in the community.

But there is also the problem of numbers. For every 100,000 people in this country there are 50 adult prisoners serving sentences at any one time. For most of Western Europe this figure is between 17 and 38. Yet the number of receptions in England and Wales is one of the lowest. In other words, the size of our prison population is a result of average sentence *length*, and would be reduced dramatically if terms of imprisonment reflected those elsewhere in Europe (Fitzmaurice and Pease 1982). In his evidence to the Home Affairs Committee in 1981, the Home Secretary stated that 'research has failed to show that measured by reconviction rates a long prison sentence is any more effective than a short one' (House of Commons 1981: xvii). The logical solution is to tackle average sentence length, but present policies address symptoms, not causes. New prisons are being built. The capital programme which cost £24m. in 1979-80 will rise to £80m. in 1986-87. The number of staff, which was 23,881 in 1979, will increase to 32,450 in the next four years, and the total expenditure on prisons will rise from £552m. in 1983-84 to £670m. by 1986-87 (*The Times* 17 February, 1984).

Against such a background the task for the Probation Service is indeed a daunting one. When an offender is sentenced to custody the officer often experiences a sense of failure. There may be doubts about whether all community options have been pursued vigorously enough. If the offence is so serious that a custodial sentence is inevitable, there will be feelings of irrelevance and powerlessness. Not surprisingly, therefore, many probation officers feel that through-care is little more than a token gesture of 'society's apology for hurt inflicted' (Davies 1974: ix). Official policy, both at local and national level, may provide little encouragement and in some cases is depressingly equivocal, as in the Home Office's 1984 Statement of National Objectives and Priorities which states that: 'Sufficient resources should be allocated to through-care to enable the Service's statutory obligations to be discharged. . . . Beyond that, social work with offenders released from custody can only command the priority which is consistent with the main objective of implementing non-custodial measures for offenders who might otherwise receive custodial sentences' (Home Office 1984b: 5).

Despite such statements, the case for through-case is undeniable, both in terms of the Probation Service's current policy objectives and its tradition of 'advise, assist, and befriend'. Alternatives to custody do not begin and end with the social inquiry report. If the Service is committed to working with those most at risk of custody then reconviction figures clearly indicate that it should be focusing its attention on those currently in prison. But through-care, by definition, cannot be broken down into convenient administrative categories. Parole, for example, is a statutory duty and provides an alternative to custody, yet it may well be dependent on a release plan which has only emerged because of an investment by the probation officer and prisoner throughout the sentence. And if parole is not granted, should such work be abandoned?

Corden and others have demonstrated that isolated prisoners represent a particularly 'poor bet' for parole. They are often homeless, and a high proportion suffer from poor health and mental illness. Although they have usually been imprisoned for less serious offences, they are very likely to return to prison (Corden and Clifton 1981; Corden, Kuipers, and Wilson 1978). Yet, as the authors demonstrate, it is possible to provide consistent and effective help at the point of release. To regard this group as a low priority brings into question not only the Service's humanity but also its sense of strategy.

But there is another, more fundamental reason for offering through-care to all prisoners. We are often told that, detention centres apart, the impact of imprisonment should be felt through the loss of liberty, and that 'men come to prison as a punishment and not *for* punishment' (Sir Alexander Paterson, quoted in Hawkins 1974: 100). But what is omitted is the obligation it places on all of us to ensure that the damaging effects of imprisonment are mitigated wherever possible and this points to a unique role for the Probation Service based on its knowledge of, and access to, the community.

Minimizing damage

Communities provide a context in which people establish roles and a sense of identity – a context which is removed by imprisonment. Prisoners become institutional property, and the person is only confirmed through the distorting mirror of the prison world. Thus the institution acts as a double-edged sword, eroding and sometimes severing the ties with the community, but also undermining the very skills necessary for survival beyond the wall.

In saying this it is important to distinguish institutional processes from the people. It does not help to blame the prison staff. Now that the reforming ideal behind Prison Rule no. 1 – 'to encourage and assist [prisoners] to lead a good and useful life' – is generally regarded as redundant, there is confusion about what is expected of staff and what they should be held accountable for. In the absence of any guiding principle, it is not surprising that the task is often reduced to 'security' – where success is measurable, and where failure is often accompanied by public censure.

There is an alternative however. King and Morgan's concept of 'humane containment' has attracted considerable support and it is but a small step to move on to the more active principle of 'minimizing damage' as an aim to be shared by both the Prison and Probation Services – in the interests of the prisoner and, ultimately, the community.

1. IN THE PRISON
The institution would be responsible for:

(a) the day-to-day welfare of inmates;
(b) assistance in maintaining and developing survival skills which assist prisoners on release;
(c) ensuring that there are effective channels of communication between the prisoner and family, friends, and community agencies.

In such a re-alignment of roles prison staff would take over some of the functions currently being undertaken by seconded probation officers. The potential for this has already been demonstrated through several of the Social Work In Prisons schemes (e.g. Crook 1982) and by Priestley and Maguire's social skills courses (Priestley *et al.* 1984).

2. IN THE COMMUNITY

For the probation officer in the field, work would be directed towards:

(a) sustaining and developing community links with the prisoner;
(b) confirming the prisoner's individuality.

The probation officer would initiate joint strategies with the prisoner which identify the likely damaging effects of imprisonment and attempt to mitigate these. Particular attention needs to be paid to important events during the sentence, and to identifying the available and potential support in the community, including perhaps residents and other prisoners' families (Matthews 1983). In this way the community can be kept alive through letters, visits, and the exchange of information. But equally important, individual work undertaken by the probation officer needs to convey the basic social work values of respect for the individual and his or her rights (BASW 1976 and 1980), notably through a commitment to joint decision-making and by ensuring that all assessments are shared with the client.

Involvement

3. WORK ON THE BOUNDARY

These changes would demand a more integrated approach on the boundary between prison and probation. Hitherto the Probation Service has relied on specialists. A shared aim would challenge the two services to co-operate at all levels:

(a) to ensure that the community dimension is represented in the prison at times of review, allocation, assessment for home leave and hostel selection, and prior to release;
(b) to help the prison identify community resources to enable it to carry out its task as defined above, including such areas as welfare rights, accommodation, advice on domestic matters, and certain training facilities.

Probation resources could be used in the prison if they related to release. For example, the provision of a group for life-sentence prisoners wanting to look at the implications of supervision on licence. All of this work could be undertaken by probation officers based in the field but with a liaison role which could replace the present institutional focus of seconded officers.

Finally, tasks and roles built around the idea of minimizing damage

how much prisoner involvement

mean little unless there is some means of ensuring consistency and accountability. Pressure is mounting within prisons for a charter of rights (Downes 1983: 26). A Council of Europe document is being promoted by 'Justice' (Justice 1983) and NACRO have recently put forward some minimum standards for prisons (Casale 1984), an idea which already had some support within the prison system (Dunbar 1983).

In the Probation Service, minimum standards have been produced in at least one department and the idea is being promoted within NAPO (NAPO 1984). Because the standards are realistic and measurable they provide a means of challenging the kind of inconsistent practice referred to at the beginning of this chapter, and introduce an element of genuine accountability. It is encouraging that this development should start with a group of offenders who are least able to make demands on the Service – thus affirming that, although they may be temporarily removed from the community, prisoners remain citizens.

'The first principle is to see the guilty as people, which they were before they were guilty, and will be when they are no longer so, and which they are in the midst of it all. Their humanity is the principle thing about them. Their guilt is a temporary state.'

(Brian Phelan 1985)

© *1987 Tony Raban*

References

BASW (1976) *A Code of Ethics for Social Work*. Birmingham: British Association of Social Workers.
——— (1980) *Clients Are Fellow Citizens*. Birmingham: British Association of Social Workers.
Casale, S. (1984) *Minimum Standards For Prison Establishments*. London: National Association for the Care and Resettlement of Offenders.
Catchpole, R. (1974) *Key to Freedom*. Guildford: Lutterworth Press.
Cohen, S. and Taylor, T. (1972) *Psychological Survival*. Harmondsworth: Penguin.
Corden, J. and Clifton, M. (1981) Helping Socially Isolated Prisoners. In S. Fairhead (ed.) *Persistent Petty Offenders*. Home Office Research Study no. 66. London: HMSO.
Corden, J., Kuipers, J., and Wilson, A. (1978) *After Prison, Papers in Community Studies*, no. 21. Department of Social Administration and Social Work, University of York.

Crook, B. (1982) A Future For Shared Working. *Prison Service Journal* 48: 15–17.

Davies, M. (1974) *Prisoners of Society*. London: Routledge and Kegan Paul.

Downes, D. (1983) *Law and Order: Theft of an Issue*. London: Fabian Society.

Dunbar, I. (1983) Purposes of Imprisonment. In *A Prison System For The 80's and Beyond*. London: National Association for the Care and Resettlement of Offenders.

Farrington, D. and Morris, P. (1983) Do Magistrates Discriminate Against Men? *Justice of the Peace* 147(38): 601–03.

Fitzmaurice, C. and Pease, K. (1982) Prison Sentences and Population: A Comparison of Some European Countries. *Justice of the Peace* 146: 575–79.

Giller, H. (1983) Residential Services and Justice. In A. Morris and H. Giller (eds) *Providing Criminal Justice for Children*. London: Edward Arnold.

Goffman, E. (1970) *Asylums*. Harmondsworth: Penguin.

Hawkins, G. (1974) The Ideology of Imprisonment. In L. Blom-Cooper (ed.) *Progress in Penal Reform*. London: Oxford University Press.

Heidensohn, F. (1975) The Imprisonment of Females. In S. McConville (ed.) *The Use of Imprisonment*. London: Routledge and Kegan Paul.

Hermann, H. (1974) A Prisoner's Perspective. In L. Blom-Cooper (ed.) *Progress in Penal Reform*. London: Oxford University Press.

Home Office (1953) *Report of the Committee on Discharged Prisoners' Aid Societies* (the 'Maxwell Report'). London: HMSO.

—————— (1963) *Report of the Advisory Council on the Treatment of Offenders: The Organisation of After-Care*. London: HMSO.

—————— (1979) *Committee of Enquiry into the United Kingdom Prison Services* (the 'May Report'). London: HMSO.

—————— (1980a) *Young Offenders*. London: HMSO.

—————— (1980b) *The Reduction of Pressure on the Prison System*. London: HMSO.

—————— (1983a) *Report on the Work of the Prison Department*. London: HMSO.

—————— (1983b) *Report of HM Inspector of Prisons*. London: HMSO.

—————— (1984a) *Tougher Regimes in Detention Centres*. London: HMSO.

—————— (1984b) *Probation Service in England and Wales: Statement of National Objectives and Priorities*. London: HMSO.

—————— (current edn) *Statutory Rules and Other Information for the Guidance of Prison Officers*. London: Home Office.

97

Home Office Circular 130/1967 (1967) *The Role of the Prison Welfare Officer*. London: HMSO.

House of Commons Home Affairs Committee (1981) *The Prison Service*, vol. I. London: HMSO.

Howard League for Penal Reform (1979) *Losing Touch*. London: Howard League.

JUSTICE (1983) *Justice In Prisons*. London: Justice.

King, R. and Morgan, R. (1982) The Prison System: Prospects for Change. *Howard Journal* 21: 94–104.

King, R., Morgan, R., Martin, J.P., and Thomas, J.E. (1980) *The Future of the Prison System*. Farnborough: Gower.

Lord Windlesham (1984) *Penal Policy and Public Opinion*. BBC Radio 3, 17 December, 1984.

Matthews, J. (1983) *Forgotten Victims – How Prison Affects the Family*. London: National Association for the Care and Resettlement of Offenders.

MIND and NCCL 1985 Report on Holloway Prison. *Guardian* 29 July, 1985.

NAPO (1984) *The Future Provision for the Through-Care Needs of Prisoners*, Consultative Paper PD 1/84. London: National Association of Probation Officers.

Othen, M. (1975) Prison Welfare: Time to Think Again? *Probation Journal* 22(4).

Parker, T. (ed.) (1973) *The Man Inside: An Anthology of Writing and Conversational Comment by Men in Prison*. London: Michael Joseph.

Parliamentary All-Party Penal Affairs Group (1980) *Too Many Prisoners*. Chichester: Barry Rose.

Phelan, B. (1985) *Knockback*. BBC 2, 27 January and 3 February, 1985.

Priestley, P. (1972) The Prison Welfare Officer – A Case of Role Strain. *British Journal of Sociology* 23(2): 224–34.

Priestley, P., McGuire, J., Flegg, D., Hemsley, V., Welham, D., and Barnitt, R. (1984) *Social Skills in Prisons and the Community: Problem-Solving for Offenders*. London: Routledge and Kegan Paul.

Sapsford, R.J. (1978) Life Sentence Prisoners: Psychological Changes During Sentence. *British Journal of Criminology* 18(2): 128–47.

The Times (1984) £23 More For Prison Plans. 17 February.

Thomas, H.A. (1982) The Road to Custody is Paved with Good Intentions. *Probation Journal* 29(3): 93–7.

Thomas, J.E. (1977) The Influence of the Prison Service. In N. Walker and H. Giller (eds) *Penal Policy-Making in England*. Cambridge Institute of Criminology.

Thorpe, D. (1983) De-Institutionalization and Justice. In A. Morris and H. Giller (eds) *Providing Criminal Justice For Children*. London: Edward Arnold.

Walker, H. and Beaumont, B. (1981) *Probation Work: Critical Theory and Practice*. Oxford: Basil Blackwell.

Worrall, A. (1981) Out of Place: Female Offenders in Court. *Probation Journal* 28(3) 90–3.

6 The changing face of probation in the USA

Douglas R. Thomson

For the past half century, probation in the United States of America has recurrently surfaced as a visible topic of popular and public policy interest. A dozen years ago, probation was enshrined by the National Advisory Committee on Criminal Justice Standards and Goals as 'the bright hope for corrections' (NACCJSG 1973: 311). More recently, the determinate sentencing debate, alleged public dissatisfaction with sentencing and correctional practices, and research evidence and policy analysis countering coerced rehabilitation have rekindled interest in probation.

While the import of this contemporary focus on probation should not be exaggerated, especially compared with interests in more sensational criminal justice issues, probation in the USA is the subject of re-examination. This chapter samples that scrutiny, analyzes public policy disputes regarding probation, and estimates its viability in the face of challenges.

Some caveats are in order. First, probation in the USA is not a homogeneous enterprise. There are thousands of departments operating variously under the auspices of federal, state, or local units of government. Some departments deal only with adults, some only with juveniles, some with both. Some units supervise parolees as well as probationers. Further differentia include whether officers are responsible for both pre-sentence investigations and supervision, and whether departments are located in the executive or judicial branch of government. Salary and education levels for entry to the occupation vary widely across units. Some departments consist of one or two part-time officers while others are staffed by hundreds of line officers organized in a multi-level hierarchy, supported by hundreds of clerical workers and specialized units.

Second, little is known in any systematic sense about what actually happens in these departments and in the work-lives of their probation officers. A characteristically low-visibility enterprise, probation has not been the subject of much research, compared to such sibling occupations as police, public welfare, or prison guards, or to such distant wealthy relatives as doctors or lawyers.

Third, whether there even is a national probation enterprise in the USA is an open question. If one exists, it is as a kind of construct more or less defined and shared by a loose-knit confederation of academic researchers and policy analysts and probation entrepreneurs.

There are some organizational vehicles, particularly for practitioners, through which probation is represented at the national level. The American Probation and Parole Association (APPA) has about 3,000 members (of whom about 2,300 are from the USA, with most of the rest from Canada) from the nearly 50,000 administrative, managerial, and operating probation officers at federal, state, and local levels in the USA. The National Association of Probation Executives (NAPE), founded in 1981, seeks to represent the interests of probation administrators. The National Institute of Corrections (NIC), an agency of the federal government, provides some technical assistance, training, and policy development support to probation as well as to parole, community corrections, jails, and prisons.

Two other items of evidence of a national probation enterprise are professional media of communication and a modest body of standards, policy analysis, and reseach directed at probation. The media consist mainly of *Perspectives*, the APPA newsletter, and *Federal Probation Quarterly*, a journal published by the Administrative Office of the United States Courts primarily for federal probation officers, but read by many state and local probation officers (Thomson and Fogel 1981). The knowledge base includes American Bar Association (ABA), NACCJSG, National Conference of Commissioners on Uniform State Laws (NCCUSL), and American Corrections Association (ACA) standards for probation.

While these factors suggest that it is possible to address probation at the national level, and to agree on some general elements constituting probation work, it probably is more difficult to do so here than in England with its centralized service. Hence we shall examine ideological and institutional concerns, but with reference to how these concerns pose survival and domain challenges to probation. These challenges fall into three broad classes of issues – normative, technological and economic, and institutional legitimacy and organizational control – with most discussion focused on the first. The chapter finishes with an assessment of probation's prospects amidst these challenges.

Normative issues

Probation in the USA exists in a normative environment of uncertainty, confusion, and controversy. Prominent landmarks of this environment include criminal sentencing, punishment, rehabilitation, incapacitation, and crime. While these landmarks started to become problematic in public consciousness over a decade ago, probation remained an unnoticed feature of the landscape until the last few years. A brief history of recent American penological ideology should illumine probation's current problematic situation.

From the progressive era of the last part of the nineteenth century through the 1960s, professional commitment to the rehabilitative ideal was virtually unchallenged. This commitment faded rapidly during the 1970s in the face of several assaults. First, there was a normative front which questioned the assumptions of rehabilitation as a pre-eminent goal for criminal sentencing. Critics such as Fogel (1975) and von Hirsch (1976) followed the American Friends Service Committee (AFSC 1971) attack, on ethical and moral grounds, on the indeterminate sentence, sentencing based on perceived offender characteristics, and coerced involvement in rehabilitative programmes. Although their reform proposals varied, these authors generally advocated a return to sentencing based on criminal offence, determinate sentences, and voluntary participation in rehabilitation programmes. Hence, their proposals sometimes are called neoclassical. Soon some of their basic assumptions were appropriated by analysts, such as van den Haag (1975) and Wilson (1975), who wanted to maintain a predictive focus in sentencing, as in the rehabilitative ideal. Their prediction, however, would be based on perceived likelihood of criminal behaviour and called for sentences emphasizing restraint of the offender. These analysts proposed restraint primarily for purposes of deterrence and incapacitation. Hence, this was a substantially different programme than that proposed by the neoclassicists who emphasized punishment based on desert and intended to reaffirm society's normative order. Nevertheless, the two positions soon became confused by the public as well as by many scholars. The more easily understood, publicly appreciated, and viscerally accepted policy goals of the incapacitationists quickly dominated political agenda, and eventually produced many sentencing reforms inconsonant with neo-classical principles and ignored or subverted the more wide-ranging political and economic objectives of some of the neoclassicists, notably the AFSC.

The normative front was greatly augmented by a cumulating and well-publicized empirical front. It presented research evidence questioning the efficacy of correctional rehabilitation programmes. The most telling work was that of Martinson and his colleagues (Lipton, Martinson, and Wilks 1975). The Martinson group had the advantages of timeliness and an aggressive publicity effort. Teasers appeared in popular magazines while the book was in preparation, and Martinson appeared on a television programme ('60 Minutes') with a large national audience. Although the book, which analysed 231 correctional programme evaluations produced from 1945 through 1967, presented a carefully worded conclusion ('With few and isolated exceptions, the rehabilitative efforts that have been reported so far have had no appreciable effort on recidivism' (Lipton, Martinson, and Wilks 1975)), and Martinson subsequently repudiated more extreme renditions of this conclusion (Martinson 1979), it became a reference point for widespread claims that 'nothing works'.

While a subsequent analysis by the National Academy of Sciences of the Martinson and colleagues research pronounced it sound (Sechrest, White, and Brown 1979), there has been a strong countercyclical trend in recent evaluations. These studies find correctional programmes effective when adequately implemented and appropriately directed toward amenable client groups (Ross and Gendreau 1980). Nevertheless, professional and popular support for the rehabilitative ideal waned substantially and appears not to have recovered appreciably. Thus, public opinion polls indicate that identification of rehabilitation as the preferred 'main emphasis in most prisons' declined from 73 per cent of respondents in 1970 to 44 per cent in 1982, although it maintained its position as the most frequently preferred goal (Brown, Flanagan, and McLeod 1984: 261).

The third front in the assault on the rehabilitative ideal has its base in the political economy of the nation. Some American criminologists have applied O'Connor's (1973) analysis of the fiscal crisis of the state to recent criminal justice reforms (Scull 1977; Cullen and Wozniak 1982). In such formulations, these reforms are superstructural adaptations to fundamental economic and political contradictions. Frequently, these critics view the normative and empirical attacks on the rehabilitative ideal as ideological, i.e. justifications for what has been mandated by material circumstances and political responses to them. Allen (1981) reaches a similar conclusion based on a functionalist analysis. He notes that the rehabilitative ideal depends on two cultural conditions: belief in human malleability and availability of material resources.

More prosaically, we observe possible sources of the attack on the rehabilitative ideal in the politics of the control of street crime. As many analysts have noted, the province of the criminal law is primarily the behaviour of individuals, rather than corporate entities, and of working class individuals at that rather than of individuals controlling the means of production (Pashukanis 1978). Thus, some would suggest that the attack on rehabilitation reflects increased class conflict (Reiman and Headlee 1981).

Neo-classicism and probation

We return now to neo-classicism since it has dominated recent discussion in the USA of probation's mission. Neo-classicism is a penological philosophy emphasizing volition, equity, proportionality, and fairness. It assumes offender responsibility in criminal behaviour, yet recognizes that probabilities of criminal choice are affected by life chances. Generally, neo-classicism accommodates the tension inherent in this position by two mechanisms. At the policy level, it differentiates action regarding penal justice from action regarding distributive justice. At the practice level, while demanding punishment it supports ameliorative services but prohibits coercing offenders into receiving them.

Equity means that like criminal harms shall be punished in like degree.* Proportionality means that punishments are gauged to the amount of criminal harm inflicted so that greater harms are punished more severely than lesser harms. Fairness means that punishment inflicted shall not exceed the criminal harm caused. This is the limiting condition stated in the oft misunderstood Biblical injunction about 'an eye for an eye, and a tooth for a tooth'.

Neo-classicism is frequently called by other names such as just deserts, retribution, commensurate deserts, or the justice model. It differs from utilitarian schools of sanctioning such as rehabilitation (or medical model or reintegration), incapacitation (or isolation or surveillance), or deterrence (specific or general). It differs from another moral school with which it is popularly confused, i.e. vengeance, by virtue of the limits neo-classicism imposes on punishment. One can observe this link in the USA by tracking the relationship of the due process and justice model movements, with the latter nudged by the former.

Table 2 depicts distinctions and overlaps among criminal sentencing purposes subsumed under due process guarantees. It identifies five major instruments of achieving sentencing purposes, and relates each to its primary sentencing goals. Each instrument has its own unique set of primary goals, yet shares one or more of them with at least one other instrument. All instruments and goals are construed as directed toward the same ultimate outcome, social defence or community protection. This is coextensive with purposes of criminal law. Whether such purposes serve mainly as a mask for class domination and exploitation is left undefined, since that is an empirical issue,

---

*Note that this 1) allows for differentiation within offence category by harm caused, 2) suggests the desirability of targeting harms caused by delicts other than street crimes, and 3) requires a range of penalties calibrated in terms of onerousness.

Table 2   *Purposes of Criminal Sentencing*

state involvement in client biography	instrument, means, or proximate cause	primary goal, end, effect, or impact	ultimate outcome
low		normative affirmation/ boundary definition	
.	punishment	normative integration	
.	reparation or restitution	moral requital	
.		reform, or embracing of responsibilities, or socially desirable behaviour	
.	social treatment, intervention, service, or assistance	rehabilitation, or development of stake in conformity	social defence, or community protection
.	surveillance	control incapacitation	
.	restraint	specific deterrence, or avoidance of pain or negative consequences	
. high		general deterrence, or general prevention and attitude-formation	

as well as an ideological one.

This renaissance of neo-classicism poses a domain challenge for probation. It long has been defined in terms of the rehabilitative ideal. State-enforced rehabilitation directed to (or at) individual delinquents and criminals has been prominent throughout the history of probation and associated institutions such as juvenile court, parole, training schools, and correctional facilities. We observe the pervasiveness of the concept in the language itself, e.g. in the word 'corrections'.

The issue then is whether probation and neo-classicism are on a collision course. In short, how can, does, or will probation – the epitome of the rehabilitative ideal – fit into a desert-based sanctioning system without losing its historical and normative identity? Some imply, using moral and empirical arguments, that probation should and can cling to its rehabilitative heritage (Empey 1979). Others state that probation should and can shift to a more retributive stance (McAnany, Thomson, and Fogel 1984). This debate has been joined and this chapter will not develop it much further, but presents it as a challenge for probation's future and as an orienting framework for two other major normative challenges confronting probation.

Challenges from the left, challenges from the right

The leftist critique of probation· is largely implicit. Since left criminologists view probation, like the criminal law itself, as so much superstructural smoke, they have not wasted much effort critiquing it. This neglect seems especially appropriate given probation's marginal status even in the perception of those who take the criminal law seriously as a subject for study and an arena for action.

A leftist critique may mean little more than concluding that probation is not worth mentioning. Beyond this, we can infer leftist positions from articles by Marxist and radical criminologists attacking and defending the justice model.

Clarke (1978) recognizes differentiation within the USA justice model movement which he characterizes as the 'radical-left' and 'liberal-right' factions. In either case, he construes the justice model as an ideological response to underlying economic contradictions which allows a 'cutting-loose from the treatment ethic'. Reiman and Headlee (1981) present a similar argument revealing some of the grudging acceptance by Marxists of the marginal utility of a rehabilitative, rather than a justice, approach to corrections. They argue that the fundamental inequities of capitalistic societies render impossible the pursuit of justice within the bounds of extant social relations. While they have no confidence in the rehabilitative ideal as a liberating force, they suggest that its treatment regimes buffer against state power at best, and at worst, do not provide the kind of legitimation for state domination that the 'so-called justice model' does.

Radical criminologists view the justice model more benignly and emphasize instead the dangers of state abuses traditionally imputed to the rehabilitative ideal. While the radicals also recognize the justice model as epiphenomenal, they find inaccuracies in Marxist critiques, e.g. identifying fixed sentencing and the death penalty as necessary constituent elements. Pending more sweeping social transformations, they find it less repressive than indeterminacy and less abusive of discretion than the treatment model is (Humphries 1984). While silent on probation, their position suggests that they might be critical of its lack of standards governing discretion in setting conditions and supervising, and would consider justice model probation as a minor contribution to efforts to reduce repression in the application of criminal law.

But both Marxists and radicals are cognizant of the destructive implementation problems the justice model has encountered. Cullen and Wozniak suggest some of the sources of these difficulties (1982: 24):

'From the left, radicals continued to assert that true criminal justice and real solution to the crime problem await the establishment of true social justice. However accurate this claim, the notion that the penal crisis will be alleviated by mass insurgency against the capitalist order struck some as beyond reach and most as un-American. While on the surface more pragmatic, the liberals' agenda proved to be equally ineffectual and, in the end, more dangerous. As an alternative to state-enforced therapy, the liberals proposed a "justice model". . . .

'However, this model contained two central and corrupting flaws. First, while liberals had traditionally preached about the irrationality and inhumanity of punishment, now they were providing retribution with a fresh legitimacy. Second, the linchpin of the justice model is that prison terms would become less repressive. Yet who might we expect to gain from advocating the parsimonious use of imprisonment? Could it reasonably be anticipated that politicians would proudly announce to their electorate that they were prepared to do justice by getting easy on crime? Similarly, would the average citizen on the street feel more comfortable knowing that offenders would now be winning early release from the penitentiary?'

These flaws point to two major strategic errors. First, justice model proponents virtually ignored probation in their discussions of equitable sentencing and correctional practices. Punishment was equated with incarceration. By default, probation emerged from the debate as leniency, despite some efforts to bring it into a continuum of gradated sanctions, e.g. by recasting it as 'mandatory supervision' (Fogel 1975). Second, they did not present a searching analysis of what underlying fairness in penalty scales meant. Thus, they did not directly confront the issue of public receptivity to various types and quantities of penalties. Perhaps, like Cullen and Wozniak, they assumed a degree of vengeance in the public that cumulating research suggests is overstated (Cullen, Clark, and Wozniak 1984).

As the justice model argument developed, it began to address these deficiencies. In particular, a 1980 NIC grant to Fogel and his colleagues at the University of Illinois at Chicago marked the inclusion of probation in the justice model debate, resulting in a book on the subject (McAnany, Thomson, and Fogel 1984) and stimulating other studies of the law and justice contexts of probation.

Although these sectarian disputes about the justice model may seem remote from probation concerns, they do pose a domain challenge for probation. The challenge comes in the form of an opportunity.

By virtue of its base in community, its history of humanitarianism, and its location as an agency of law, probation is in a unique position to adopt and develop justice model principles. Thus, it seems in some ways well-suited to confront the crime control/risk prediction/selective incapacitation threat by stressing the commonweal advantages of an approach that seeks normative integration via modest but proportionate penalties, or of one that seeks reparation or requital (*Table 3* and accompanying discussion, pages 116–17).

But justice model principles have not been widely embraced by American probation. On the contrary, there has been a virulent reaction by some probation leaders (Helber 1984). Even when justice model principles are given lip service, it is often in the context of a total package that disparately combines moral and utilitarian conceptions of probation.

There are three likely reasons for probation's rejection or corruption of the justice model. First, probation practitioners are pragmatic. They generally have little patience for the jurisprudential fine points of the justice model vs. crime control model vs. medical model dispute. Rather, they seek wise strategic choices to bolster their embattled institution and occupation. Sometimes this means straw man arguments against the justice model. Sometimes this means co-opting it.

Second, probation is insular. Since the justice model has been promulgated primarily by persons external to probation, they cannot appeal effectively to in-group solidarity. That they are not part of the club facilitates derision of their ideas as unrealistic and unworkable.

Third, probation is weak politically. Hence, it cannot take the moral high road or lead a reform movement. Given probation's institutional and occupational weaknesses, it is prudent to be pragmatic. Given the insecurities associated with probation's still nascent professionalization effort, insularity also may be prudent until such time that the occupation can endure external scrutiny and interchange. Insularity regarding deliberations about its future is reasonable in view of the environmental invasion probation organizations suffer as their work is shaped by judges, attorneys, social service agencies, and funding and legislative bodies.

Since justice model proponents have not yet established themselves in positions of moral entrepreneurship (Becker 1972) so that they can be efficacious in seeing their reforms to fruition, why should probation entrust its future to them? Instead, justice model initiatives seem to be following the dismal path worn by earlier criminal justice and other social reform efforts which have yielded regressive effects (Austin 1982). Thus, if the justice model opportunity is to be appropriated successfully by USA probation, it likely will be by some departments whose local circumstances and leadership permit such mystical ministrations. For the rest, the justice model legacy is likely to be one of the strategic gains obtained via co-optation (e.g. adding just deserts as a third layer to the probation cake built with control and assistance layers), or of the enhanced occupational solidarity generated by perceiving a common enemy.

We turn now to the challenge from the right which probation has not used the justice model to counteract. The critique of probation from the right is decidedly more vocal and explicit than that from the left. Significantly, rightist critiques focus on probation itself and tend to avoid any critical scrutiny of the justice model. Instead, the right has appropriated the language of the justice model to further its own utilitarian ends. This tactic and the visibility of rightist critiques are a major source of leftist critiques of the justice model, and of popular – and scholarly – confusion of the justice model with deterrence and with incapacitation approaches to sentencing and penalties. Such confusion is understandable given occasional lack of clarity by proponents about justice model moral goals; retrospective perspective as contrasted to the utilitarian goals and prospective perspective of the crime-control-through-sentencing school; the labyrinthine and convoluted nature of such jurisprudential arguments; and the marked success of the right in co-opting justice model ideology.

Thus, rightist critiques of probation do not require much elaboration. They portray probation as leniency, 'crime's second chance', 'a slap on the wrist', an alternative to sentencing and punishment. Such portrayals feed off rehabilitation justifications for probation.

These negative portrayals follow with proposals emphasizing probation's control functions and capabilities. These include intensive supervision, coerced therapy, case classification based on risk and need assessments, and accountability of probation and probationer. This contrasts with justice approaches which emphasize probation as punishment, which looks backward and attempts to repair harm done rather than controlling future behaviour based on predictions of risk.

There are several cross-cutting issues in all of this:

- prediction vs. description;
- crime control vs. norm affirmation;
- humanitarianism vs. accountability;
- discretion vs. due process;

- fear of crime vs. fear of tyranny;
- punishment defined in terms of incarceration.

The consequences for probation are as follows:

- probation defined as not penal, but recognized as penal;
- this was in the wake of probation being defined as not authentically or effectively rehabilitative;
- thus, between these two attributions, probation was left without a compelling identity;
- probation has now been cast as a penal alternative;
- but this is frequently misunderstood (often by probation practitioners) or misappropriated (by those interested in incapacitation or the chimera of crime control);
- the challenge is to answer whether definitions of penological situation in general can shift to a focus that is retrospective and moral rather than predictive and utilitarian, and if so, to decide whether probation can make the same shift.

This discussion points toward two underlying concerns which cut across the various political philosophies portrayed. These are the issues of professionalism and community. They are central to probation's future.

Professionalization

Probation leadership in the USA long has embraced professionalism as an image for its occupation and professionalization as a strategy for occupational enhancement. While these efforts have not dealt adequately with the conceptual and pragmatic issues of professionalization in bureaucracies (Scott 1969), and follow the tradition of occupations seeking greater power and prestige for themselves, they epitomize probation's desire to be taken seriously – by community groups, communications media, government funding authorities, other human services occupations, and the legal professionals (defence counsel, prosecutors, judges) with whom – and often for whom – probation works.

But recent developments in rethinking probation have made the professionalization effort even more problematic. In particular, some view the justice model as a threat to professionalization. Inasmuch as justice model initiatives seek limitations on probation officer discretion, this suspicion is understandable.

Such fears are not grounded in an appreciation of recent justice model proposals (Thomson and McAnany 1984). These proposals 1) recognize that justice requires human interaction and evaluation, 2) make the probation officer a central actor in pursuing justice via the pre-sentence investigation, and 3) call for constraining discretion via documenting individual sentence rationales and referring to them for precedents to ensure equity and proportionality.

This is not entirely theoretical. In Minnesota, for example, where a desert-based sentencing guidelines system (von Hirsch 1983) has been conscientiously implemented, probation officers are considered the 'guidelines experts' (Minnesota Sentencing Guidelines Commission 1984). In California, one of the effects of determinate sentencing legislation was an increase in the influence probation departments have in the sentencing process, as a result of pre-sentence investigations which are more closely linked to sentencing considerations. These reports changed toward emphasizing information regarding current offence and prior record and de-emphasizing information regarding offender's social and psychological history and circumstances (Lipson and Peterson 1980: 19).

Effects on probation work of justice model reforms will depend on the environment into which they are introduced as well as on the content of the reforms themselves. Introduction of such reforms in juvenile probation in Washington State may have depressed officer morale since the determinate sentencing introduced is perceived as taking power from probation and giving it to the prosecutor, and as an abrupt shift from the work philosophy to which juvenile probation officers are accustomed. Thus justice model proponents suggest that applications in juvenile court will be different from those in criminal court (Thomson and McAnany 1984).

How can justice model proposals limit probation officer discretion while enhancing probation professionalism? The answer lies in an appreciation of the meaning of rules and of trust as used in defining professions. Rules must be distinguished from procedures, and trust from indifference. Justice model rules constraining probation are principles which structure discretion. They are not operational procedures creating clerical specialists. Hence they are comparable to an attorney's rules of practice, not to an assembly-line worker's rigid regimen prescribed by de-skilling regimes (Braverman 1975).

Thus these rules require that some trust be reposed in probation officers. The warrantors of this trust include appropriate professional socialization and collegial supervision. Under a justice model regime, socialization and supervision would be taken seriously because probation officers would be entrusted with matters of significance and visibility: crafting thoughtful sentence recommendations and facilitating sentence compliance.

Yet there is room in the justice model probation family for members of varying size and personality. Thus extravagant expectations apply to those gregarious relatives who invest their energy in extensive mediation efforts, aggressively pursuing justice. They do not apply to the self-contained relatives who conscientiously discharge their duties as officers of the court, conserving state authority while allowing conflicts to devolve to their parties, communities, and the institutions that have spawned them (Christie 1977, 1981).

Probation's base in community

The second major domain challenge that current normative reconsideration raises is probation's community context. Again the issue is larger than probation. Writ large, the issue is the relationship of punishment to social structure, and how the former is legitimated by the latter. Such broad and important topics of enquiry can only be alluded to in the present forum.

In particular, we return to a fundamental sociological distinction raised by Tonnies (1887), that of the difference between community and society. Regarding sanctioning systems, it seems that discipline would be associated with community and punishment with society. Thus the prototype of the legitimacy and efficacy of discipline is primary groups such as family, school, and peer group. As roles become segmented, value systems more heterogeneous, and differential group interests more articulated, discipline is replaced by punishment. Punishment emerges as a more disinterested approach to sanctioning with due process controls limiting the state's authority.

This issue poses a major problem. Probation long has been cast as a community function. This has been a theme from its volunteerist origins through rehabilitation as community reintegration to justice model formulations. Yet the limited focus of punishment (retrospective and proportionate) and its due process boundaries suggest that justice model probation will be seriously constrained as a community function.

There are several ways of dealing with this conundrum. One is suggested by Duffee's (1980) application of community theory to criminal justice reform. Applying community theory to probation, he suggests ways in which it might vary across community types (Duffee 1984b). Thus he identifies the following associations of probation organization with community structure: external probation in the disorganized area, community-placed probation in the fragmented community, community-run probation in the solidary community, and community-based probation in the interdependent community.

In related work, Harlow (1984) concluded that the integrity of justice model probation could be maintained by implementing it only in communities willing to accept it in relatively pure form without much compromise with discordant principles. This community theory work reminds us that punishment, like probation, is not monolithic, and requires definition, elaboration, and interpretation in terms of particular community structures. It is here that probation departments can serve well in articulating penal justice in particular communities.

A second response to the problem posed is to note that justice subsumes punishment, not the reverse. Even though justice model proponents like to note that they are focusing on penal justice rather than distributive or social justice, they also often leave ajar the door for progress toward larger social purposes as incidental benefits (Thomson and McAnany 1984).

One version of this approach allows for utilitarian purposes as long as they are limited by retributive considerations (Morris 1974). This is not simply a matter of taste, however, but is contingent on the particular probation function involved. Thus I have suggested that the broader child welfare mandate of the juvenile court validates transcending strict desert boundaries (Thomson and McAnany 1984). Harlow (1984) has criticized such pluralistic implementation of justice model probation as denying its fundamental principles. But Duffee (1984b) and Nelson, Segal, and Harlow (1984) have stressed the importance of crafting probation's functions and mission to community context. This would seem to permit a range of justice model manifestations within the broader range of probation types, assuming that the purpose of a prescriptive model is to provide guiding principles rather than a confining and inflexible doctrine. Community theorists cannot have it both ways.

The final response to the community nexus problem is suggested by my colleague, Patrick McAnany, who has often noted the affinity of desert and rehabilitation. Kidder's (1975) discussion of the moral requital function of punishment is perhaps the most widely known rendition of this link. This position affirms that the offender's payment of debt earns readmission with full rights and responsibilities to the community which has punished the person, and that in the process a positive construction of moral character is reaffirmed. Thus, inasmuch as there is any rehabilitation, it is moral, not psychological or physical. It is voluntary and a latent function of the sentence, not its purpose. But the key point is that moral requital requires a community to do the requiting and readmission. It may be worth examining what role given probation departments can play in this process. Some probation departments in the USA seem to be redefining their functions in justice model terms, or at least incorporating the justice model as a newly visible mythic element (Dinsmore 1983). Such developments should be monitored in terms of the impetus for such change (e.g. responsiveness to fiscal crisis, conformity with sentencing reforms such as determinate sentencing or sentencing guidelines, or increased attention from various community interest groups), and in terms of the consequences that differential community linkages have for individual and collective functions of punishment.

Probation mission alternatives to the justice model

This is but one way of posing the normative challenge to probation. But determinate sentencing is currently under attack as research cumulates and the positive functions of discretion are reaffirmed (Goodstein, Kramer, and Nuss 1984). Hence it is conceivable that this challenge will fade.

While under ordinary circumstances, a preoccupation with defining appropriate mission would be unnecessary or overly scholastic (Scott 1981), probation's current crisis suggests that it is worthwhile. There are several alternatives for probation's mission competing with the justice model.

First, there is the reaffirmation of rehabilitation. But can paradise be regained? Is humanitarianism enough? Can it masquerade as pragmatism under the searchlights of research and public accountability? What about humanitarianism and the victims' rights movement? What about social justice?

Second, there is probation as control. Intensive probation supervision is the exemplar. It reminds us that service provisions are used to control. Yet one can integrate a control approach within a just deserts framework (Morris 1974), although the practical difficulties of doing so are enormous. Probation as control is politically attractive to conservatives (crack down on criminals by making probation tougher and more effective) and liberals (keep a lid on prison populations by making probation tougher and more effective). But it poses the dangers of net widening and excessive expansion of state control. It poses other questions too: Can it achieve its promise? Does probation as control overpromise? Does it heighten control versus assistance tensions?

Third, there is the 'balanced service' approach long favoured by probation practitioners (Harlow and Nelson 1982), but criticized by an array of analysts who want purposes ranked. The chief advantages of this approach, in that it seeks to integrate law enforcement and rehabilitation functions, are that it allows for flexibility in planning, managing, and practising probation, and it appeals to diverse constituencies. It also suggests the desirability of research that would examine the realities of probation in terms of behavioural impacts as perceived by probationers (Duffee 1984a). A major disadvantage is that it understates the law context of probation and how changes in corrections law demand a fundamental transformation of probation's identity (Cohen and Gobert 1983, McAnany 1984). It also is subject to the problems of its constituent elements as presented in the preceding two paragraphs. Related to the first flaw, balanced service has conventionally been a two-dimensional affair, featuring false dichotomies of public safety versus offender service, crime control versus social services, and cops versus social workers. Thus balanced service has tended to ignore justice and has therefore been incomplete, although this seems to be changing as retrospectivity and moral concerns have become subjects of polite public discourse. Hence balanced service some day may mean probation's navigating its way among public safety, offender service, and justice interests, among crime control, social services, and moral requital efforts, and among cop, social worker, and officer of court occupational identities. There is some evidence that this is the kind of balance that probationers perceive (Allen 1984).

Fourth, there is probation as local community option (Duffee 1984b). This is in large measure what we have today, although its proponents would make the definition of mission more self-conscious and visible (Nelson, Segal, and Harlow 1984), and tailor it more conscientiously to departmental and community circumstances. This approach is attractive in terms of its pluralistic appeal, its focus on community empowerment and probation as stakeholder, and its feasibility. But it begs the question. Granted that American probation's mission cannot be defined at a national level, any more than law enforcement's mission could be (Wilson 1968), it will be defined in one way or another in thousands of departments across the nation. Discussion at the national level can help define the options for local consideration, and propose guidelines for choosing a mission. Absent such discussion, probation's mission at the local level will likely be what is most convenient for fitting into that jurisdiction's prevailing criminal justice operations and accommodating the personnel, technology, and training provisions already in place in or desired by its probation department.

Fifth, there is probation abolition (Parnas 1976). Recent research (Petersilia *et al.* 1985; Haynes and Larsen 1984), uninformed media interest, and prison industry privatization interests make this a greater possibility than it perhaps has ever been. Yet probation is entrenched and is showing some strength as a profession. Media interest tends to fade, the alternatives to probation are unproven, expensive, or pose serious questions regarding civil liberties, and the research is subject to challenge. For example, the study by Petersilia *et al.* concerns California counties which have been hard hit in their probation departments by the real estate tax recession initiatives of recent years, resulting in probation caseloads as high as 300 probationers per officer. Moreover, the study focused on recidivism as its outcome measure, turning the assessment of probation into a technical and utilitarian matter while virtually ignoring political and moral considerations.

The Haynes and Larsen study makes assumptions about the relationship between arrest rates and criminal behaviour which may be as good as anyone else's assumptions, but are no more compelling. It is perhaps more important that the cost comparisons are based on existing programmes and hence do not incorporate the costs of new construction.

From this review of the normative challenges to probation's future, we are left with two conclusions to temper any forecasting: 1) probation belongs to the public as well as to the profession, and 2) probation is a community function. Thus, probation's mission will be defined by the extent and type of public involvement and the degree to which probation punishment and other functions are validated by its community. The mission and function questions posed to the profession and the public are suggested by *Table 3* which represents change considerations in terms of probation's history and its contemporary sentencing context. The issues for communities are whether their probation organization should and can remain rehabilitative (cell a), and if not, whether it should move in the direction of just deserts, either holistically (cell b) or in a narrower due process sense (cell d), or in the direction of crime control (cell c). The issue at the national level is how probation as an institution will move. Analytically, we will want to know how stability or mobility affect probationers, communities, probation practice, organizations, the profession, and the institution.

Probation in light of crime as American mythology

To understand ambivalence about probation, we should recognize the extent to which crime and its control function as a myth in the USA (Quinney 1984). Crime taps into general feelings of malaise and distrust of governmental and other societal institutions, romanticism about an imagined past, a frontier sense of justice, fears associated

Table 3
Varieties of probation mission in context of sentencing goals and probation practice

	purpose of sentencing	
focus of probation	*utilitarian* *(crime control)*	*moral* *(justice administration)*
resocialization	(cell a) rehabilitation	(cell b) requital
penalties	(cell c) surveillance	(cell d) reparation

with race and ethnicity, class, and immigration and new worlds, a longing for empowerment, and a quest for community. Crime as myth tells more about our collective experience and identity, about our hopes and fears, and our capacities for hatred and for love than it does about the social policies we would fashion given the opportunity.

Hence, a recent study (Thomson and Ragona 1984) illustrates that presenting crime policy issues in the context of information about criminal cases and sentencing options reveals a temperate American public. In fact, the public emerges as less vengeful and more receptive to probation than political élites appear to realize as evidenced by their legislation. Such evidence suggests that probation can not only survive, but define and maintain its domain with integrity.

Technological and economic issues

While much discussion of recent years has focused on normative arguments regarding probation in the USA, its survival is also challenged by technological and economic issues. The challenges of technique appear in forms such as family therapy, behavioural contracting, and caseload classification and management systems. The larger phenomenon they represent is the rationalization of probation work. This involves greater bureaucratization of probation even as it augments claims to professionalization of probation. What suffers is the linking of probation with community. This threatens probation since it requires either legitimation by its community context or neglect and de facto permission to function as a low visibility, low impact enterprise. Rationalization, however, severs community linkages and threatens to make probation effectual. This creates a worst of both worlds situation, of the type that the worst of the rightist critiques proposes. This rationalization of probation work has been augmented by the fiscal crisis of the last few years, including social

117

service cutbacks associated with the current upturn in the business cycle.

Like many other encroaching phenomena in the USA, recent fiscal threats to, and responses by, probation originated in the state of California. A strong state correctional association and the interests of a public administration research centre at the University of Southern California, with funding from the National Institute of Corrections, produced several sophisticated analyses of the crisis and how probation could respond (Fitzharris 1979, 1981; Harlow and Nelson 1982). These reports proposed strategies for cutback management, constituency building (nurturing networks of support), stakeholder (those with interests in the organization) identification, and probation marketing that challenged probation aggressively to confront the economic crisis. The legacy of these efforts seems to be a probation enterprise in California with a capacity for efficacious political action rarely encountered in probation in the USA.

Despite these efforts, probation has been devastated. While criminal justice expenditures in California increased by 30 per cent (in constant dollars) from 1975 to 1983, probation expenditures declined by over 10 per cent. Yet during this period, probation's caseload increased from 211,103 to 243,791 yielding decreases in per probationer expenditures of nearly 25 per cent (from $2,060 to $1,600 in 1982 dollars) (Petersilia *et al.* 1985). Even more striking has been the 29 per cent decrease in the number of probation agency employees.

This economic crisis in California was precipitated by an initiative which drastically reduced property taxes, a major source of county probation funding. There was much concern that tax revolt would spread across the nation, and that probation departments and other public agencies soon would have to make the difficult choices confronting their counterparts in the West. For a time, there was some evidence of similar movements elsewhere but the threat has receded. The recent economic upturn in the USA may explain part of this. But the sweeping social service cuts by the Reagan Administration had already overwhelmed the tax revolt landscape and shifted attention for the moment to cuts in federal, rather than state and local, agencies.

Hence, probation has been spared – for now. However, it is reasonable to expect that probation will again be confronted by significant survival and domain challenges as the result of economic forces. If the California experience is replicated nationwide, probation will have difficulty holding its own compared with other criminal justice and other public agencies. In fact, Fitzharris (1981) found that this was happening in other states during their budget cutbacks. These prospective developments suggest the potential strategic value of probation's pre-emptive turn to intensive probation supervision, caseload classification, and other programmes of rationalization, and public safety emphasis. The fascinating questions the answers to which we will not know for some years are these: Are these efforts enough? Are they self-destructive? What other domain shifts will probation undertake to ensure survival? Do justice principles provide a viable alternative route to survival?

Institutional legitimacy and organizational control issues

Our discussion to this point implies a substantial degree of public interest in probation. This assumption is problematic. We turn now to fundamental questions of legitimacy and control. Who care about probation in the USA? Who controls and will control it? Who are the stakeholders? What are the prospects for reform?

Few care. Those who do tend to be either practitioners and fellow-travelling academics or those who seem intent on trashing the enterprise as we know it. There is little in between that is not inert. Probation's survival and form will depend on which of these two forces is dominant over the long run. A critical strategic matter here may be which of the two is more successful in energizing and mobilizing the middle.

More concretely, we can say that probation in the USA tends to be controlled by actors in local environments. Typically, these are the legal professionals of the courthouse – judges and prosecutors mostly, but also defence counsel. Law enforcement, jails, and social service agencies operate more on the periphery of local influence as do some cities' civic groups whose impact is episodic and felt at the institutional rather than the managerial or operational levels (Scott 1981). In some jurisdictions, state probation or corrections departments are influential stakeholders in probation. Moreover, there is a trend toward centralization as state subsidies and definitions of probation increase and state funding supplants local funding.

American probation's relationship with its environment is dualistic. Probation controls the details of work functions once they have been defined. But there is an absence of internal control over the larger issues of legitimating myths, division of labour, and rationalization of work.

Some probation officers fear that emphasis in recent years on community resource management and brokerage may harbour disastrous consequences for probation. They suggest that continuing delegation by probation of its responsibilities to other agencies will leave probation departments vulnerable to attack as agencies which do too little and can readily be eliminated. Such predictions may underestimate probation's core significance as a legal institution in which is reposed authority of the judicial branch of government. Despite the current rush to privatization in the USA, it remains a fundamental principle of democracy that governments cannot delegate their legitimation to private entities. Basic constitutional limits apply to the state's delegation of its coercive authority. Attempts to sever the link between court-imposed sanctions and their execution appear politically untenable, apart from any consideration of countervailing powers such as judicial interests, the claims of probation as an occupation, political patronage, and the logistical need for someone to do the court's 'dirty work' (Hagan, Hewitt, and Alwin 1979) of ensuring that punishment is administered.

Prospects for survival

What can we conclude about American probation's future? Will it survive? Will it flourish?

The prospects appear good. Culturally, probation is quintessentially American. It is pragmatic, optimistic, easy, and cheap. It allows observers to be optimistic or cynical. It invites tinkering, and it does not fight back. Probation is both low profile and capable of adapting to and incorporating new institutionalized myths (Meyer and Rowan 1977) while maintaining substantial control over daily activities, at least once crises pass and reforms are made routine. Restitution, intensive supervision, and caseload management are contemporary programmatic examples of this adaptive capacity.

In addition, the prevailing political economy of the American criminal justice sector requires probation or a functional equivalent. There is no likely functional equivalent on the horizon. Perhaps some deep-rooted sense of the interactional requirements of justice has prevented a system of fines from replacing probation. Or perhaps pragmatic considerations of the difficulties of collection and the desirability of supervision and threat control provided by probation have carried the day. In any event, the numbers of American probation officers, advances in unionization, the sensitizing effect of recent fiscal cutbacks, growth of professional associations, cultural legitimacy, and increased governmental entrenchment via state centralization suggest that probation in the USA will continue at least to survive.

But a major threat to prosperity, if not to survival, may be the allure of overreaching, of promising too much. The clearest recent evidence of this possibility is intensive supervision. But other institutions and organizations survive and flourish despite a lack of substantive achievement on output criteria, or even in the absence of output criteria (Meyer and Scott 1983). In this regard, the greatest threat to American probation may be its willingness to embrace inappropriate outcome criteria such as recidivism. But there is evidence that recent threats to probation have made its managers more astute and sophisticated (Harlow and Nelson 1982). Thus a group that has always been pragmatic with regard to internal operations is now perhaps more realistic, shrewd, and efficacious in how it presents its activities and capabilities to external constituencies.

As long as courtroom work groups require a means of sanctioning and controlling offenders without incarcerating them, there will be a place for probation. As long as prisons and jails are full, probation will not be closely scrutinized or held uncomfortably accountable. Finally, probation will not experience transforming reform until the criminal justice sector of which it is a part does, and that is unlikely to occur until long-term demographic shifts reduce prison populations or unforeseen political and economic changes provide new legitimating myths.

© *1987 Douglas R. Thomson*

Note: I appreciate the contributions of Patrick D. McAnany and David Fogel in assessing a draft of this chapter.

References

Allen, F.A. (1981) *The Decline of the Rehabilitative Ideal: Penal Policy and Social Purpose*. New Haven, Conn.: Yale University Press.

Allen, G.F. (1984) *Correctional Directions in Federal Probation: Analysis of the Probationers' Experiences and Attitudes*. Ann Arbor, Mich.: University Microfilms.

American Friends Service Committee (1971) *Struggle for Justice*. New York: Hill and Wang.

Austin, J. (1982) The Unmet Promise of Alternatives to Incarceration. *Crime and Delinquency* 28(3): 374–409.

Becker, H.S. (1972) *Outsiders*. 2nd edn. New York: Macmillan.

Braverman, H. (1975) *Labor and Monopoly Capital*. New York: Monthly Review.

Brown, E.J., Flanagan, T.J., and McLeod, M. (eds) (1984) *Sourcebook of Criminal Justice Statistics, 1983*. US Department of Justice, Bureau of Justice Statistics. Washington, DC: US Government Printing Office.

Christie, N. (1977) Conflicts as Property. *British Journal of Criminology* 17: 1–19.

——— (1981) *Limits to Pain*. Oslo: Universitetsforlaget.

Clarke, D. (1978) Marxism, Justice, and the Justice Model. *Contemporary Crises* 2 (January): 27–62.

Cohen, P. and Gobert, J.J. (1983) *The Law of Probation and Parole*. Colorado Springs, CO: Shephard's/McGraw-Hill.

Cullen, F. and Wozniak, J. (1982) Fighting the Appeal of Repression. *Crime and Social Justice* 18: 23–33.

Cullen, F.T., Clark, G.A., and Wozniak, J.F. (1984) *Explaining the Get Tough Movement: Can the Public be Blamed?* Unpublished paper.

Dinsmore, J. (ed.) (1983) *Change: A Juvenile Justice Quarterly*. V(4).

Duffee, D.E. (1980) *Explaining Criminal Justice: Community Theory and Criminal Justice Reform*. Cambridge, Mass.: Oelgeschlager, Gunn, and Hain.

——— (1984a) Client Biography and Probation Organization. Chapter 10 in P.D. McAnany, D. Thomson, and D. Fogel (eds) *Probation and Justice: Reconsideration of Mission*. Cambridge, Mass.: Oelgeschlager, Gunn, and Hain.

——— (1984b) The Community Context of Probation. Chapter 12 in P.D. McAnany, D. Thomson, and D. Fogel (eds) *Probation and Justice: Reconsideration of Mission*. Cambridge, Mass.: Oelgeschlager, Gunn, and Hain.

——— (1984c) Models of Probation Supervision. Chapter 6 in P.D. McAnany, D. Thomson, and D. Fogel (eds) *Probation and Justice: Reconsideration of Mission*. Cambridge, Mass.: Oelgeschlager, Gunn, and Hain.

Empey, L.T. (1979) From Optimism to Despair: New Doctrines in Juvenile Justice. Foreword to C.A. Murray and L.A. Cox, Jr *Beyond Probation: Juvenile Corrections and the Chronic Delinquent*. Beverly Hills, Calif.: Sage.

Fitzharris, T.L. (1979) *Probation in an Era of Diminishing Resources*. Sacramento, Calif.: Foundation for Continuing Education in Corrections.

——— (1981) *Economic Strategies in Probation: A Handbook for Managers*. Sacramento, Calif.: California Probation, Parole, and Correctional Association.

Fogel, D. (1975) '. . . We Are the Living Proof . . .' *The Justice Model for Corrections*. Cincinnati, Ohio: Anderson.

——— (1984) The Emergence of Probation as a Profession in the Service of Public Safety: The Next Ten Years. Chapter 3 in P.D. McAnany, D. Thomson, and D. Fogel (eds) *Probation and Justice: Reconsideration of Mission*. Cambridge, Mass.: Oelgeschlager, Gunn, and Hain.

Goodstein, L., Kramer, J.H., and Nuss, L. (1984) Defining Determinacy: Components of the Sentencing Process Ensuring Equity and Release Certainty. *Justice Quarterly* 1(1): 47–73.

Greenberg, D.F. and Humphries, D. (1982) Economic Crisis and the Justice Model: A Skeptical View. *Crime and Delinquency* 28(4): 601–09.

Hagan, J., Hewitt, J.D., and Alwin, D.F. (1979) Ceremonial Justice – Crime and Punishment in a Loosely Coupled System. *Social Forces* 58: 506–27.

Harlow, N. (1984) Implementing a Justice Model in Probation. Chapter 13 in P.D. McAnany, D. Thomson, and D. Fogel (eds) *Probation and Justice: Reconsideration of Mission*. Cambridge, Mass.: Oelgeschlager, Gunn, and Hain.

Harlow, N. and Nelson, E.K. (1982) *Management Strategies for Probation in an Era of Limits*. Berkeley, Calif.: Bay Area Research Center, School of Public Administration, University of Southern California.

Harris, M.K. (1984) Rethinking Probation in the Context of the Justice Model. Chapter 1 in P.D. McAnany, D. Thomson, and D. Fogel (eds) *Probation and Justice: Reconsideration of Mission*. Cambridge, Mass.: Oelgeschlager, Gunn, and Hain.

Haynes, P. and Larsen, C.R. (1984) Financial Consequences of Incarceration and Alternatives: Burglary. *Crime and Delinquency* 30(4): 529–50.

Helber, N.L. (1984) President's Message on Administering Justice, Raising Children and Other Problems with Simplistic Solutions. *Perspectives* 8(4): 3.

Humphries, D. (1984) Reconsidering the Justice Model. *Contemporary Crises* 8: 167–73.

Kidder, J. (1975) Requital and Criminal Justice. *International Philosophical Quarterly* 15: 255–78.

Lipson, A.J. and Peterson, M.A. (1980) *California Justice Under Determinate Sentencing: A Review and Agenda for Research*. Santa Monica, Calif.: Rand.

Lipton, D., Martinson, R., and Wilks, J. (1975) *The Effectiveness of Correctional Treatment: A Survey of Treatment Evaluation Studies*. New York: Praeger.

McAnany, P.D. (1984) Mission and Justice: Clarifying Probation's Legal Context. Chapter 2 in P.D. McAnany, D. Thomson, and D. Fogel (eds) *Probation and Justice: Reconsideration of Mission*. Cambridge, Mass.: Oelgeschlager, Gunn, and Hain.

McAnany, P.D. and Thomson, D. (1984) *Equity and Effectiveness in*

Responding to Probation Violations: A Guide for Managers. Boulder, Colo.: National Academy of Corrections.

McAnany, P.D., Thomson, D., and Fogel, D. (eds) (1984) *Probation and Justice: Reconsideration of Mission.* Cambridge, Mass.: Oelgeschlager, Gunn, and Hain.

Martinson, R. (1979) New Findings, New Views: A Note of Caution Regarding Sentencing Reform. *Hofstra Law Review* 7: 244–52.

Meyer, J.W. and Rowan, B. (1977) Institutionalized Organizations: Formal Structure as Myth and Ceremony. *American Journal of Sociology* 83: 340–63.

Meyer, J.W. and Scott, W.R. (1983) *Organizational Environments: Ritual and Rationality.* Beverly Hills, Calif.: Sage.

Minnesota Sentencing Guidelines Commission (1984) *The Impact of the Minnesota Sentencing Guidelines: Three Year Evaluation.* St Paul, Minn.: Minnesota Sentencing Guidelines Commission.

Morris, N. (1974) *The Future of Imprisonment.* Chicago, Ill.: University of Chicago.

National Advisory Committee on Criminal Justice Standards and Goals (NACCJSG) (1973) *Report on Corrections.* Washington, DC: US Government Printing Office.

Nelson, E.K., Ohmart, H., and Harlow, N. (1978) *Promising Strategies in Probation and Parole.* Washington, DC: US Department of Justice.

Nelson, E.K., Segal, L., and Harlow, N. (1984) *Probation Under Fiscal Constraints.* Washington, DC: National Institute of Justice/NCJRS.

O'Connor, J.F. (1973) *The Fiscal Crisis of the State.* New York: St Martin's.

Parnas, R. (1976) Legislation to Abolish Probation. *California Correctional News* 30(4).

Pashukanis, E. (1978) *Law and Marxism: A General Theory.* London: Ink Links.

Petersilia, J., Turner, S., Kahan, J., and Peterson, J. (1985) *Granting Felons Probation: Public Risks and Alternatives.* Santa Monica, Calif.: Rand.

Quinney, R. (1984) Myth and the Art of Criminology. Acceptance Speech for Edwin H. Sutherland Award, American Society of Criminology, 36th Annual Meeting, Cincinatti, Ohio.

Reiman, J.H. and Headlee, S. (1981) Marxism and Criminal Justice Policy. *Crime and Delinquency* 27(1): 24–47.

Ross, R.R. and Gendreau, P. (1980) *Effective Correctional Treatment.* Toronto: Butterworths.

Scott, W.R. (1969) Professional Employees in a Bureaucratic Structure. In A. Etzioni (ed.) *The Semi-Professions and Their Organization: Teachers, Nurses, Social Workers*: 115–23. New York: Free Press.

———— (1981) *Organizations: Rational, Natural, and Open Systems*. Englewood Cliffs, NJ: Prentice-Hall.

Scull, A. (1977) *Decarceration: Community Treatment and the Deviant – A Radical View*. Englewood Cliffs, NJ: Prentice-Hall.

Sechrest, L., White, S.O., and Brown, E.D. (eds) (1979) *The Rehabilitation of Criminal Offenders: Problems and Prospects*. Washington, DC: National Academy of Sciences.

Thomson, D. (1982) *The Social Organization of Enforcement Behaviors in Probation Work*. Ann Arbor, Mich.: University Microfilms.

———— (1984) Prospects for Justice Model Probation. Chapter 4 in P.D. McAnany, D. Thomson, and D. Fogel (eds) *Probation and Justice: Reconsideration of Mission*. Cambridge, Mass.: Oelgeschlager, Gunn, and Hain.

Thomson, D. and Fogel, D. (1981) *Probation Work in Small Agencies: A National Study of Training Provisions and Needs*. Chicago: Centre for Research in Law and Justice, University of Illinois at Chicago.

Thomson, D. and McAnany, P.D. (1984) Punishment and Responsibility in Juvenile Court: Desert-based Probation for Delinquents. Chapter 5 in P.D. McAnany, D. Thomson, and D. Fogel (eds) *Probation and Justice: Reconsideration of Mission*. Cambridge, Mass.: Oelgeschlager, Gunn, and Hain.

Thomson, D. and Ragona, A.J. (1984) Fiscal Crisis, Punitive Content, and Public Perceptions of Criminal Sanctions. Paper presented at Annual Meeting of Academy of Criminal Justice Sciences, Chicago.

Tonnies, F. (1964) *Community and Society (Gemeinschaft und Gellschaft 1887)*. East Lansing, Mich.: Michigan State University Press.

van den Haag, E. (1975) *Punishing Criminals: On an Old and Painful Question*. New York: Basic Books.

von Hirsch, A. (1976) *Doing Justice: the Choice of Punishments*. New York: Hill and Wang.

———— (1983) Commensurability and Crime Prevention: Evaluating Formal Sentencing Structures and Their Rationale. *Journal of Criminal Law and Criminology* 74(1): 209–48.

Wilson, J.Q. (1968) *Varieties of Police Behavior: The Management of Law and Order in Eight Communities*. Cambridge, MA: Harvard University Press.

———— (1975) *Thinking about Crime*. New York: Basic Books.

Wright, K.N. (ed.) (1981) *Crime and Criminal Justice in a Declining Economy*. Cambridge, Mass.: Oelgeschlager, Gunn, and Hain.

PART II

Issue and community-based practice

In the opening Chapter 7 David Walton discusses the accommodation, employment, and educational needs of offenders against a backdrop of the continuing recession and poorer social conditions for the most disadvantaged. The identified issues are closely interrelated but do call for separate strategies by the Probation Service. Walton looks at the link between homelessness and offending and outlines specific initiatives by the Service in both the voluntary and statutory sector. He warns, however, that the efforts of staff in special projects are necessarily limited and ameliorative and need to be fused with broader strategies in housing. In noting that most offenders are unemployed Walton asks whether probation officers should help them find work or cope with unemployment, particularly where the job market is exhausted. As with homelessness, he finds links between unemployment and crime and gives examples of probation controlled initiatives as well as the government sponsored job creation schemes. Lastly, Walton examines the basic educational needs of offenders – to cope with low levels of literacy and numeracy, lack of qualifications and practical skills. Responses to the problem are illustrated from the prison setting, probation centres, and the work of voluntary organizations like NACRO. The search for basic provision in the form of housing, employment, and education offers a way out of offending but should, Walton reminds us, also take into account individual choices if personal dignity is to be retained.

In Chapter 8 Robert Purser, a director of an alcohol advisory service and a former probation officer, describes the links between mood altering substances and offending. First, he plots the growth of alcohol related offences in a society where alcohol consumption has risen rapidly. He notes the high levels of alcoholism related to a handful of studies on prisoners, people on probation, and youth crime. Following the move away from a disease model of thinking, Purser outlines the progress that has been made by probation officers in setting up alcohol education groups that help clients to re-learn drinking behaviour. He discusses a range of programmes for drinkers with multiple and serious problems, as well as for the impaired driver. He develops a strong advocacy for an alcohol strategy in which management invests time and money in training, support services, and links with other agencies. The same lessons apply to drug taking. Purser briefly sketches its relationship to offending within a context of high youth unemployment and an increased supply of drugs.

Richard Green in Chapter 9 draws on his direct experience of working in a multi-racial area of Birmingham and his own research study. Green argues that traditional probation approaches to black people in trouble have identified them as a problem rather than understood the problems of black people. Part of this misunderstanding lies in the ideology and practice of the Service, the drive to integration rather than to social justice, poor training especially in the area of racial awareness, and a colour-blind approach which fails to recognize that white and black offenders may require different responses. Green calls for a new response which acknowledges that racial disadvantage is a major factor in black crime. He cites two project examples from Birmingham which are specifically addressed to the cultural and social needs of blacks who are at risk in terms of their encounters with the criminal justice process. He ends by suggesting that even though the programmes on offer are relevant to the needs of blacks they throw up further dilemmas, which as yet remain unresolved.

In Chapter 10, John Harding follows up and develops in more detail the theme of reparative justice already referred to in Part I, Chapter 6 by Douglas R. Thomson. He briefly traces the history of reparation and looks to reasons for its revival over the past twenty years. The movement is inseparably linked to a better understanding of victimization levels in society, the need for supportive action both practical and legislative, coupled with the search for accountable measures that hold offenders in the community rather than in prison. Harding discusses the principles of reparation and the assumed benefits and pitfalls for the offender, the victim, the public, and criminal justice personnel. He illustrates practice from a range of examples both in the United Kingdom and the USA, giving particular emphasis to mediation, where victim and offender are drawn together in the presence of a third party to resolve conflicts and reach an agreement. Lastly, Harding looks at the future potential of reparation for probation and criminal justice and the switch it represents from principles of retribution to conciliation and restoration.

Rule 37 of the Probation Rules 1984 empowers probation officers to take part in crime prevention projects. Successful responses to crime in communities relies heavily on agencies working together. Vivien Stern in Chapter 11 describes the importance of the inter-organizational approach based on a number of demonstration programmes set up by NACRO over the past five years. Ms Stern begins by outlining the limitations of the criminal justice system in combating the consequences of crime, noting in particular that despite the rapid rise in law and order expenditure, recorded crime levels continue to rise and detection rates to fall. She records the change in focus to crime prevention, and the need for co-ordinated strategies that link agencies with residents on estates who suffer the heaviest impact of crime – vandalism, petty theft, and loss of morale. Examples are drawn from NACRO's work on fifty-eight estates in England and Wales, with key emphasis given to the involvement and participation of residents. The second illustration concerns NACRO's juvenile crime consultancy groups in ten areas. There, the focus is on information gathering, understanding the impact of crime, and the responsibility of the agencies to provide facilities that contain and reduce crime. Ms Stern concludes with a discussion on the issues arising from the inter-agency approach, both the advantages and the pitfalls, and challenges agencies, such as probation, to understand the social impact of crime by making closer links with those who are most exposed to its effects.

In the concluding Chapter 12 John Hill argues that with a shift in focus from the treatment of the individual offender to a concern for the social basis of crime, a number of practices have evolved often with no common rationale or test of measurement as far as effectiveness is concerned. He identified two major strands in community-based work, one related to crime reduction and the other involving individuals from the community after a crime has been committed – the victim, the offender, and local mediators. Hill takes a critical look at these two areas and concludes that much of crime reduction work by the Probation Service is concerned with improving the quality of life for offenders, which in itself can be a stabilizing factor in preventing a return to crime. He suggests that there are a number of possibilities arising out of community involvement in the consequences of crime, not least the reduction of conflict between parties in dispute. Evaluation here is focused on qualitative factors such as attitudes, opinions, and feelings of the participants. Finally, Hill stresses the need for the Service to be clear about its objectives when embarking on community-based work so that the task of evaluation is quite explicit.

7 The residential, employment, and educational needs of offenders

David Walton

Introduction

In recent years, the traditional 'one to one' casework approach to clients' needs has been subjected to increased scrutiny and become the object of some scepticism. While still acknowledging the need for individualized casework with many offenders, the Probation Service has also had to develop an understanding of the collective needs of its clients and changes in demands which have consequently been placed upon it. The Probation Service has therefore looked for tangible areas of action which can be part of a more comprehensive strategy of intervention towards providing for some of offenders' most urgent and basic needs such as accommodation, employment, and education.

To some extent this change can be attributed to trends in social work theory and training, and the expectation that the Probation Service should provide a range of credible 'alternative to custody' facilities and programmes which are relevant to the needs of both offenders and courts. However, the most pressing reasons for change have stemmed from the deterioration of economic and social conditions in the late 1970s and the 1980s, and the consequent need to offer tangible responses which seek to ameliorate some of the harsher effects of the recession on the lives of many offenders.

For example, increasing awareness of the disadvantaged position of low-income single people in the housing market, worsened by cutbacks in housing investment, has heightened the Probation Service's awareness of the need to penetrate housing systems and to promote the development of various forms of provision which are appropriate to the needs of single homeless offenders. Similarly the effects of the recession on the extent of unemployment experienced by offenders has necessitated the involvement of some probation areas in employment-creation programmes of the type promoted by Manpower Services Commission (MSC). In the educational sphere there has been involvement in activities ranging from schemes with vocational training aspirations, to those which acknowledge the likelihood of continuing unemployment and hence seek to enhance clients' abilities to cope with low income and enforced leisure time.

A brief scan of the 'Index of Probation Projects' for 1982–83 provides a crude but quantifiable picture of the scale and diversity of Probation Service activity in these areas of need. A figure of approximately 640 projects is revealed, although this is probably a considerable underestimate of the actual position. Numerically the most significant areas of project activity are residential schemes; approximately 400 projects provide 6,000 bed places for offenders. The remaining 240 projects cover a wide spread of schemes catering for employment and educational needs in the widest sense, such as education schemes, day centres, employment projects, literacy and numeracy schemes, motor projects, social skills groups, sports and leisure groups. On the face of it, this list arguably constitutes an impressive testimony to the enterprise of the Probation Service in its attempts to develop and exploit new or different methods of working with offenders. Viewed from a wider perspective it can be seen as only scratching the surface of the needs and problems of offenders in the 1980s, representing an average merely of about twelve such projects to each probation area in England and Wales. However, it must also be acknowledged that the number of probation managed or promoted 'projects' is not the sole measure of the Service's response; of at least equal importance is the extent to which other resources in the mainstream of society, such as housing, vocational training, adult education, are made accessible to offenders by the Service. The interplay, and often tensions, between strategies which emphasize an offender-specific and project-based approach as opposed to a more generalistic approach embracing mainstream provisions, will be seen to be a frequent theme of this chapter.

Whatever the arguments and counter-arguments relating to this particular debate, action against accommodation, employment, and education problems on the part of the Probation Service must be seen as legitimate and relevant in the context of current government-defined objectives and priorities for the Service as they relate to the development of 'alternative to custody' provisions. For as a Home Office study of the prison population in the south-east of England suggests, as many as a third of the prisoners in the sample could have been suitable candidates for diversion from custody, if suitable provision for employment and other problems had been available (Home Office 1978).

Having noted some of offenders' collective needs in the context of present-day society's economic and social realities, and having attempted to quantify in broad terms the Probation Service's response to that situation, we must also acknowledge the impact of this state of affairs on individual probation officers' day-to-day dealings with their individual clients. The combined impact of homelessness, unemployment, educational disadvantage, and under-achievement are probably to be most vividly seen amongst many of the residents of offender hostels. As Bill Jones, warden of a probation hostel, has stated:

'There has always been a social distance between staff and residents. But now the residents seem to be falling further away from us. The staff are all in employment, whereas only one of the sixteen residents has a job. Staff have the wherewithall, the money and the confidence to go out for an evening in company. Not so the residents. Their world has become much lonelier. When there was work they were part of another group of people and often the younger ones would get a great deal of parenting from the foreman or the canteen lady. . . .

'There seems to be little realization from others that when there is large scale unemployment it is the like of our clients who get clobbered. We are still asked the same questions about how many in the hostel, how many working, how many re-offending? No one will tell us what we need to do even to begin to reinstate our residents in society. . . . The sense of futility is as real to the staff as it is to the clients.' (Jones 1985)

Residential needs of offenders

By 1985 there were about 400 offender accommodation facilities, either managed directly by the Probation Service in the form of approved probation and bail hostels or by voluntary agencies and housing associations, providing almost 6,000 bed places. This number of places represents growth of approximately 30 per cent since 1981.

OFFENDING AND HOMELESSNESS
As these figures indicate, in recent years the Probation Service has become increasingly aware of the high rate of homelessness amongst offenders specifically, and single people generally, and the role it should play in the development and support of accommodation services. As a national average it has been estimated that between 20 and 30 per cent of the Probation Service's clients are homeless or unsuitably housed, and the majority of these are single. Studies have also shown that up to 55 per cent of persons discharged from prison have a housing problem and the likelihood of their subsequent reconviction is appreciably greater. Similarly, studies of single homeless

people have repeatedly revealed that a significant proportion of the single homeless have been in custody at some stage (35 per cent in a 1982 study funded by the Department of the Environment). The causal relationship between homelessness and offending may often be complex and possibly indirect, and may in some instances be associated with other factors such as personality and social adjustment. However, the high levels of representation of offenders amongst the homeless is clear and provides ample justification for the involvement of the Probation Service in the housing and residential arena.

CHANGING EXPECTATIONS AND CHANGING PROVISION
This increasing incidence of homelessness among offenders has not only expressed itself in terms of a demand for more bed places in offender accommodation projects; there has also been a stronger and clearer vocalization of the type of accommodation that is aspired to and required by homeless offenders. As a generalization it can be stated that over the past ten years the phrase 'offender accommodation' has grown into a wider concept of provision which goes beyond the traditional 'hostel' with residential staff. Offender accommodation now also includes a wider spectrum of facilities such as private lodgings schemes, small group homes, cluster bedsit schemes, supported flats (normally with non-residential staff), and some access arrangements to normal fair rent accommodation provided by housing associations and local authority housing departments. The 1977 Housing (Homeless Persons) Act, while of only marginal direct benefit to the single homeless, has nevertheless encouraged more purposeful attempts on the part of proba-tion to achieve access to council housing for homeless offenders, with some limited success.

This broadening of the range of offender accommodation in the country has reflected consumer demand and the views of probation staff as to the style of accommodation their clients require and are capable of managing. A study of short-term prisoners at Winson Green Prison in Birmingham (Stanton 1982) explored the prisoners' and their proba-tion officers' opinions, as to the sort of accommodation they required following release from prison. The survey's findings endorsed other studies both local (Hill 1980) and national, that the predominant demand was for more independent forms of accommodation, such as supported cluster flats schemes and normal housing. Unmet accom-modation needs of women offenders and young black offenders have also been recognized in some areas and greater priority has been given to the development of schemes for these groups. This trend away from conventional hostel provision towards smaller and more independent units should not be interpreted as discrediting the work and contribution of the longer established hostels. Hostels are still the bedrock of the offender accommodation system. The need still remains to perform certain specialized functions such as emergency accommodation and to provide for certain groups with special needs, such as the disturbed young offender, the mentally ill, the alcoholic, the heavily institutionalized older recidivist, and to provide accommodation for the more serious or persistent offender with a more specific supervisory and supportive expectation from the courts as in the case of the approved probation/bail hostels. The aim in recent years has been to provide a more balanced range of provision so as to enhance and emphasize flexibility and choice in the range of accommodation options available to offenders in the community.

CHANGES IN HOUSING FINANCE

The trends and developments so far described have not been instigated by the Probation Service alone. The voluntary sector has had to both promote and adapt to change. Following the 1974 Housing Act, housing associations have had greater incentive with the financial backing of the Home Office, Housing Corporation, and Department of Environment, to become involved in the provision of 'shared housing' for 'special needs' groups such as offenders. However, the increase has been one of quality as well as quantity. Much of the offender accommodation that has become available in recent years has been of a much higher standard, which reflects the concern of the Probation Service and voluntary agencies to enhance the housing welfare and dignity of homeless offenders.

OFFENDER ACCOMMODATION AND THE CRIMINAL JUSTICE SYSTEM

As we have seen, housing resettlement has become a legitimate and central objective for the Probation Service and voluntary agencies, in their work with homeless offenders. In addition, however, the expectations of the criminal justice system, in particular the courts, have been of equal importance. Housing resettlement needs of offenders may in fact be a central preoccupation for the courts also. A probation order, made in respect of relatively minor offences committed by a homeless person, with a condition 'to reside where directed by the probation officer' may represent the court's concern for the welfare of the individual; and constitute an attempt to ensure that the offender having been placed initially in supportive hostel accommodation may then be better able to move on to more independent and permanent accommodation within the duration of the probation order. The needs and expectations of penal establishments are also relevant in this context, and voluntary sector projects continue to perform their longer established role of tackling the resettlement needs of homeless discharged offenders on statutory or voluntary after-care licence.

OFFENDER ACCOMMODATION AS AN ALTERNATIVE TO CUSTODY
Courts will of course often be preoccupied with matters other than the housing needs of the offender. Over the past ten years the Probation Service has increasingly sought to offer the courts various credible sentencing options and relevant provisions in the community, in respect of offenders who might otherwise have received a custodial sentence. Offender accommodation facilities have therefore needed to adjust and keep pace with this trend, to ensure that they can play a full part in the Service's 'alternative to custody' strategy.

APPROVED PROBATION AND BAIL HOSTELS
The sector of the offender accommodation system which provides the courts with the most obvious (but not exclusively so) alternative to custodial sentence or remand is made up of the approved probation and bail hostels, of which there are now 100 in England and Wales.
   'Alternative to custody' does not mean a substitute form of custody. The approved hostels can however offer courts some reassurance, where it is required, of a level of supervision and support which is more extensive and intensive than could normally be expected in the open community. The most fundamental aspects of the approved hostels operation which underpin these aims, are the specific condition of residence within the probation order, and the staffing levels (higher than those normally to be found in other offender accommodation projects) which can ensure adequate cover twenty-four hours a day, seven days per week.
   In recent years the role of the bail hostels and the ability of probation hostels to accept persons on bail when necessary has been given increased prominence by the Probation Service. This has been pursued as a means of increasing courts' confidence in the provisions of the 1976 Bail Act (which require courts to grant bail unless there are clear and specific reasons as to why it should not be granted), and also as part of the Service's strategy to encourage the use of non-custodial disposals by courts, by using the bail bed places as gateways to longer-term offender accommodation placements in the probation hostels or elsewhere.

DIVERSION FROM THE CRIMINAL JUSTICE SYSTEM OF THE
HOMELESS DRUNK OFFENDER
Under the provision of the 1972 Criminal Justice Act the police are
empowered to take drunk offenders to a centre designated for this
purpose under the Act, for the purpose of 'drying out' and sobering
up. This process is intended to be an alternative to the all too familiar
time consuming and expensive cycle of court appearance, fine, and
subsequent imprisonment for non-payment of fine. Drying out
facilities, such as the Leeds Detoxification Centre and the Birmingham 'Wet Shelter', offer the drunk the opportunity to sober up under
humane and controlled circumstances, with the possibility of follow-
up action and advice especially for those who are homeless. Regrettably, it currently appears unlikely that government funding will be
forthcoming for any more such initiatives in this neglected area of
social policy and need.

Probation interest in and commitment towards these schemes is
indicative of a wider recognition of the relatively high incidence of
problem drinking among many of its clients, and the possible causal
connections between this and offending and homelessness. It is for the
homeless drunk offenders, in whom this interplay of factors is seen in
extreme form that inner-city probation teams have to develop specific
strategies involving liaison with a number of agencies and facilities,
including night shelters, drying-out facilities (in the few instances
where they exist), and longer-term rehabilitative hostels.

PROBATION LINKS WITH VOLUNTARY PROJECTS
Different probation services have evolved different organizational
structures for dealing with offender accommodation issues and
homeless offenders, depending on the scale of the problem and the
diversity of residential and housing provision to be dealt with. Some
degree of functional specialization has become a common feature of
many services' responses. More particularly the development of the
'liaison probation officer' role has become, virtually without excep-
tion, a central feature of services' arrangements for linking with
voluntary accommodation projects.

Liaison probation officers provide vital operational, advisory, and
monitoring links with the voluntary projects. If these tasks are to be
pursued fully they can often prove to be time consuming, but are
nevertheless essential if the full benefits of these valuable and
relatively cheap community resources are to be realized by the Service
and the courts.

DEVELOPING THE PROBATION SERVICE'S HOUSING STRATEGY

The point has already been made that the Probation Service's responsibility towards homeless offenders must go beyond the promotion and management of offender-specific residential projects into a more strategic approach, which attempts to encourage a broader understanding of the needs of single homeless people and the development of appropriate housing policies towards this group. In certain probation areas there are good examples of ways in which probation and/or NACRO housing development staff have worked towards the establishment of district council level forums; these aim to provide for greater co-ordination, joint planning and action between voluntary agencies and statutory departments, such as Housing, Social Services, DHSS, as well as the Probation Service.

HOUSING AND WELFARE RIGHTS

The development of greater access opportunities for homeless offenders to mainstream housing provision has had to be pursued against the backcloth of an increasingly complex array of welfare and housing rights issues and various changes in their administration instituted by the government. Examples of this include the problematic introduction of the housing benefit system to a wider range of claimants, including some hostel dwellers; limitations on the approval of DHSS furniture grants to homeless claimants wishing to move into their own unfurnished accommodation; proposed ceilings and time limits on DHSS payments for claimants under twenty-five years old in certain board and lodging establishments. Greater attention has also recently needed to be given to the hardship experienced by clients living in sub-standard housing, hostels, and lodgings, normally in 'multiple occupation', and the relevance of environmental health legislation to any action strategies designed to tackle such deficiencies.

HOUSING RESETTLEMENT AND SOCIAL WORK

Changes of the sort described above have meant that probation officers working with the single homeless require information and training on welfare and housing rights if their clients' position in the housing market is not to become further disadvantaged. Additionally, housing resettlement and social work goals have had to be integrated and, where necessary, reconciled with each other. Probation officers engaged in this area of work have had to develop an awareness of the need to assess individuals' ability to cope with their own tenancy; recognize the significance, in the eyes of housing agencies, of individuals' previous housing and rent payment record; and develop learning opportunities in survival skills such as budgeting, cooking, housekeeping.

Employment needs of offenders

The fundamental dilemma for the Probation Service when considering the implications of current levels of unemployment and their impact on offenders is to decide whether it should primarily address itself to the employment needs or the unemployment needs of offenders. Should the Probation Service's approach be primarily based on the belief that eventually 'real' job opportunities will emerge and therefore it must ensure that offenders receive whatever skills training is necessary for the acquisition of those jobs? Or should the Service accept the strong likelihood that a very substantial proportion of its clients will always be among the ranks of the long-term unemployed, and therefore that emphasis must be given to an approach which seeks to provide legitimate and acceptable alternatives to conventional employment in the form of 'occupation'? If such occupation, whatever its nature and content, is to be of any real value it must be seen by the unemployed individuals as being of some relevance to their needs and aspirations as defined by themselves. This dilemma and the tensions that surround it will be seen in this section to underly virtually every aspect of the Probation Service's perceptions of unemployed offenders' employment needs, and its attempts to tackle those needs.

Frequent or long-term unemployment among offenders is not a new phenomenon. The effects of the current economic recession have, however, greatly escalated the levels of unemployment among the working population overall, and consequently for offenders also. This again poses a dilemma for the Probation Service. Should it differentiate between the 'old' unemployed and the 'new' unemployed? The 'old' unemployed are composed of individuals who for whatever reasons of disadvantage, handicap, or personal choice would rarely acquire and retain long-term employment on the normal open job market. On the other hand, the 'new' unemployed have, or are capable of acquiring, work-related skills which would be marketable in the event of appropriate employment opportunities emerging. In its response the Probation Service is having to attempt to understand and distinguish between the needs of those two broad groups and tailor its strategies accordingly. That response has also to take account of the possibility that, as NACRO (Crow 1982) states in its submission to the House of Lords Committee on Unemployment, 'Even the ending of the present recession is unlikely to solve the problem since fundamental changes in the nature of the labour market mean a decrease in those areas of employment where traditionally many offenders have been most likely to find work'.

Overall the scale of the problem now faced by the Probation Service is immense. In the early 1970s it was generally known to be the case that 30 to 40 per cent of clients of the Service were unemployed. Now that figure stands at an overall average of about 70 per cent, with about half of these falling into the long-term (the 'old') unemployed group. Various studies (for example, Hill 1981) have shown that in particularly disadvantaged areas, such as parts of the Midlands and the North, probation clients were four times more likely to be unemployed than the rest of the economically active population, and that the impact of this trend is disproportionately higher for black clients.

UNEMPLOYMENT AND OFFENDING

Various studies (as summarized by Crow 1982) have established a relationship between rising unemployment and rising crime. That relationship is, however, a complex one, and any interpretation of overall unemployment and crime rates should take into account other factors such as age, type of offence, regional factors, and nature of unemployment (for example, short- or long-term). The causal link between unemployment and crime is revealed as being particularly strong in respect of crime against property and among younger age groups. Although reasons for higher incidence of criminal convictions amongst unemployed people are many and varied, two key factors are opportunity and motive. In simple terms unemployed people have ample time and opportunity to plan and execute certain crimes, particularly against property, and, more important, the frustrations and boredom associated with unemployment and low income may provide a motive for committal of crimes which lead to financial gain. Viewed from this perspective it is self-evident why the Probation Service should be involved in the promotion and management of schemes which attempt to provide constructive and satisfying activity, and special employment programmes designed to act as alternatives to unemployment.

UNEMPLOYMENT, CRIME, AND RACE

In recent years public attention has been drawn to apparently higher rates of criminality amongst black youths in certain urban areas, but studies (for example, Stevens 1979) on this aspect of youth offending patterns strongly suggest that this higher level of offending by black youths, where in evidence, reflects the higher levels of unemployment experienced by black youths in comparison with white youths.

UNEMPLOYMENT AND CUSTODY
At both remand and sentence stage unemployment may be a crucial factor in determining whether a custodial or non-custodial decision is made by courts. Custodial reception rates show a strong correlation with unemployment rates (Crow 1982). This has been a trend seen in previous decades and is in evidence in the current recessionary period, although some observers have suggested that certain 'alternative to custody' provisions such as community service orders, which have been increasingly used by courts during the course of this decade, have served to retard, to some extent, the rate of increase in custodial receptions (Roberts 1983).

UNEMPLOYMENT, RELEASE FROM CUSTODY, AND RECONVICTION
Several studies (summarized by Crow 1982) have shown that a depressingly predictable pattern of unemployment among short-term prisoners leads to other problems such as homelessness, social isolation, and the increased likelihood of further petty crime. Not surprisingly, surveys of prisoners' own opinions have revealed employment and decent accommodation as their most fundamental and urgent requirements, if successful resettlement into the community is to be achieved.

PROBATION RESPONSE
So far in this section we have reviewed the extent of disadvantage experienced by offenders in the job market and the close interrelationship between offending and unemployment and custodial sentencing; and the consequent hardship, boredom, and apathy which are likely to follow from these factors. Additionally it has had to be recognized that while unemployment has always been a crucial problem for many offenders, these problems have been further exacerbated by the currently high level of general unemployment.

In reviewing the range of services provided for unemployed offenders by the Probation Service and other agencies such as NACRO and APEX, it is useful to distinguish between those services which were beginning to emerge during the 1970s as mainstream probation provisions, and those which have developed during the 1980s mainly as part of MSC-promoted responses to the unemployment levels created by the recession.

MAINSTREAM PROBATION DEVELOPMENTS

Community service
The introduction in the 1970s of the community service order was of considerable significance, as the Probation Service was faced with

having to deal directly with the work-related problems of some offenders who even at a time of relatively full employment could not acquire and retain steady jobs because of educational, social, or personal difficulties. Conversely, in spite of apparently indifferent or bad work records, many such offenders were discovered to be capable of carrying out a wide range of demanding and socially useful tasks, through the mixture of direction and support contained within community service. Since then the role of community service as an alternative to custodial disposal and/or as an alternative to unemployment has probably become more complex as the numbers of unemployed offenders appearing before the courts has increased. The crucial point, however, for the purposes of this chapter is that the inception of community service orders did constitute a significant growth point for the Probation Service whereby it recognized its capacity and mandate to pursue various tasks which were relevant to the community and also relevant to the needs of some unemployed offenders.

Day care schemes
Alongside the growth of community service, interest in other developments gathered momentum, such as sheltered workshops, day training/activity centres, drop-in centres, informal activity groups which were all, to varying degrees, of relevance to unemployed clients. This spectrum of provision seeks to meet the needs of unemployed offenders in different ways. Workshops and day activity centres can offer clients with poor employment records a relatively sheltered environment within which they can gain a sense of achievement and routine at their own pace. Alternatively, such facilities can act as a means of enhancing clients' job prospects on the open job market by increasing self-confidence and basic social and life skills, including numeracy and literacy, and by some specific vocational skills development. The work programmes in such centres are varied but may include activities such as wood and metal work, car mechanics, and furniture renovation. Attendance for many will be as a condition of a probation order, and care has to be taken by the Service to ensure that such statutory orders are made by the courts only in respect of offenders who would otherwise be likely to receive a custodial sentence.

Drop-in centres and informal activity groups also perform a variety of relevant functions in respect of unemployed clients. They may in fact be attempting to meet needs which would be more appropriately met by the establishment of, if resources were available, a workshop or activity/training centre. However, the proper role of drop-in centres and informal activity groups within a wider spectrum of day provision, is generally recognized as enhancing the support available to unemployed clients, by the provision of activities which are educative in the broadest sense. These small-scale schemes may act as a relatively unstructured sanctuary and social base for the long-term unemployed, or as a staging post for those who can have some realistic expectation of obtaining work at some stage in the future.

Development of work creation programmes
Since the late 1970s and early 1980s the developing range of offender-specific provision described in the last section can be viewed alongside a broader range of employment creation and training provision as promoted by the MSC. A seemingly never-ending and constantly changing stream of schemes has emerged from the MSC, such as YOP, STEP, WEP, CEP, and currently the Youth Training Scheme (YTS) and Community Programme (CP). The true purpose and political motives that lie behind these government-promoted schemes has of course been a matter of considerable national debate and the Probation Service has had to take account of a range of views.

The Service has to some extent exploited these provisions but the bulk of developments for offenders has been undertaken by voluntary agencies such as NACRO and APEX. In the case of NACRO, by 1984 it was running eighty CP schemes providing over 7,000 work places, and forty-six YTS schemes providing about 2,400 work places predominantly for offenders. Voluntary agencies and probation areas which have taken on the management of CP and YTS schemes have aimed to provide work-based programmes with some training inputs, as allowed for under the terms laid down by MSC. YTS schemes have tended to provide training in workshop-based trade skills such as plumbing, electrics, catering, computer literacy, followed by job placements. CP schemes have been mainly involved with providing project work in areas such as environmental improvement and community service. To varying extents there has been some scope for job related training in areas such as basic literacy and numeracy, health and safety, and self-presentation skills for job search purposes. There are many serious limitations to these MSC programmes, in particular the twelve-month time limit imposed on an individual's participation, low wages, and often the availability of part-time work only. Nevertheless they have gone some way towards providing constructive occupational opportunities, and the schemes mentioned above, run by offender-linked agencies, have on the whole been well used by unemployed offenders.

The involvement of clients in these types of MSC schemes often involves protracted negotiations with agencies such as DHSS, Inland

Revenue, housing benefit offices, especially at the entry and departure stages, relating to the individual's welfare rights and income maintenance. Consequently, as was previously noted in relation to homeless clients and their entry into the housing system, unemployed clients also require detailed welfare rights advice and advocacy from probation officers, when their entry into this sector of the job market is being planned.

OVERALL PROBATION STRATEGY TOWARDS UNEMPLOYMENT
We have now reviewed the range of responses that the Probation Service has or can be involved with in dealing with the needs of unemployed offenders. These responses have ranged from, at one extreme, offender-specific provisions such as community service orders; through a variety of support and training facilities for unemployed offenders such as day activity and drop-in centres; job search and placement schemes for offenders on the open market; to, at the other extreme, engagement with schemes that are not necessarily offender specific, of the type promoted by MSC. Faced with such a wide array of possible provisions it is necessary for the Probation Service to draw these together into a coherent strategy for the Service's response towards unemployment.

The essential components of an overall strategy have been stated by the Association of Chief Officers of Probation (ACOP) (1985) as follows:

1) To know what facilities exist which may benefit unemployed clients.
2) To know clients and understand their needs well enough to refer them appropriately to existing services, within and outside the Probation Service.
3) to maintain an effective liaison system with such facilities.
4) To provide or encourage provision of facilities specially developed for those of our clients who are so under-achieving that they are not able to make effective use of the normal pattern of facilities, even when referral and liaison systems are working well.
5) Maintain awareness in the community among employers, sentencers, and other key groups as well as the general public about the problems and needs of offenders in the context of severe unemployment levels.

Educational needs of offenders

It will have been apparent from the previous section that there is a close relationship between employment and educational needs of many offenders. Educative inputs, be they for the purpose of training for work, education for enforced leisure, or improving basic and life skills, were seen to be frequent features of the services', and related agencies', work with unemployed offenders. For this reason, therefore, this section is shorter and needs to be read within the context of the previous section on employment. It will also become apparent that educational needs of offenders has not been identified as a distinctive issue in its own right to the extent which homelessness and unemployment have been, and this appears to be reflected in the paucity of research studies in this area.

EDUCATIONAL NEEDS AND OFFENDING
The link between offending and educational under-achievement is normally presented as an indirect one involving unemployment which, as discussed in the previous section, has various links with offending. Put simply, educational under-achievement limits individuals' abilities to find secure employment even at times of relatively high employment and reduces their opportunities to obtain legitimate rewards from society, and this may therefore encourage a predisposition towards criminal activity.

LEVELS OF EDUCATIONAL NEED AMONG CLIENTS OF THE
PROBATION SERVICE
Direct observations by probation officers on the low levels of formal educational qualifications among their clients clearly reveal a high level of educational under-achievement. There is some evidence to suggest, however, that the true extent of under-achievement among clients is not always detected. While it is common practice within the Service to discuss and record formal educational background at the social inquiry report stage, problems of literacy and numeracy are much less likely, perhaps not surprisingly, to be detected. At other points in the criminal justice system, such as receptions into young offender institutions, more formal screening and assessment processes do take place and predictably reveal high levels of educational disadvantage and under-achievement. Similarly, NACRO reported in 1984 that 60 per cent of persons joining their CP employment schemes had no educational qualifications and 80 per cent had no recognized vocational qualifications; of the younger people joining the YTS schemes 81 per cent had no educational qualifications and 65 per cent had been involved, to varying degrees, in school truancy, and over half had need for improvement in basic literacy and numeracy.

EXISTING EDUCATIONAL PROVISION FOR OFFENDERS

In 1982 both NACRO and the Conference of Chief Probation Officers reported on surveys that had been conducted in England and Wales on education provision and social/literacy/life skills projects for offenders. These included schemes that were specifically designed for, or had special arrangements for access by, offenders. Overall, approximately 200 schemes were being run for offenders by the Probation Service, education departments, or voluntary organizations in forty-seven of the fifty-six probation areas. Most of these schemes involved between twelve and twenty students at a time, amounting to 2,500 in all. Nearly all schemes were reported as being over-subscribed with increasing referrals. Virtually all of the schemes were focused on basic education. The limited extent of special training for staff in these areas was noted. Use of volunteers as tutors and aids was a common feature of the schemes.

The schemes operated in a number of settings such as hostels, colleges, community centres. It is important to note that 33 per cent of probation areas had developed explicit links with penal institutions as a central feature of the education schemes; 45 per cent with hostels; and over 50 per cent with day centres. It may be that the apparent concentration of more disadvantaged clients in these particular settings has stimulated staff into focusing more specifically on clients' collective needs.

The reference to penal institutions' educational work is important in this context as it is well recognized that, with a few notable exceptions, such penal-based activity does not have effective links with community-based educational provision. Hence any educational experience that the client has had the benefit of while serving his or her sentence is not reinforced following release. A NACRO report, *Bridging the Gap* (1981), makes specific and critical reference to this aspect of education for offenders and ascribed significant roles to the Prison Education Department, the Probation Service, and local education authorities for the achievement of greater co-ordination and co-operation.

The surveys also reported that educational schemes frequently started as a response to the high level of unemployment among probation clients, and the role of NACRO in stimulating and supporting these enterprises had been important in many cases. The inception of schemes has tended to reflect and rely upon the energy and determination of individuals rather than on policy initiatives by probation or education services, and there has been a need for probation management to take account of this developing area of work and provide support as appropriate.

Since 1982 most developments of education work with offenders have taken two broad routes. First, as described earlier in the section on employment needs, day provisions such as day centres and drop-in centres have frequently included educational activity in their programmes, and secondly, NACRO under the MSC Voluntary Projects Programme, has established twelve local projects for offenders and non-offenders who wish to take up education and training opportunities locally. These projects have three main components: advice and information; provision of basic education; and the involvement of volunteers, many of whom are also unemployed.

OBJECTIVES AND PURPOSES
It is apparent that there is considerable scope for further promotion and development of educational schemes for offenders. However, as a means of guiding such future activity, it is important to be clear about objectives and purposes particularly with reference to the precise role that the Probation Service should be performing. Stated at its most fundamental level the purpose of educational activity with offenders can be seen as being embodied in Prison Rule no. 1: 'The purpose of the training and treatment of convicted prisoners shall be to encourage and assist them to lead a good and useful life.' Notions of 'good and useful' may be easy enough to perceive in terms of the general expectations of society and the courts, but it is also incumbent upon the Probation Service to understand and vocalize the needs and aspirations of offenders themselves. It is therefore vital that any educational scheme that the Probation Service is associated with emphasizes and provides ample scope for offenders to express their own views, both at initial and later stages, as to what they see their needs as being and what type of educational experience will be relevant to those needs. Such an approach is essential if voluntary commitment and motivation on the part of the individual is to be stimulated and sustained.

As previously stated, the fact of unemployment has frequently emerged as the stimulus to the development of educational schemes for offenders. The dilemma that this trend has posed is whether such schemes should primarily aim to help offenders cope with unemployment or increase their chances of obtaining work. The objectives of schemes have therefore often had to attempt to straddle both of these expectations, in addressing themselves towards a spectrum of needs – ranging from ongoing tuition in basic skills, life quality enhancing activities, employment enhancement skills, vocational training, and higher academic achievement.

It is clear that, even if resources allowed, it is neither feasible nor desirable for offender education groups to embrace fully this spectrum of needs and expectations. While recognizing the validity of itself directly providing certain elements, especially at the more basic end of the spectrum, the Probation Service must also assume a co-ordinating and promotional role in devising a broader strategy, which brings together various education agencies and links them with offenders. Direct recruitment of individual offenders into educational institutions without a preparatory phase will often show an unrealistic expectation and many offender education groups place great emphasis on the confidence-building aspect of their work, so that offenders feel better able subsequently to opt for more formal mainstream educational opportunities.

Conclusion

A number of broad themes have emerged from this chapter and in this final section some of these are given particular prominence.

ECONOMIC AND SOCIAL HARDSHIP
The introduction to this chapter argued that the recession and conse-quential hardship of the late 1970s and 1980s was the primary pressure on the Probation Service to develop a range of practical responses which addressed themselves towards the accommodation, employment, and educational needs of offenders. This assertion would seem to be largely correct. However, the Service's responses, while prompted by the recession, could not be realistically described in any way as providing real solutions to the fundamental causes or effects of the recession. At best they have ameliorated some of the harsher effects of economic and social disadvantage. Many would argue that the types of schemes and activities described in this chapter are initiatives which the Probation Service should in any event, regardless of current economic circumstances, have been engaged in. For as has been frequently pointed out, many of the Service's clients have always been considerably disadvantaged in the housing, employ-ment, and educational spheres.

THE OFFENDER SPECIFIC VS. THE GENERALIST APPROACH
It follows from the above that much of the offender specific activity, such as offender accommodation and day centres, which we have reviewed in this chapter have essentially reflected the offender's posi-tion at the margins of mainstream society, and arguably have even reinforced that position. Such an assertion is not unduly negative and defeatist, although at first sight it may seem so, but merely realistic.

Such realism underlies the constant need to recognize that Probation Service activity in these areas of offender disadvantage must always seek to identify and maintain connections with related interests in the broader community, if opportunities for integration into mainstream provisions are to be achieved. Hence the Service's strategies must encompass, and strike a balance between, offender-specific and generalist approaches.

THE PREVENTION OF RE-OFFENDING

In the current climate of 'alternatives to custody' strategies it has to be recognized that for many external observers the prevention of re-offending is a crucial expectation of the Probation Service's, and related agencies', work generally and, more specifically, of accommodation, employment, and educational schemes. The extent to which reconviction rates are monitored varies greatly between different types of schemes. Such monitoring, if it is to be meaningful, must be both detailed and comparative. Considerable detail is required if precise assessments can be made about changes in frequency and seriousness of offending, distinguishing longitudinally between the period of time that the individual is a recipient of the scheme's services, and the period after departure from the scheme. It is only with such information that valid comparisons can be made with the extremely limited effect of penal institutions on reconviction rates.

INDIVIDUAL CHOICE

Alongside the objective of prevention of re-offending, the types of projects described in this chapter quite properly give equal priority to objectives which in essence deal with the enhancement of quality of life, with individuals' abilities to cope with the pressures of modern day living, and with the exercising by the individual of some degree of personal choice. However, critics can and do argue that such schemes are often inadequately resourced and do not provide the level of service and degree of opportunity that the individual aspires to and feels entitled to. Such criticisms clearly carry a certain validity but nevertheless the concept of individual choice remains an essential and widely held value within the Probation Service. As Roberts (1983) has put it: 'Perhaps the most important issue is that any opportunity which helps the offender to help himself, to exercise his own choices about which scheme is right for him, has benefits beyond the simple one of providing useful and hopefully gainful occupation – it restores the dignity that only personal choice can offer.'

© *1987 David Walton*

References

ACOP (1985) *Summary of responses to employment questionnaire, Spring 1984 and consequent recommendations for practice in probation areas.* Wakefield: Association of Chief Probation Officers.

Barfield, G., Cook, A., and Dunkley, E. (1984) *Four years on: an evaluation of the Greencoat House Education Group* (October). Birmingham: West Midlands Probation Service.

CCOP, Working Party on Employment of Offenders (1982) *Social/Literacy/Life Skills Work and Projects* (June). Conference of Chief Probation Officers.

Crow, I. (1982) *Submission to the House of Lords Committee on Unemployment* (September). London: National Association for the Care and Resettlement of Offenders.

Dunkley, T. (1984) Probation and the Community. Unpublished paper, West Midlands Probation Service.

Hill, J. (1980) *A survey of the accommodation needs of clients referred to the Kent Street After-Care Unit.* Birmingham: West Midlands Probation Service.

————— (1981) *A survey of unemployment amongst probation service clients in the Birmingham North area* (March). Birmingham: West Midlands Probation Service.

Home Office (1978) *A survey of the south east Prison Population*, Research Bulletin no. 5. London: HMSO.

Jones, B. (1985) In Residence: 'When I get out of here . . .'. *Social Work Today* 16(19).

NACRO (1981) *Bridging the Gap.* London: National Association for the Care and Resettlement of Offenders.

————— (1982) *Education for Offenders and Ex-Offenders in the Community.* London: National Association for the Care and Resettlement of Offenders.

————— (1983a) *Report of the Review Group on the Residential Voluntary Sector.* London: National Association for the Care and Resettlement of Offenders.

————— (1983b) *Unemployment, Training and Resettling Ex-Offenders. A Response to the MSC Consultative Document 'Towards an Adult Training Strategy.'* London: National Association for the Care and Resettlement of Offenders.

NPRIE (1982–83) *An Index of Probation Projects.* London: National Probation Research and Information Exchange.

Pearce, A. (1985) Education for Prisoners and Ex-Prisoners. *West Midlands Probation Service Staff Bulletin.*

Roberts, J. (1983) Unemployment Amongst Offenders: The Probation

Service Response. Paper delivered at the Midland Regional Staff Development Office Workshop in December 1983.

Stanton, A. (1982) *Survey of Short-Term Prisoners in Winson Green Prison.* Birmingham: West Midlands Probation Service.

Stevens, P. (1979) Predicting Black Crime. Home Office Research Unit Bulletin no. 8. London: HMSO.

8 Responding to the drink/drug-using offender

Robert Purser

This chapter emphasizes the links between mood-altering substances and offending. It plots the growth of alcohol-related offences in a society where alcohol consumption has risen rapidly. Initiatives for problem drinking clients are discussed, as is the growth in confidence of probation officers in dealing with such clients. The issue of drug-taking and its relationship to offending is briefly sketched, within a context of high youth unemployment and an increased supply of drugs.

Why the concern?

Why is there concern about alcohol and offending? Clearly laid down in the British system of justice is the concept of intent and of an individual's responsibility for offending behaviour. Excessive drinking is neither a defence nor a mitigation. Yet it is widely recognized that a substantial proportion of offenders appearing before the courts had not intended to break the law. However, at the end of an evening's drinking the effects of alcohol (reduction of inhibition and diminution of judgement) together with some peer group pressure and the perception of a criminal opportunity may result in an offence being committed. It does seem that the consumption of alcohol is an increasingly significant factor in the rising number of offences. The following analysis (based on Prins 1980) is an attempt to clarify the complicated relationship between an offender's alcohol use and offending behaviour.

Alcohol and its relationship with crime

1. *Offences against the Licensing Law* related to the manufacture, distribution, and sale of alcohol. Generally these laws are concerned to regulate alcohol consumption. Examples of this offence include:

(i) the licence – serving under-age drinkers; serving after hours; serving an intoxicated person;

(ii) the drinker – drinking under age;

(iii) the parent – giving alcohol to a child under five except on medical orders.

2. *Offences related to behaviour which specifically mention alcohol,* usually where alcohol consumption involves an element of risk:

(i) being incapable or disorderly in a public place having consumed sufficient alcohol to be judged drunk;

(ii) driving a car with a blood alcohol level over 80 mg per 100 mls;

(iii) being in contravention of occupational regulatory laws, for example, driving a train under the influence of alcohol.

3. *Offences committed while under the inhibiting effects of alcohol:*

(i) where the disinhibiting or judgement affecting properties of alcohol have played a part in the decision-making process, for example, where an argument has led to an assault because of the lessening of an individual's self-control;

(ii) where the disinhibiting effect of alcohol was used by the offender to obtain 'dutch courage' in order to commit the offence, for example, by someone needing to drink before carrying out a burglary.

4. *Offences committed while the offender is in a psychotic state* – the psychosis being induced by alcohol. An example is an assault committed when in this state of mind.

5. *Offences not committed while intoxicated,* but resulting from an alcohol problem:

(i) a drinker stealing provisions because the family money has been spent on alcohol;

(ii) a drinker stealing alcohol to consume;

(iii) a drinker stealing items to sell to obtain money to buy alcohol.

This classification can be useful in avoiding an over-simplified view of drinking problems, by identifying the various causational relationships. It might be used as a basis for estimating the extent of alcohol-related problems in a team's caseload as well as exploring with the individual client how drinking may be involved with crime.

The last ten years – the growth of a response to people with alcohol-related offences

Probation officers since the mid 1970s have become increasingly aware of the significance of excessive drinking as a factor in criminal behaviour. This has led to a mushrooming of locally based initiatives to improve the Probation Service's response to such offenders. Previously, problems with alcohol were seen as a marginal concern involving only the single homeless alcoholic offender. Now most probation officers are coming to recognize that excessive drinking may be a factor in their clients' problems. Gone are the days when only one member of the office needed expertise in the field of alcohol abuse. It can now be seen that all officers need the knowledge and skills to work effectively with clients and their patterns of drinking.

The problems of increasing consumption

During the years 1962–82 the consumption of alcohol in England and Wales doubled – with beer increasing by 22 per cent, wines by 240 per cent, and spirits by 95 per cent. By 1983 the British were spending more than £13,400 m. on alcoholic drinks, which amounts to £35m. every day.

Linked with this increasing consumption has been an increase in the indicators of alcohol abuse (see *Tables 4, 5, 6*).

Table 4   *Mortality – cirrhosis of the liver*

	1970	1983	% increase
male	806	1,111	37.8
female	764	1,073	40.4
total	1,570	2,184	39.1

Source: Office of Population Censuses and Surveys (OPCS).

Table 5 *Admissions to mental hospitals (relating to main and underlying diagnosis involving alcohol)*

	1970	1983	% increase
male	6,648	11,575	74.1
female	2,060	5,631	173.3
total	8,708	17,206	97.5

Source: DHSS.

154

Table 6 *Drunkenness offences and proceedings against motorists*

	1973	1983	% increase
proved drunkenness offences	99,274	109,724	10.5
proceedings against motorists for drink-driving	65,248	98,000	50.1
total	164,522	207,724	26.3

Source: Christian Economic and Social Research Foundation; Chief Constables' Reports 1984.

The official estimate of the number of people with drinking problems in the United Kingdom has been given as 740,000 (Donnan and Haskey 1977) but this may be an under-estimate. A survey, *Drinking in England and Wales* (Wilson 1980), confirmed the seriousness of the size of the problem and indicated that the greatest amount of harm was in the eighteen to twenty-four age group.

The notion is widely held that the vast majority of the population drink sensibly and that a small minority are alcoholics. It is now understood that a society's drinking is more usefully viewed as a continuum, ranging from those who drink nothing, through those who drink small quantities, those who drink moderately, to those who drink heavily. There can, therefore, be no hard and fast dividing line between safe and hazardous drinking, with factors such as gender, social situation, and state of health interacting. However, there is widespread agreement with guidelines put forward in the report of the Royal College of Psychiatrists, *Alcohol – Our Favourite Drug* (1986); this has joined with the Health Education Council in recommending the levels of consumption set out in *Table 7* as a reasonable guide. (It should, of course, be noted that for people with particular problems in health or other areas of life, no drinking may be the appropriate recommendation.)

It is obvious from this evidence that the problem of rising consumption is taking a toll, yet society's attitude to the use of alcohol is not one of real concern. Perhaps this is because we, as consumers of alcohol, subscribe to media images which show people of high status, sexuality, and life-style enjoying drink. We are not confronted by the reality of excessive drinking and its harmful side.

Moving away from the disease model

Although the disease model of alcoholism has held sway since the 1950s it has perhaps not been helpful to probation officers in their practice. It has focused too much on the heavily dependent drinker,

155

Table 7   *Drinking guidelines*

	women	men
harmful drinking	35 units per week or more	50 units per week or more
hazardous drinking	14–34 units per week	21–49 units per week
safe drinking	less than 14 units per week	less than 21 units per week

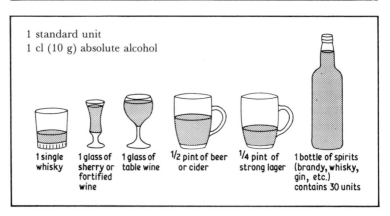

1 standard unit
1 cl (10 g) absolute alcohol

1 single whisky | 1 glass of sherry or fortified wine | 1 glass of table wine | ½ pint of beer or cider | ¼ pint of strong lager | 1 bottle of spirits (brandy, whisky, gin, etc.) contains 30 units

drawing attention away from working with people at an early stage of a drinking problem. Officers saw the problem as one of referral to the medical profession for treatment rather than having the confidence to see that they were already equipped to help. Clients perceived themselves as powerless over their drinking rather than capable of learning to understand the reasons for their drinking. In the last ten years new approaches in understanding drinking and drinking problems (Heather and Robertson 1981 and 1986) have done much to encourage probation officers. These approaches have been based on seeing drinking as learned behaviour which, like other behaviours, is capable of change.

The incidence of alcohol-related crime

Many of the studies into the incidence of alcohol-related crime have been crude measures fraught with problems of definition. Often they have been carried out by 'practitioners' rather than independent researchers so that accepted knowledge is based on 'received wisdom' rather than empirical research.

Despite these problems probation officers are well aware of the relationship between alcohol abuse and crime and the following brief descriptions of recent studies may act as a guide to informed discussions.

Jeffs and Saunders (1983) (see *Table 8*) interviewed 1,209 people arrested in a south coast resort in May to September 1979 and found that 64 per cent admitted consuming alcohol in the four hours preceding the commission of the offence for which they were arrested.

Table 8

	total number of arrests	number and % reporting alcohol intake	
drunkenness	183	183	100%
drink-driving	83	83	100%
criminal damage	112	99	88%
breach of peace	71	59	83%
assault	151	118	78%
theft	368	151	41%
miscellaneous	167	62	37%
burglary	74	19	26%
total	1,209	774	64%

Source: Jeffs and Saunders (1983).

They found that 46 per cent of all arrests occur during the hours of 10pm–2am and that 90 per cent of persons arrested during this time reported drinking in the four hours preceding their offence. Of the under-25 year olds arrested (72 per cent of the total), 68 per cent had been drinking during the preceding four hours. The study also found that the heaviest drinking age group was the 18–20 year olds. However, it is notable that as many as 65 per cent of the under-18 year olds admitted consuming alcohol prior to the arrest.

A study by Morris and Murphy (1973) at the magistrates' court in Ealing suggested a minimum of 10 per cent of people appearing before the court were either 'alcoholic' or were 'at risk' of becoming so.

A small study of the magistrates' courts in Hereford and Worcestershire in 1982 showed 28 per cent of male offenders' offences were definitely alcohol related, while 22 per cent of female offenders' offences were alcohol related (Hereford and Worcestershire Probation Service 1982).

Knapman (1982) carried out a survey of the incidence of alcohol-related problems in probation officers' caseloads in Northamptonshire and found that 47 per cent of offenders had an alcohol-related problem. He found that adult probation clients drank 60 per cent

above the average for the population, were four times more likely to
get drunk and nine times more likely than the general population to
be classified as having a drink problem. He also found that one-third
of probation clients under eighteen had a drink problem.

The Institute of Health Studies at Hull University has carried out
a similar study using clients of the Humberside Probation Service and
concluded that 33 per cent of all offenders are problem drinkers, 17
per cent of all offenders are 'hard-core' problem drinkers (that is,
problem drinkers with medium to high dependence). They also found
that 19 per cent of male offenders drank more than fifty units weekly
(three times as much as that estimated for the male population of
England and Wales) and 13 per cent of female offenders drank more
than thirty-five units weekly (ten times as much as that estimated for
the female population of England and Wales) (Taylor 1985).

The Home Office estimated that 5,000 prisoners in 1967 (14 per
cent of the then prison population) had 'serious drink problems'. In
a Home Office survey of south-east prisoners in 1972 some 25 per cent
of the sample (excluding civil prisoners and those with life sentences
or unconvicted) had a recorded drink problem (Bruun 1982). Such
problems have been shown to be particularly prevalent among short-
term prisoners, where 40 per cent of one sample had previous convictions for drunkenness. In 1979 the Chairman of the Parole Board in
his annual report (Home Office 1980) drew attention to the finding
that 50 per cent of applicants for parole, where the offence was
murder, had been drinking before the offence was committed.

In a study (Fairhead 1981) of a sample of fifty persistent petty
offenders at Pentonville Prison, which examined the social disadvantage of men serving sentences of less than twelve months and with five
or more previous convictions, thirty-five were 'habitual heavy
drinkers'.

Wilson, in his survey *Drinking in England and Wales* (1980),
concluded that the heaviest drinkers were likely to be: (a) male; (b)
under thirty; (c) unmarried; (d) spending several evenings out a week.
Interestingly, the British Crime Survey (Hough and Mayhew 1983)
finds that it is just this group who are most likely to assault others. The
effects of alcohol in this equation cannot be ignored.

The cost of alcohol-related offending

Holtermann and Burchell attempted to estimate the annual cost
attributable to alcoholism and other forms of alcohol misuse in a
Government Economic Service Working Paper (1981). They found
the costs to the police, judiciary, prisons, and Probation Service

particularly difficult to estimate because of the lack of suitable data on which to base this costing. Using evidence given to the Blennerhassett Committee on drink driving, on the amount of police time taken in breathalyser tests and processing drink-drive arrests they estimated that in 1977 prices the costs imposed upon the police due to non-accident and drunkenness offences in 1975 was in the order of £2.39m. whilst the rest of the costs of prison sentences for all offences of drink and drugs amounted to £870,000 (1977 prices) (Holtermann and Birchell 1981).

Chambers (1984) projected the cost savings of an experiment in West London where drunkenness offenders were cautioned only and calculated a saving in court costs of £4.75m. in London, or in national terms £9.84m. per annum. He calculated that the saving in police time would gain an operational capacity of an extra ninety-six officers for the metropolitan police areas. No-one has calculated the cost of alcohol-related crime to the Probation Service.

One may conclude that the lack of research into the cost of alcohol-related offending, where the costs are clearly so great, reflects the conspiracy of government and society to cover up the negative side of alcohol use. Until this information is made available it will be difficult to engage in a balanced debate about the allocation of appropriate resources in response to the problems alcohol causes.

Points to take into consideration are:

(i) it seems probable that the more often a person offends and returns to prison the more likely he is to have an alcohol problem;
(ii) alcohol may be as significant a factor in women's offending as in men's offending;
(iii) youth crimes, particularly burglaries and offences of violence, are frequently alcohol related;
(iv) there is no aspect of the work of the Probation Service where an alcohol factor can be ignored.

Recognizing a client's drinking problem

Probation officers can recognize someone drunk at fifty paces but they often fail to make an appropriate assessment of a client at an earlier stage of the problem. Knapman (1982) surveyed probation officers and their clients in Northamptonshire and found that while 47 per cent of probation clients had an alcohol problem, officers identified 17 per cent only. However, in other research, probation officers compare favourably with general practitioners and social workers in this respect (Cartwright, Shaw, and Spratley 1975).

The main purpose of this chapter is to encourage probation officers to feel confident when working with clients who have drink-related problems. Providing officers have sufficient knowledge of the effects of alcohol, the skills to apply when working with problem drinkers, supportive supervision, and are able to refer to specialized services when necessary, then they are as well equipped as any other professional worker.

A client may not link his drinking with the problems resulting from it, or it may be too painful to face up to the consequences of drinking. Other clients have accepted the risks of being caught rather than lose the perceived benefits of drinking. On some occasions it may be that the probation officer finds it difficult to ask direct questions about their client's drinking because of such factors as lack of confidence and insufficient training.

To overcome this officers should develop practices which ensure that drinking problems are recognized. These may include:

(i) making a careful note, in diary form, of the previous week's drinking;
(ii) looking out for some of the common indicators of alcohol abuse (see *Table 9*)

Often a client will be aware that there is an alcohol problem and is waiting to be prompted. It is a matter of asking the right question at the right time. Patience and persistence will often pay off!

Working with problem drinkers

Having recognized a client's drinking problem it is important to develop a relationship of mutual trust so that drinking can be openly discussed. This will be assisted by an open and non-judgemental attitude which will help to rebuild the individual's confidence. It is first necessary to understand the events surrounding an individual's drinking. This will include an appreciation of the person's life-style and will go on to look in detail at:

(i) the events leading up to a drinking occasion;
(ii) the factors making up the drinking situation, obtained from answers to the following questions: where did the drinking take place; in whose company; what time of day; what drink; how much alcohol; what effect; how was the occasion limited; what meaning did the drink have;
(iii) the consequences of drinking including an appreciation of the benefits as well as the harm which occurred.

Beyond these practical issues lies the meaning which the individual

Table 9 *Common indicators of alcohol abuse*

social	familial	psychological	physical
financial (debts, rent arrears, inexplicable poverty)	psychological complaints in spouse – especially anxiety and depression	anxiety – symptoms of all kinds – especially shakiness	gastritis
legal (shoplifting, taking and driving away, assault)	psychological and behavioural problems in children (enuresis, aggressive behaviour, anxiety, poor school work)	depression	burns
work (deterioration in work performance, absenteeism, frequent changes of job)		overdose	accidents (at home, work, and on the road)
accommodation (eviction, frequent changes of residence)	marital disharmony (may include sexual problems)	sexual problems, including impotence	flu-like symptoms
aggressive behaviour (fights)	wife battering	drug abuse – especially of sedatives and tranquillisers	obesity in young males
home (neglect, bottles lying around)	child abuse		

Source: Harwin (1979) *Social Work Today* 10(41).

attaches to his or her own drinking. Everyone drinks for his or her own good reasons and part of the counselling process must be to understand that meaning.

The next step is to work out how drinking relates to other parts of the person's life and its links with other life problems.

(i) Excessive drinking may have led to debt, family, or marriage problems. Tackling the drinking may help resolve the other problems.

(ii) Excessive drinking may be a poor coping strategy for other underlying problems (for example, by the woman who is drinking to cope with the departure of her grown-up children, or by the spouse who drinks to deny an unhappy marriage). Spending time on the underlying problems may be necessary before the alcohol problem can be tackled.

(iii) The relationship between drinking and other problems is so complex that causal relationships cannot be identified. Progress may only be possible by concentrating on one problem so that the others are seen in relationship to it.

(iv) The individual uses other problems as a strategy for avoiding the alcohol problem. The client may say 'If only my financial situation were easier . . .'. It is usual here to confront the client with the alcohol problem to avoid time being wasted.

It is helpful to explore the implications for a client in changing his or her drinking, with particular emphasis on the negative consequences. The following matrix may be of use:

	excessive drinking	*abstaining/controlled drinking*
advantages/benefits	1	1
	2	2
	3	3
disadvantages/problems	1	1
	2	2
	3	3

For a successful outcome it is essential that the client is in full agreement with goals set out and the methods used to achieve them. For example, the goal may be to avoid drinking which leads to offending or to ensure that drinking does not harm the family budget or the client's health. For those abstaining, alternatives to drinking situations will have to be worked out and for those who are controlling their drinking ways of maintaining this have to be agreed.

In assisting the client to realize these goals it will be necessary to build up new support structures. These may include the use of volunteers and group activities. For single homeless clients specialist accommodation and day-centres will be vital. A thorough knowledge of local resources is necessary and this may be available through the local Alcohol Advisory Service or Council on Alcoholism. A national guide to services is available published by Alcohol Concern (1986). However, for the majority of problem drinkers referral to a specialist agency will not be necessary and the number requiring hospital treatment may be as low as 5 per cent. However, the possible medical needs of problem drinkers should be borne in mind and where necessary referral to the general practitioner be made.

Developing initiatives within the Probation Service

Recently a series of imaginative and valuable new initiatives have been developed within the Probation Service. These must be seen as supplementary to the essential work of all probation officers in responding to those with drinking problems in their own caseloads. These new projects provide a focus for consciousness raising, and an opportunity for training as well as providing a valuable service for the client. Like all new initiatives they need to be carefully evaluated and a wide debate needs to take place about certain ethical issues. Some of these projects incorporate a measure of control and coercion.

(i) *Alcohol education groups*

Since 1980 a number of experimental groups have been established, targeted at offenders in the early stages of a drinking problem. Early groups were started in Dundee (Robertson and Heather 1982), Coventry (Bailey and Purser 1982), and Reading (Goodman and Scott 1982), based on the same general principles:

(a) using an educational model where those attending are given factual material on alcohol and drinking;

(b) bringing about an understanding of drinking based on the idea that drinking is a behaviour that can be changed;

(c) teaching the social skills necessary to deal with drinking problems.

The groups run for six to eight sessions within the context of a short probation order or during a deferred sentence. This approach raises the use of the 'special condition' clause. A number of groups use a special condition, for example, to attend six weekly sessions in a sober state. Critics argue that imposing a special condition clause may lead to a higher tariff sentence if the person re-offends. Critics also argue that probationers should not attend groups under duress. I see no evidence to suggest that re-offending after completing the special condition clause leads to higher tariff sentences. In answer to the 'duress' issue my experience is that many clients openly say they would not have attended the group voluntarily but that, with hindsight, they were pleased that they had to attend. The majority find it a valuable experience. Furthermore, the clear conditions laid down focus the attention of the court, the client, and the Probation Service on the alcohol problem. All parties involved are seen to be attempting to tackle the problem and to be intervening in a positive way.

(ii) *Alcohol groups for offenders with a more serious problem*
Initiatives of this sort have taken place in Corby (Hamson *et al.* 1983), Clacton (Stewart 1984), Oxford (Goodman 1983) and provide longer term support with a focus on mutual sharing, and learning new problem-solving skills. These groups may be integrated into general community provision – if it exists. Research on the Corby project suggests a significant reduction in the rate of re-offending.

(iii) *Alcohol groups for drink driving offenders*
The Probation Service's practice has been to neglect this group of clients except when involved in other crime or at risk of going to prison. Yet the Department of the Environment (Blennerhassett Report) (1976) suggested that many drinking drivers offended as a result of an underlying drinking problem and made a series of pro- posals involving the screening of repeated drink drivers. Some alcohol education groups have taken drink drivers, but an important deve- lopment in the Hampshire Probation Service has been the estab- lishment of groups specifically for drinking drivers (Martin 1986).

(iv) *Initiatives for offenders with multiple life problems including homelessness and alcoholism*
Recent developments in provision for this most deprived group of offenders began in the late 1960s. Particular attention was given after the publication in 1971 of the Home Office report *Habitual Drunken Offenders*. In practice most developments have taken place in the voluntary sector, but many have either been initiated by or significantly contributed to by probation officers or the Proba- tion Service. These initiatives have been blighted by the lack of a proper funding basis. More recently the work by Suzan Fairhead

(1981) at the Home Office Research Unit has suggested that a co-ordinated multi-disciplinary approach to working with this group of offenders is necessary. Cities where there are examples of good practice include Leeds, Manchester, Oxford, and Coventry. The services here include some of the following components:

(a) *Day-centre provision* This may be for probation clients solely or as a more general community provision, providing a welcoming environment where tea and food are available as well as bathing and washing facilities. A day-centre can often act as a 'shop front' affording access to other specialized services, as well as providing educational opportunities, social work, and welfare rights service.

(b) *Detoxification service* These places provide a temporary shelter for those needing to be detoxified where any medical needs can be attended to. They may be either units specializing in diverting drunkenness offenders from the courts as in Leeds or Manchester (Kessel *et al.* 1984) or part of a general community provision. Hashimi, Otto, and Shaw (1985) have comprehensively reviewed these projects. It is of considerable concern that government, through the Home Office and the DHSS, has now withdrawn funding from detoxification centres, leaving this aspect of dealing with alcohol problems to the police. There is an urgent need to persuade government of the short-sighted nature of its present policy. 'Out of Court', a group sponsored by a wide range of concerned organizations, such as the Association of Chief Police Officers, the Central Council of Probation and After-care Committees, and the National Association of Probation Officers, campaigns for alternatives to the police and prison cell for offenders, and for an adequate government response.

(c) *Emergency accommodation* Facilities need to exist for those temporarily homeless who do not fall within the provisions of the Homeless Persons Act. It is increasingly recognized that large night shelters are unsuitable for this task and that provision should be through small establishments, where careful assessment of the individual's housing and social needs can be made.

The inclusion of the single homeless within the terms of the Homeless Persons Act would do much to reduce the crisis of homelessness faced by many people. Organizations including the Campaign for the Single Homeless People (CHAR) and Shelter campaign for this change.

(d) *Supportive long-term accommodation* Most single homeless offenders live without a sense of continuity and roots. Good long-term accommodation fosters a sense of belonging. It is necessary to offer a variety of housing, for example, bedsitters, 'dry' houses (where there is a clear understanding that drinking is not permitted), and group homes (where residents set their own rules).

(e) *An active probation response*   This involves probation officers in providing a service which seeks out those homeless problem drinkers who wish to change their situation, either when they appear in court or when they are in contact with another agency. It may involve putting together a package of support in conjunction with other agencies.

(f) *A co-ordinated inter-agency approach*   To provide an effective service for those requiring several agencies there needs to be close liaison between agencies. This will ensure that clients receive the service they require and that there is no duplication of effort.

(v) *The compulsory use of Antabuse*
A new and controversial development has been the use, as yet only in inner London, of the drug Antabuse, which is administered as a condition of a probation order to those with a serious alcohol problem (Brewer 1982). Antabuse, in the absence of alcohol, passes through the body with only small side effects. In contact with alcohol it produces an extreme response of nausea, heart palpitation, and severe headache. The aim is to provide the client with a daily chemical reminder not to drink alcohol. This approach raises some crucial issues:

(a) Can a court, through a probation order, compel the administration of medication?

(b) What is the legal responsibility of the Probation Service in administering such a drug should there be side effects, or a fatality linked to drinking?

(c) Can it be argued that the end, a client not drinking, is justified by the means – compulsorily administering a drug?

An equally important question arises from the lack of facilities for homeless people, including problem drinkers, in many urban areas. It can be argued that adequate community facilities supported by intensive probation work would provide an equally effective service without the ethical misgiving which the compulsory administration of Antabuse causes.

(vi) *New approaches in custodial settings*
The closure of the alcoholic unit in Wakefield Prison in 1975 demonstrates the scanty attention paid to problem drinkers in prison, apart from the widespread visiting carried out by Alcholics Anonymous groups. However, three recent developments are noteworthy:

(a) An experiment at Low Moss Prison, Glasgow (Ditton and Phillips 1983) segregated alcohol-related offenders in an alcoholic unit where, while a normal prison routine was adhered to, meetings were held to discuss alcohol problems and plans on release. It was found that those attending the unit did rather better than the others in terms of not getting into so much trouble within the prison and having a lower reconviction rate.

(b) A number of large city prisons have attempted to link problem drinkers with agencies on release. Generally the results of these schemes have not been encouraging.

(c) Recently alcohol education groups or social skills groups with an alcohol component have been started in youth custody centres and prisons, which are often attended immediately prior to release.

Omissions

Despite the growth of special projects little has happened within the divorce court relating to alcohol problems. As alcohol problems are considered to contribute significantly to marital breakdown it is to be hoped that some experiments in this area might take place. Finally, and ironically for the Probation Service, Aquarius, a voluntary alcohol agency in Birmingham, recently appointed a court worker to identify and work with problem drinkers in the precincts of Birmingham Magistrates' Court.

The role of the Probation Service in the prevention of alcohol-related problems

Much of the work of the Probation Service takes place after the conviction of the offender, on an individual basis. With some exceptions little is done by the Probation Service in the prevention of alcohol problems in society. Outlined below is a strategy by which the Probation Service, along with other agencies, may become partners in the prevention field.

(i) *National prevention policies*

It is now generally recognized that the level of alcohol-related harm is proportional to the amount of alcohol consumed in a society (Royal College of Psychiatrists 1986). An increase in consumption will lead to an increase in harm. Although the price of alcohol is an important factor, it is not easy to work out how to reduce the level of harm and how to develop an effective preventive strategy on alcohol problems. Simplistic answers which fail to appreciate the positive role of alcohol in society or which do not have the backing of public opinion will be counter-productive.

The Royal Medical Colleges in 1984 formed 'Action on Alcohol Abuse'. It is beginning to provide a powerful focus for this debate. The Probation Service, through its national organizations (the Central Council of Probation Committee, the Association of Chief Officers of Probation, and the National Association of Probation Officers), should be active in this. Government clearly has a central role in prevention policies and its responsibilities are spelt out in the Central Policy Review staff report *Alcohol Policies* (Bruun 1982). This report remains unpublished and officially secret, though it is available from Sweden. In 1982 it was followed by a discussion document published by the DHSS called *Drinking Sensibly*. In this, government abrogates its responsibility for the leading and co-ordinating on alcohol policy, giving primacy to economic forces and responsibility to individuals for decisions about drinking.

In 1986 proposals have been put forward by government for a national 'Alcohol Forum', which would bring together agencies concerned with the problems of alcohol abuse, such as Alcohol Concern, with representatives of the drinks trade and government. It is unclear whether this forum will provide the opportunity for the development of a co-ordinated preventive strategy, or will come to be a talking shop with no real commitment by government and the trade to achieve a reduction in the incidence of alcohol problems.

(ii) *Local prevention strategies*
Despite the lack of centralized action by government the possibilities for developing local action are much more encouraging. Research at the Institute of Health Studies at Hull University, which has just been published, draws together a wide range of proposals for the reduction of alcohol-related problems (Tether and Robinson 1986). This publication is fully supported by the DHSS as the source book for tackling alcohol problems in Britain.

(a) *Action through the licensing law* Although our licensing law is in general in need of revision, the IHS group suggests that it could be made much more effective. The group proposes that each area should have a licensing forum comprising representatives of the magistrates, police, health services, the local authority, the drinks trade, and the Probation Service, where local policy can be agreed and particular problems addressed.

(b) *Action through preventive policing of the licensing law*   One function of the licensing law is to protect individuals and society. An experiment by the Devon and Cornwall police in a resort town, where licensees were informed that the police would pay particular attention to the enforcement of the licensing law, backed up by regular visits by the police, was carefully monitored by Jeffs and Saunders (1983). In comparison with a control town a drop in crime of 15 per cent was found during the experimental period.

(c) *Action by inter-agency co-operation*   Concern about city centre weekend crime, usually on the part of drunken young people, has led the Home Office Research Unit, in conjunction with the police, to look at this type of crime. A study from the north-east of England suggests that co-operation between the police, magistrates, local authorities, and drinks trade can lead to proposals which produce a city centre environment less conducive to crime. These various approaches suggest that each Probation Service with its committee can promote a strategy to prevent alcohol-related crime by action at both a local and a national level.

The task of management

Management has the responsibility of ensuring that every probation officer is able to respond to the variety of problem drinkers on his or her caseload and is adequately supported and resourced. The first task is to be clear about the level of need: the extent and nature of drink-related problems in each team's caseload has to be established.

(i) *Training*

An essential accompaniment to this responsibility is the provision of training so that the probation officer feels confident of recognizing and working with problem drinkers. Encouragingly, many probation officers attended the Summer Schools run by the Alcohol Education Centres and several regional training officers have run courses. Additionally, a number of county services run courses for their staff. The course run by Nottinghamshire Probation Service is an excellent model, involving team delegates developing areas of knowledge. Another approach is locally based multi-disciplinary training, which involves workers from the health, social services, and voluntary sectors.

Training should, as far as possible, be local and involve specialist workers from the nearby alcohol services. It should be organized to take into account the needs of officers in their day-to-day practice. Training should also be provided for managers to enable them to monitor the response to problem drinking, support and supervise probation officers in their work with clients. Furthermore, managers need to be assisted in monitoring the effectiveness of the service offered to problem drinkers. The Probation Service also has the responsibility for ensuring that pre-qualification training courses contain adequate coverage in working with problem drinkers.

(ii) *The development of services*

The Probation Service must be fully involved in consultations about the development of services. This may be through co-option to the relevant Health and Social Services joint care planning team or through other local co-ordinating structures. Much of the development in the voluntary sector, through councils on alcoholism and alcohol advisory services, dry houses, and day-centres, has been as a result of Probation Service initiatives. In areas with inadequate or non-existent specialized alcohol services the Probation Service should work with other agencies to develop them.

(iii) *The co-ordination of services*

The Probation Service should play its part in ensuring that all local agencies work together in the provision of services, training initiatives, and the prevention of alcohol problems.

(iv) *Employee alcohol policies*

Probation management and unions should develop policies and procedures so that employees are given the opportunity to receive help for an alcohol problem (Health and Safety Executive 1981). Alcohol Concern run a workplace service division established to advise on workplace service policies and practices.

Other drugs and their relationship to offending

The phenomenon of 'drug consciousness' which has overtaken British society during the mid 1980s will, no doubt, be studied by future social historians. As this chapter is being written it is impossible to ignore anti-drug campaigns in the local press, health education media campaigns, together with the rapid development of local services sponsored by the DHSS, and it is tempting to join in this hyperbole. Yet, in relation to alcohol problems, heroin misuse remains a relatively small-scale problem. Home Office figures show that 235 people died from drug abuse in 1984, whereas Action on Alcohol Abuse have estimated that over 25,000 people die each year from alcohol abuse. However, it is the rapid growth in drug problems which is of serious concern, spurring every department of the state into coordinated action. In the context of this rapidly changing use of drugs and the evolving views on appropriate responses, this section can present only a brief over-view of the relationship between drug use and offending and the task of the probation officer in relation to this changing social trend.

The drugs considered in this section can be divided into two groups: (a) drugs such as heroin, amphetamines, barbiturates, cocaine, and cannabis, whose possession is against the law; (b) substances taken for their mood-altering properties which are not illegal, for example, solvents and cough-mixture.

Why a particular drug is deemed illegal by British law, while another is not, provides a fascinating topic of study and in recent years an impor-tant debate has taken place concerning the legalization of cannabis and the control of solvents. Media images exploit the use of alcohol as a social cohesive and the use of drugs as a force towards disintegration.

Both images are over-simplifications. In fact, the most frequent users of mood-altering drugs are women who are prescribed tranquillizers to cope with the symptoms of stress. However, these large numbers of women, whatever their other life problems, do not become clients of the Probation Service. We need to look elsewhere for those whose drug use is a factor in offending.

Youth culture and drug taking

Over the last two decades certain groups within the youth culture have used drugs to symbolize their antagonism towards authority, parental lifestyles, and the establishment. These symbolic gestures have been determined by the peer group, the availability of a drug, its price, and the tolerance of society. However, they have been limited in time generally to the period of the individual's youth. But since the mid 1970s youth unemployment has risen markedly, making possible the development of new sub-cultures expressing alienation, anger, and frustration in relation to authority. To symbolize these attitudes, whose causes change from time to time, the sub-cultures use a variety of drugs.

Plant (1985) carried out a study following up 1,000 young men and women to examine their patterns of alcohol, tobacco, and illicit drug use three years after leaving school. He noted that whilst illicit drug use at school predicted later alcohol as well as drug use, alcohol consumption was not in itself predictive. He expressed particular concern about the high level of illicit drug use found amongst the young unemployed.

The availability of drugs, especially heroin, has grown apace since the mid 1970s, drawing in greater numbers of users. Media reports suggest that city housing estates where unemployment is high are experiencing a rapid growth in heroin use. People here find themselves at risk of being drawn into conflict with the law.

Drugs and offending

The research outlined below tells us that many drug users have had criminal records, suggesting that drug abuse is a step along an individual's path to criminality.

Prins (1980) reported that in a study of heroin addicts in a London prison, carried out by James in the late 1960s, 44 per cent had appeared before a juvenile court and 76 per cent had been convicted by a court before addiction. Gordon (1973) published a study of male, multiple drug users, who had started their drug taking before the age of twenty-one, and found that 92 per cent had court convictions and 48 per cent had been convicted before using drugs. Grimes reports that in a group of addicts that he studied 29 per cent were on probation (Grimes 1977).

Mott (1981) in a review of the literature came to the following conclusions:

'(i) About two-thirds of male opiate users have been convicted of offences before they become notified.

(ii) Their reconviction rates during follow-up periods of between two and five years, while they remain in receipt of prescriptions for opiates, may be higher than expected when their age and number of previous convictions are taken into account, because of the proportion convicted exclusively of drug offences.

(iii) While remaining in receipt of prescriptions for opiates they are likely to be convicted of drug offences and the majority of these offences will involve opiates, but the longer they continue to receive prescriptions the less likely they are to be convicted exclusively of drug offences.

(iv) A reduction in licit opiate use is accompanied by a reduction in convictions for any type of offence.

(v) Their non-drug offences, at any time, consist mainly of theft offences, and they are not likely to be convicted of offences involving violence against the person.'

Prins (1980) puts forward a three item classification of drugs and crime:

(i) Offences against Acts of Parliament established to control the possession, distribution, and consumption of drugs;

(ii) offences committed to obtain drugs, either by breaking into pharmacies, or to obtain money for the purchase of drugs;

(iii) offences due to the ingestion of drugs; these may include public order offences, assault, and damage to property.

While these categories are similar to those for alcohol and crime, the illegal nature of many drugs results in users being more likely to be in conflict with the law. Unlike the case with alcohol, possession of the drug may be more serious than an offence committed to obtain it or due to the ingestion of the drug. Additionally the cost of maintaining the habit will result in all but the most affluent having to commit crimes to produce the considerable funds necessary.

The scale of illegal drug use

The official statistics on illegal drug use derive from two sources – doctors treating opioid addicts and the agencies of law enforcement.

The fact that such use is illegal of necessity makes the interpretation of Home Office statistics fraught with dangers, and therefore such statistics are more useful in showing trends rather than as an accurate measure of drug use. None the less it is quite clear from the figures of narcotic addicts notified to the Home Office that there has been a massive rate of increase in drug use, and especially heroin use (see *Table 10*).

Table 10

yr	heroin addicts	total addicts
1953	60 (approx.)	290
1963	237	635
1973	847	1,496
1983	4,787	5,866
1984	6,611	7,410

Source: Institute for the Study of Drug Dependence (ISDD) (1985).

The true scale of use is probably several times these figures. Whereas during the mid 1970s law enforcement agencies felt that the illegal use of drugs was essentially under control, the present concern is that the growth of use is now out of control.

Working with the drug abuser

To work with an offender who uses drugs the probation officer will need a basic understanding of the drug, its normal effects, addictive properties, and sub-cultural meanings. A helpful publication on this topic is available from the Institute for the Study of Drug Dependence. A close liaison with a local medical or specialized drug service is important, but the essential work by the probation officer will be in the setting up of mutually agreed goals and the establishment of a positive, trusting relationship seeking to achieve them. In some areas this individual work is supported by self-help groups.

The DHSS released £3m. in 1984/85 as pump-priming money for services for drug abusers, and in 1986 released further monies to regional health authorities for the development of services. District health authorities are now obliged to draw up plans for local services for drug abusers and these will now be subject to inspection by the Health Advisory Service, which is responsible for ensuring the adequacy and quality of services. The Advisory Council on the Misuse of Drugs published a major report in 1982 in which it recommended that each area should have a drug advisory committee on which the Probation Service should be represented. These local committees can actively monitor the nature and the size of drug problem and make recommendations concerning prevention, services, and training, as well as ensuring good inter-agency co-operation.

Conclusion

The theme of this chapter has been that alcohol and drug use are so significantly interlinked with law breaking that it is essential that the Probation Service takes positive action in response to it. This must involve clear policy objectives with regard to alcohol and drug use by the Probation Service, adequate pre-qualification and post-qualification training, skilled supervision, and the opportunity for the development of properly evaluated client work.

There is growing evidence that this is beginning to happen and there must therefore be initiatives in the sharing of good practice, and the encouragement of innovative approaches. Initiatives must not be solely dependent upon the enthusiasm of an individual, but on the commitment of all levels of the Probation Service. With evidence of a growing convergence of theoretic approaches to understanding drinking, drug taking, and other behaviours (Orford 1985) it can be anticipated that a broader spectrum of alcohol related offending can be dealt with effectively by the Probation Service.

Yet the social context within which the Probation Service operates is continually evolving different views on order and law and the offender. Similarly, social attitudes to mood-altering substances are changing. Currently tobacco use is seen as harmful to the individual and the community, while there has been a steady growth in alcohol use and the use of illegal drugs. Britain in the mid 1980s remains staggeringly complacent about the harmful effects of alcohol while in the grip of a moral panic about the use of illegal drugs. Social attitudes are reflected in the attitudes of probation officers, and therefore necessarily have an impact on how practitioners define the factors in offending.

It is, therefore, essential that individual probation officers and the Service collectively evolve a critical view of our use of alcohol and drugs so as to be involved in the debate about the provision of appropriate services and in the development of preventive strategies both at local and national level.

Throughout its history the Probation Service has found itself at the sharp end in dealing with alcohol and drug-related offending. Current trends suggest that this is unlikely to change but the growth in the understanding of alcohol and drug use has substantially improved our ability to respond to it.

© *1987 Robert Purser*

References

Advisory Council on the Misuse of Drugs (1982) *Report of the Working Party on Treatment and Rehabilitation.* London: DHSS.

Alcohol Concern (1986) *Alcohol Services: A Directory for England and Wales.* London: Alcohol Concern.

Bailey, H. and Purser, R. (1982) *Coventry Alcohol Education Group. Report on the First Twelve Months.* Coventry and Warwickshire Council on Alcoholism.

Barr, A. (1984) The Ideologies of Despair: A Symbolic Interpretation of Punks' and Skinheads' Usage of Barbiturates. *Social Science Medicine* 19(9).

Brewer, C. (1982) Probation with Antibuse: A New Chance for Alcoholic Offenders? *Probation Journal* 29.

Bruun, K. (1982) Alcohol Policies in the United Kingdom. University of Stockholm.

Cartwright, A.K.J., Shaw, S.J., and Spratley, T.A. (1975) *Designing a Comprehensive Community Response to Problems of Alcohol Abuse.* Maudsley Alcohol Pilot Project. London: DHSS.

Chambers, A. (1984) Cautioning: The Metropolitan Police

Experiment. Paper given at a joint Out of Court/FARE/Avon Council on Alcoholism Conference.

Department of the Environment (1976) *Drinking and Driving – Report by the Departmental Committee* (Blennerhassett Report). London: HMSO.

DHSS (1982) *Drinking Sensibly*. London: HMSO.

Ditton, J. and Phillips, C. (1983) *An Exploratory Assessment of the Positive Rehabilitation Potential of the Alcohol Unit at HM Prison Low Moss*. Unpublished thesis, Department of Sociology, University of Glasgow.

Donnan, S.P.B. and Haskey, J. (1977) Alcoholism and Cirrhosis of the Liver. *Population Trends* 7(18). London: OPCS.

Fairhead, S. (1981) *Petty Persistent Offenders*. Home Office Research Studies. London: HMSO.

Gardin, A. (1973) Patterns of Delinquency in Drug Addiction. *British Journal of Psychiatry* 122.

Goodman, P. (1983) Probation and the Chronic Drinker. *Probation Journal* 30(3).

Goodman, P. and Scott, J. (1982) Trouble through Drink – a Probation Response to Drink-related Problems. *Probation Journal* 29(4).

Gordon, A.M. (1973) Patterns of Delinquency in Drug Addiction. *British Journal of Psychiatry* 122: 205–10.

Grimes, J. (1977) *Drug Dependency Study – A Survey of Drug Addicts Attending for Treatment*. London: HMSO.

Hamson, C., Knapman, E., Mallett, J., and Smith, M. (1983) *Corby Alcohol Therapy Group 1979–81 Report*. Northampton: Northamptonshire Probation Service.

Harwin, J. (1979) Recognition of Alcohol Problems. *Social Work Today* 10(41).

Hashimi, L., Otto, S., and Shaw, S. (1985) *Problem Drinking Experiments in Detoxification. Report of the Detoxification Evaluation Project*. London: Bedford Square Press/National Council of Voluntary Organizations.

Health and Safety Executive (1981) *The Problem Drinker at Work*. London: HMSO.

Heather, N. and Robertson, I. (1981) *Controlled Drinking*. London: Methuen.

——— (1986) *Problem Drinking – The New Approach*. Harmondsworth: Penguin.

Herefordshire and Worcestershire Probation Service (1982) *Report to Staff Conference*. Unpublished.

Holtermann, S. and Burchell, A. (1981) *The Costs of Alcohol Misuse*. Government Economic Service Working Paper. London: DHSS.

Home Office (1971) *Habitual Drunken Offenders – Report of the Working*

Party. London: HMSO.

—— (1980) *Report of the Parole Board 1979*. London: HMSO.

Hough, M. and Mayhew, P. (1983) *The British Crime Survey – Home Office Research and Planning Unit Report*. London: HMSO.

Institute for the Study of Drug Dependence (1985) *Official Statistics on the Misuse of Drugs*. London: ISDD.

Jeffs, D. and Saunders, W. (1983) Minimizing Alcohol-related Offences by Enforcement of the Existing Licensing Legislation. *British Journal of Addiction* 78(1).

Kessel, N., Makenjuola, J., Rossall, C., Chand, T., Flore, B., Redmond, A., Rees, D., Gordon, M., and Wallace, P. (1984) The Manchester Detoxification Service. *The Lancet* 14 April.

Knapman, E. (1982) Unpublished M.Sc. thesis, Cranfield Institute of Science and Technology.

Lewis, R. (1985) The Illicit Heroin Market. *Probation Journal* 32(2).

Martin, J. (1986) A Course for Drivers Convicted of Drink/Driving. *Justice of the Peace* 150(12): 182–84.

Morris, R. and Murphy, E. (1973) *Alcohol Offenders, Court and Community*. London: Helping Hand Organization.

Mott, J. (1981) Criminal Involvement and Penal Response. In G. Edwards and C. Busch (eds) *Drug Problems in Britain*. London: Academic Press.

Orford, J. (1985) *Excessive Appetites: a Psychological View of Addictions*. Chichester: John Wiley.

Plant, M. (1985) *Alcohol, Drugs, and School Leavers*. London: Tavistock.

Prins, H. (1980) *Offenders, Deviants, or Patients*. London: Tavistock.

Robertson, I. and Heather, N. (1982) An Alcohol Education Course for Young Offenders. A Preliminary Report. *British Journal of Alcohol and Alcoholism* 17(1).

Royal College of Psychiatrists (1986) *Alcohol – Our Favourite Drug* (2nd edn. of the report *Alcohol and Alcoholism*). London: Tavistock.

Shaw, S., Cartwright, A., and Spratley, T. (1978) *Responding to Drinking Problems*. London: Croom Helm.

Stewart, A. (1984) Clacton Problem Drinkers Group. *Probation Journal* 31(2).

Taylor, D. (1985) Summary of the Results of the Humberside Probation Client Caseload Survey. In M. Backhouse, I. Gurevitch, and S. Silver (eds) *Problem Drinkers and the Statutory Services*. Hull: Humberside Probation Service.

Tether, P. and Robinson, D. (1986) *Preventing Alcohol Problems*. London: Tavistock.

Wilson, P. (1980) *Drinking in England and Wales*. London: Office of Population Censuses and Surveys/HMSO.

Further Reading

Advisory Committee on Alcoholism (1978) *Pattern and Range of Services for Problem Drinkers*. London: HMSO.
Collins, J.J. (1982) *Drinking and Crime*. London: Tavistock.
Davies, J. and Raistrick, D. (1981) *Dealing with Drink*. London: BBC Publications.
Dorn, N. (1983) *Alcohol, Youth and the State*. London: Croom Helm.
Edwards, G. (1983) *The Treatment of Drinking Problems*. London: Grant McIntyre.
Edwards, G. and Grant, M. (1980) *Alcoholism Treatment in Transition*. London: Croom Helm.
Gossop, M. (1982) *Living with Drugs*. London: Temple Smith.
McConville, B. (1983) *Women under the Influence*. London: Virago.
Plant, M.A. (1982) *Drinking and Problem Drinking*. London: Junction Books.
Stimson, G. and Oppenheimer, E. (1982) *Heroin Addiction, Treatment and Control in Britain*. London: Tavistock.
Williamson, P. and Norris, N. (1984) *Personal Skills Training for Problem Drinkers*. Aquarius and Alcoholics Rehabilitation Research Group. Birmingham: University of Birmingham.

Useful Addresses

Institute for the Study of Drug Dependence (ISDD)
1–4 Hatton Place
Hatton Garden
London EC1N 8ND
Tel: 01-430-1991

Standing Conference on Drug Abuse
1–4 Hatton Place
Hatton Garden
London EC1N 8ND
Tel: 01-430-2341/2

Alcohol Concern
305 Gray's Inn Road
London WC1X 8QF
Tel: 01-833-3471

Action on Alcohol Abuse
Livingstone House
11 Carteret Street
London SW1H 9DL
Tel: 01-222-3454/5

Teachers Advisory Council on Alcohol and Drug Education
(TACADE)
3rd Floor, Furness House
Trafford Road
Salford M5 2XJ
Tel: 061-848-0351

Southern Office
202 Holdenhurst Road
Bournemouth BH8 8AS
Tel: 0202-295874

Out of Court – alternatives for drunkenness offenders
Livingstone House
11 Carteret Street
London SW1H 9DL
Tel: 01-222-3454/5

Directories

Drug Problem: Where to Get Help. BBC Drugwatch/SCODA.
Alcohol Services: A Directory for England and Wales. Alcohol Concern.

9 Racism and the offender: a probation response

Richard Green

'I would like to think that I look upon all the people I deal with as sort of colourless, classless.'

(White probation officer talking about his work with black offenders)

Introduction

Working as a probation officer and subsequently senior probation officer in the West Midlands for the past eight years has provided a number of challenging experiences. One among them is the case of a young black juvenile (the term 'black' will be used here to denote people of Afro-Caribbean origin rather than in the wider political sense) who had been released on licence from a Detention Centre. At first he came in weekly. He tended to arrive late and clearly was coming in under protest. He would sit with head bowed, staring at the floor, making the occasional monosyllabic reply to questions or sighing deeply. I tried desperately to induce some communication between us using what skills and knowledge were available to me, but never with any real success. When I called at his home invariably he was out. His parents complained bitterly about his truancy from school, refusal to attend church, and staying out until the early hours of the morning. Eventually he stopped coming into the probation office altogether and shortly afterwards got into trouble again and was sent to Borstal. I recall feeling completely frustrated and totally powerless to influence him. Colleagues talked of similar experiences and the same feelings of frustration and helplessness.

Cases like this eventually crystallized my feelings that the Probation Service was uncertain about how to deal with such young black offenders. The usual approaches were unsuccessful and it seemed that a new response was needed, though what kind of response was unclear. To give the matter more consideration I decided to make a study of the Probation Service's work with young black offenders under the guidance of Aston University. For the past six years this has

180

involved a survey of the literature on race and deviance; a detailed analysis of 138 court reports on juveniles; close observation from inside of the Probation Service's work with young black offenders; observation of the Handsworth Cultural Centre and the City and Handsworth Alternative Scheme; and in-depth interviews about race with fourteen probation officers and other colleagues in the field of deviance. The emphasis of the research was initially on the young black offenders, but eventually shifted on to the Probation Service itself. It had led me to the conclusion that the Probation Service is itself making black people a problem instead of dealing with the problems of black people.

Institutional racism and colour-blindness in the Probation Service

In 1979, as part of the research, a survey was made of social inquiry reports prepared on juveniles in Wolverhampton. It showed that in only 6 per cent of black male juvenile cases was supervision by a probation officer recommended; the equivalent figure for indigenous male cases was 23 per cent. It also revealed that while probation officers were less willing to commit themselves on whether the young blacks were likely to get into trouble again, where they did give an opinion they felt it was more likely than with young whites. Despite this feeling that the risk was greater, fewer recommendations for the long-term involvement of a probation officer with young blacks was made. The net effect was that young blacks were generally higher up the tariff ladder of sentences than similar whites at the same point in their deviant career; they were also more at risk of attracting a custodial sentence because of this.

Other researchers have reported the disproportionate number of young blacks in custodial institutions (Taylor 1981; Guest 1984). Taylor offered a number of possible explanations for why this was, but came down in favour of none in particular; Guest concluded that the disproportionate number of blacks in the youth custody system was due to the acute social disadvantage they suffered, which made them more prone to commit crime. My own conclusion is that part of the reason for the failure of the Probation Service to divert black youngsters from custody lies in the irrelevance of what it currently has to offer them. With the best of intentions, it has for a long time looked upon black and white deviants as the same; the effect, however, has been to ignore racism as a contributory factor in black deviance and thereby to disadvantage black offenders instead of helping them.

One of the difficulties with larger institutions like the Probation

181

Culture of service

Probation and the community

Service is that they develop a culture of their own into which their employees are socialized. It then becomes extremely difficult to isolate practices which are making the organization dysfunctional, because they have become so much a part of the daily routine. This process occurs more usually by default than deliberately, as Husband (1980) pointed out. However, in matters of racism it is not the good intention that counts, but the actual effect such policies and practices have on the black people these organizations are supposed to serve. It is not necessarily the case that probation officers who fail to recommend supervision for black juveniles are racists; the problem is that the ideology and practices of the Probation Service, into which they have been socialized, lead officers to conclude that black clients are unsuitable for supervision.

One aspect of this process of socialization is the failure of officers to acknowledge the different influences bearing on black and white crime. Researchers on race do not tend to work on crime and so no adequate theory of black crime has ever been available to officers. Criminology tends to be 'colour-blind', and so probation officers apply the same criminological theories to black offenders as to white. Regardless of race, offending behaviour tends to be attributed to pathological factors such as family disruptions, lack of effort at school resulting in unemployment and boredom, or an aggressive personality. However, this kind of colour-blind approach fails to recognize that the black life experience is fundamentally different from white experience in our society, and that the difference is due to racism. Structural theorists about racial disadvantage have begun to emerge. Marxist authors such as Solomos (Solomos _et al._ 1982) use a class analysis to identify the way in which race has been used as a scapegoat to divert attention from what they see as the organic crisis of British capitalism. Rex and Tomlinson (1979), on the other hand, adopt a Weberian perspective to identify black Britons as an 'underclass', a separate status group inferior to the white working class, which constantly loses out in the perpetual jockeying between groups for power and access to public resources. These structural theories have begun to influence some writers in the field of deviance; Joshua and Wallace (1983: 5) concluded that the street disturbances in Bristol in 1980 were not meaningless, inexplicable violence, which was the view promoted by the government; but rather 'a reactive attempt to gain access to state power, and to change the stance and role of the state on race'. However, to date such theories have had little impact on the work of the Probation Service in its daily dealings with black deviance. Racism is hardly ever taken into account by probation officers when writing court reports on black offenders. It was often hard to

Colour
blindness

PS doesn't differentiate and treat all the same.

distinguish from the content of those social inquiry reports surveyed during the research whether the offender was black or white, save for the occasional reference to parental origins or by the offender's name. Many liberal probation officers, like the one quoted at the beginning of this chapter, are eager not to differentiate and deliberately set out to treat everyone in the same way. Yet the way in which black people are reacted to, and the way they themselves act, is all mediated through the colour of their skin. No attempt by a probation officer to explain black crime will be adequate unless it takes radical disadvantage into account rather than simple social disadvantage.

If the situation is to change, the Probation Service has to reconsider its established practices and routines in the light of institutional racism and colour-blindness. There are a number of aspects which lend themselves to criticism, but the research highlighted five in particular: recruitment; training; professionalization; individualization, and integration.

RECRUITMENT
A survey conducted in the West Midlands Probation Service in 1979 showed that while 13.3 per cent of the county's caseload was of Afro-Caribbean or South Asian origin (26.5 per cent in north Birmingham; 22 per cent in Wolverhampton) only 9 out of 372 (2.42 per cent) probation officers were from these minority groups. Though there has been a slight improvement, these groups remain unrepresented in the Service. However, increasing their number to 13.3 per cent would not resolve the issue; that would only load the responsibility on to their shoulders and allow white officers to believe they can place the issue to one side. Nevertheless, black officers can make a significant contribution. With many white officers race as an issue is peripheral to their lives which, as the interviews with them showed, leads them to believe that the problems are minor and will pass:

'Most of the people I've spoken to about some of the race problems that exist seem to think that it is the minority, and most of the West Indian lads aren't that interested anyway, and in the main they get on really well and are doing OK.'

(white West Midlands probation officer)

'It is a similar sort of thing to a persistent offender; usually by the time he is twenty-four or twenty-five he meets a girl, tends to sort of calm down, and I've got a feeling that it is going to be multi-racial, far more acceptable in a generation's time here, and I don't think that these problems are going to be quite so prominent.'

(white West Midlands probation officer)

183

The attitude of these officers seemed to be that if ignored the whole problem would go away. However, such an attitude denies colour as a factor in the black offenders' development and sense of personal identity. This is not a mistake which black probation officers would make. Those interviewed clearly remembered incidents when they had been the victims of racist attitudes, their strength of feeling showing through:

'As a young kid when I came to England, I had never cried so much in my life in terms of prejudice: you sit on a bus and people get up next to you; or you offer somebody your seat, particularly old women, who will say to me that they don't take seats from wogs, and words I'd never heard before in my life.'
(black West Midlands senior probation officer)

For black people racism is a permanent and often central feature of their lives, not fleeting and peripheral as with white officers. Black officers are therefore more likely to identify racist practices and seek to change them. This process has begun in the West Midlands where a 'race forum' has been created to act as a pressure group.

There is no shortage of black people wanting to become probation officers. The barrier to their recruitment is the Certificate of Qualification in Social Work. The requirement for the CQSW is a prime example of institutional racism and colour-blindness: the intention to recruit better qualified people as probation officers is laudable; the effect, however, is to exclude a number of black candidates. Because of poor experiences in schools and the pressures of racism generally, fewer black candidates achieve the necessary academic qualifications that would enable them to qualify for a place on a course of professional training, especially when in fierce competition with whites who may have degrees or GCE passes. Having a universal method of entry fails to recognize the racial disadvantage suffered by black people: it purports to treat black and white the same, but in fact is colour-blind and so actually puts black people at a disadvantage. One answer might be for the Probation Service or the Home Office to establish access courses for unqualified candidates, which could be of great benefit in helping more black people to take up places on CQSW courses.

TRAINING

Once recruited into the Probation Service, the next step is to train candidates. Training on race relations issues is crucial if the Probation Service is to work effectively with black offenders. At one time professional training courses ignored race issues completely. Of those interviewed during the research who had undergone training, six had experienced no input at all on race. The rest had had some input but said it was limited in content and tended to deal with ethnicity issues.

Some courses are now attempting to address racism more directly. However, the lack of teaching on race by professional training courses in the past means that there are a number of practising probation officers whose knowledge of race issues is inadequate. Though in-service training on race is available, for a long time this also concentrated on the less contentious issue of ethnicity. One white senior probation officer interviewed who was involved in the organization of in-service training on race mentioned the need to 'approach this with a great deal of sensitivity and care, or the defences go up and you have done an injustice to people so that they go away more entrenched than when they arrived'. Her desire to deal with the issue sensitively was meant to be helpful in that beneath it lay the wish for white officers to have a positive experience about race. However, in reality such an approach would allow officers to end the course without having considered institutional racism at all. They could go away content with their knowledge on race when in fact there was an entire area which had been ignored. Black probation officers, in contrast, said they believed that institutional racism had to be examined on such training courses however painful the process was. They felt that issues of conflict, such as the problems of black officers working within a predominantly white organization, or the responses of offenders to black people in authority, had to be tackled. They were in favour of courses which heightened probation officers' awareness that the Probation Service as an organization could be a part of the problem, instead of black offenders being labelled as the problem and the race issue left alone.

PROFESSIONALIZATION

Improved training is an illustration of the Probation Service's desire to be seen as a professional organization. The Probation Service does not have an easy task in arguing for the rehabilitation of offenders, particularly at a time when there are popular fears about the increase in the crime rate and calls for harsher sentencing. As an attempt to counter such calls, as well as out of self-interest, the Probation Service is eager to improve its professional image. The additional prestige it gains from professionalization enables the Service to exert more influence within the criminal justice system to the benefit of the offender. However, professionalization is a double-edged sword in that the greater prestige which it brings can be used to hinder and retard change as well as to promote it. There was evidence from the research that a number of probation officers clearly felt threatened by their inability to relate to young blacks. Their lack of response was seen as a challenge to officers' professional competence. One senior probation officer argued that young black people made probation officers feel unsuccessful:

'I think probation officers do find it difficult and would rather not engage therefore with young black people because it makes them feel *unsuccessful*, and anything that does that to us, we would rather work in an area where we could be regarded as successful and not the opposite.'   (white West Midlands senior probation officer)

Perhaps it is a natural reaction that officers should want to work with those clients where they feel there is a reasonable chance of success. However, it could equally be argued that out of a desire to appear competent and successful, they avoid risk-taking and holding out for non-custodial sentences when faced with a doubting court. The end result of what began as an attempt to increase prestige to assist offenders could be that young blacks are disadvantaged by not being offered supervision. There was evidence of this in the reports examined, which usually contained a recommendation as to sentence, particularly in the concluding paragraph. An example is:

'It is now some two and a half years since Leroy last appeared in court. He lives in an area of high delinquency where the opportunity to commit this sort of offence is frequent. It is perhaps to his credit that he has managed not to reoffend for four years. However, if the court is prepared to view this offence as a minor setback, it may consider that Leroy is able to pay an appropriate monetary penalty from his not inconsiderable weekly pocket money.'
(report on a black fifteen-year-old)
'It is my opinion that he is in need of some structured training which at this stage might not necessarily have to be in a closed environment. The desired result may be achieved by making him the subject of an attendance centre order.'
(report on a black fifteen-year-old)
'While it is freely admitted that he has problems with his home, he must learn that the commission of anti-social acts is not an appropriate way of dealing with them. Hence, while it may seem harsh to him, it is felt that a short period at a detention centre at this stage could cause him to reconsider his attitudes and behaviour at an age when there is still time to make something of his life.'
(report on a black sixteen-year-old)

Their probation officers seemed to be blaming these young black offenders for their behaviour with little reference to the social context. One officer refers to the offender living in a delinquent area, but any thoughts on why the area might have become delinquent, or why this family found itself living there are missing from the report. Paradoxically, officers seemed to use the delinquency of their black clients as a reason to avoid the involvement of offering supervision; the challenge to their professionalism offered by such clients seemed a likely explanation for this withdrawal of service. Professionalization could help black people, but only if the Probation Service uses its prestige to place black crime in its social context and argue the case against racism. The evidence from the research was that at present it is doing exactly the opposite.

INDIVIDUALIZATION

One of the problems the Probation Service has in arguing the case against racism is that the criminal justice system deals with the offender individually. Courts do not encourage a more global perspective which views offending within a wider social context. When this has been done it has been queried by a doubting judiciary (Mathieson 1982). By definition racism operates at the level of groups: a whole section of the community is discriminated against on the grounds of its colour or cultural behaviour. If racism is to be properly understood it has to be understood at a global level. The Probation Service, however, adheres to all kinds of social work values which talk about the need to treat clients as individuals; to adopt a non-judgemental attitude and accept the individual whatever his or her deviations; and to pay attention to the individual's needs and rights. Unfortunately this ideology, laudable in itself, hinders a proper understanding of the significance of racism as a factor in deviance because probation officers are trained into an occupational perspective which makes it difficult for them to rise above individual cases.

The origins of social work culture also lie in a view of the world seen in terms of psychodynamics and psychological explanations for behaviour. These marry well with the offender-centred approach of the criminal justice system. However, probation officers regularly meet examples of racial disadvantage which properly ought not to lend themselves to offender-centred explanations. Nevertheless, their socialization into Probation Service culture leads them to conclusions drawn from family or individual pathology.

The kinds of explanations for black deviance advanced by probation officers in the reports examined during the research referred to factors such as mental illness; disruptions in the black family leading to inadequate socialization; peer group influence; and an anti-authority attitude. Few reports tried to place the offending within the social context of racism; most tended to blame black offenders for their own disadvantage. Such colour-blind explanations run the risk of seeing deviant acts committed by black people as incompetent acts, and are unlikely to make for effective work with such offenders. Probation officers need to consider the global perspective, even if they must be cautious when preparing reports for certain judges.

INTEGRATION
One reason why a more global perspective is discouraged may be that public welfare organizations do not exist solely for the benefit of their clientele. As has been suggested elsewhere (Bailey and Brake 1975:2), state welfare schemes are seen in their true perspective only when it is realized that they exist not to bring about social justice but to sustain the established situation. Probation officers stand at the intersection between the powerful and powerless; only if they can convince courts that individual deviants pose no threat to society will they be allowed to claim them as their clients. When offenders are allowed to remain in the community, the task then assigned to probation officers is to seek their clients' rehabilitation by getting them to conform to the standards of mainstream society. The question of obtaining social justice does not arise. This 'integrationist' ideology is particularly problematic when dealing with black people because of their position as an underclass in the social structure. To try to reintegrate black offenders with society as it is currently structured is to try to persuade them to accept a position of disadvantage on the basis of their ethnicity. In such circumstances, as Rex and Tomlinson (1979: 242) observed of social workers in the Handsworth district of Birmingham, the socialization of the black client seems less relevant than fighting with him against society for a better deal. Herein lies the dilemma for the Probation Service: in work with black offenders racism is a key issue and necessitates facing up to the issues raised by their position as an underclass; yet the Service's roots and traditions lie in an integrationist ideology and in treating everyone in the same way, rather than in fighting for social justice. Because the influence of the Service's roots and traditions is still strong, most of the officers interviewed during the research took the view that the appropriate response is equal treatment for all. Few white officers were in favour of special initiatives to try to deal with the additional disadvantage suffered by black offenders. They believed that such initiatives would fuel myths about black people getting preferential treatment. One white officer stated baldly that she believed the objective should be to assimilate black people so that they would become like whites, and not

to emphasize the differences. By contrast, black workers favoured special initiatives and were often involved in promoting them. One officer criticized the integrationist stance taken by some white officers:

'They're denying themselves that there are differences and in so doing it is making their job easier. Because if they acknowledge that there are differences, it is going to be more taxing on them to actually meet these differences, identify differences and meeting the needs that these differences give rise to.'

(black West Midlands probation officer)

She felt that such officers are denying that black people are different, which leads to the cultural traditions and philosophies of the white probation officer being imposed, by design or default, on the black client.

The integrationist traditions of the Probation Service are praise-worthy insofar as they seek a more tolerant response from society towards the social outcast. However, when probation officers are dealing with racial disadvantage, such traditions generate colour-blind practices within the Service which inhibit effective work with black offenders. If probation officers do not fight against the racial disadvantage experienced by their black clients then they can never hope to gain the confidence of the black community.

Producing change within an organization like the Probation Service is no easy task. Even the most caring of people can be socialized into the normal practices and daily routines fostered by its ideology, without realizing their racist implications. It then becomes hard to believe that racist practices exist and that a new response is required; all kinds of defence mechanisms operate to draw a veil over the issue. However, new responses from the Probation Service *are* required: they must leave behind colour-blind approaches and recognize the centrality of racial disadvantage to black deviance. In the next section two responses made in the West Midlands will be reviewed.

A new response

Until recently probation practice has been developed largely by whites and so based on their norms. Black people, however, belong to a socially stigmatized category, and their experience of racism produces different attitudes and responses within them as a group. This in turn requires a different response from the Probation Service. Attempts have been made in the West Midlands to provide this new response in the form of projects funded under the terms of the Inner-City Partnership Scheme. These projects differ from traditional probation practice in that they attempt to get away from the traditional colour-blind approaches which have predominated.

One of the most imaginative initiatives in the West Midlands has been the Handsworth Cultural Centre. The Cultural Centre deals with black people as a group. It operates as a community centre, using, for instance, black dance, drumming, and steel band to promote black culture in the community and, through cultural achievements, to inspire the confidence within individuals to deal better with all aspects of their lives. It also seeks to link young blacks, many of whom have never seen the Caribbean or Africa, with their cultural roots. Some have visited the Caribbean thanks to funds raised by the Cultural Centre; others have increased their knowledge through maps, pictures, and music; yet others have visited Africa to learn traditional dances. What is most striking when visiting the Centre is the feeling that it is a Centre for black people: pictures of dancers in traditional dress, maps of Africa and the Caribbean, and posters describing the lives of African kings abound on the walls. Another feature is that the staff are predominantly black, starting with the first person seen on entering – the receptionist. Most of the staff and sessional workers live locally and so know socially the users of the Centre and the rest of their families. The Cultural Centre has been very successful in providing a leisure facility within their own community which local black people feel comfortable about using. It has the added qualities of promoting a positive image of black culture (often berated by others); and using cultural activities as a device to raise the awareness of young blacks about their cultural origins and make them proud of them.

The City and Handsworth Alternative Scheme, sponsored by the National Association for the Care and Resettlement of Offenders, is another project developed initially in the Handsworth area. It originated from a white senior probation officer's concern at the large number of young blacks from the local community who were being sent into custody. It aimed to prevent this by assisting probation officers to provide the court with the most positive image possible of such offenders. In this way it hoped to secure alternative sentences, primarily probation orders. In fact, through the reluctance of probation officers to make referrals to the project, it has tended to diverge from the Service and obtain its own referrals by locating a worker within the courts. This worker contacts young blacks at court, usually as they are waiting to appear for the first time, and gives basic advice on court procedures and the advantages of having a sympathetic solicitor. Hence, CHAS tends to get involved at an earlier stage than the Probation Service, and often prepares court reports on defendants on its own initiative. It seeks to link its offenders with employment projects, courses, and accommodation facilities which have largely been developed by black people for the local black community. The advantage of such a project is that it starts by recognizing racial disadvantage as a major contributory factor in black crime. It employs workers who are sensitive to the implications of being black in a predominantly white society and can talk freely with offenders about these problems. Like the Cultural Centre it mostly employs black workers, and is located close to the community it serves.

Projects such as the Cultural Centre and CHAS are bold initiatives founded on the belief that black offenders are different. They reject the traditional colour-blind approaches of the Probation Service and place the redressing of racial disadvantage at the centre of what they are attempting to achieve. As might be expected, their new approach has not always been welcomed by probation officers. Officers who felt threatened by the challenges of their black clients have felt even more threatened by these projects. They argue that providing extra facilities for black people increases the resentment felt among whites and will only worsen race relations; that all offenders should be treated alike; that such projects do not employ professional social work staff; and that too much money and effort is being put into such projects at the expense of traditional Probation Service work.

Imaginative and inspired as they are, such projects do bring dilemmas of their own. One of the most difficult is that they ghetto-ize black people, diverting them into projects primarily designed for a single racial category. This kind of differentiation adds legitimacy to the use of skin colour to separate out one group of people from another. Taken to an extreme it could lead to systems of apartheid similar to those found in South Africa. Another dilemma is that there is a risk of developing a two-tier probation system, with black people receiving a second-class service. Projects funded by the Inner City Partnership have a limited life, and tend to employ staff without social work qualifications. It could be argued that the 'street knowledge' which black staff have is more relevant; nevertheless, the short-life nature of these projects means that the best of their recruits move on to more secure employment, or to obtain qualifications which will enable them to command a higher salary. Whatever is the case, their black clients are in danger of losing out through the lack of stability and permanency in the projects. A third area of concern is the danger of the Cultural Centre and CHAS raising the expectations of the black people they serve with little hope of their expectations being fulfilled. The Cultural Centre could produce people who are experts in African dance or steel band, and take pride in their culture and in doing something well; equally, CHAS could improve the quality of their clients' lives by keeping them out of custody, improving their accommodation, and getting them a place on a government employment scheme. However, despite all this, racism will remain a feature of their lives and they will have to battle constantly against its effects. It may be that an expert in African dance, or someone who has been on a course, still cannot obtain employment and feels the only effective way of combating racial disadvantage is by offending. Such dilemmas as these place question marks against the validity of the projects and are not easily resolved.

Conclusion

The central argument of this chapter has been that black offenders are different, and that it is racial disadvantage which makes them so. A different response is called for from the Probation Service, which needs to take a step back from its daily routines and practices to look at itself afresh in the context of institutional racism. In particular, it needs to rid itself of its traditional colour-blind approach to black deviance. The Cultural Centre and CHAS are attempts to do this, and have provided positive alternative responses which firmly locate black crime in its social context. Nevertheless, they have created dilemmas of their own which as yet remain unresolved.

© *1987 Richard Green*

References

Bailey, R. and Brake, M. (1975) *Radical Social Work*. London: Edward Arnold.

Guest, C.L. (1984) A Comparative Analysis of the Career Patterns of Black and White Young Offenders. Unpublished M.Sc. thesis, Cranfield Institute of Technology.

Husband, C. (1980) Notes on Racism in Social Work Practice. In *Multi-Racial Social Work* 1: 5–15.

Joshua, H. and Wallace, T. (1983) *To Ride the Storm: the 1980 Bristol 'Riot' and the State*. London: Heinemann.

Mathieson, D. (1982) Social Comment – An Appropriate Role for the Probation Service. *Justice of the Peace* (23 October): 660–62.

Rex, J. and Tomlinson, S. (1979) *Colonial Immigrants in a British City*. London: Routledge and Kegan Paul.

Solomos, J., Findlay, B., Jones, S., and Gilroy, P. (1982) The Organic Crisis of British Capitalism and Race: the Experience of the Seventies. In Centre for Contemporary Cultural Studies (University of Birmingham) *The Empire Strikes Back: Race and Racism in 70s Britain*. London: Hutchinson.

Taylor, W. (1981) *Probation and After-Care in a Multi-Racial Society*. London: Commission for Racial Equality.

10 Reparation: the background, rationale, and relevance to criminal justice

John Harding

'These prison bars are an incarnation not of our society, but of our world's inability to produce a workable concept of justice and penance. Here are the bars, clanging, needing paint, the facts of our sense of good and evil, arbitrary, vestigial and cruel.'

(John Cheever, *Notebooks*)

The revival of interest in the concept of reparation by governments, criminal justice personnel, the public, and the media has been the subject of much speculation and small-scale experimentation over the past five years, particularly in the United Kingdom, North America, and Europe, after centuries of neglect and abandonment. Indeed, Stephen Schafer, a Hungarian criminologist, writing in exile from London in 1960 would have been surprised by the strength of the revival over a short period of two decades. He conducted an international survey of twenty-nine countries on behalf of the Home Office, inquiring about the status of reparation. 'The general situation involves the victim of crime in a more or less hopeless position with regard to his claim for restitution' (Schafer 1960:10).

In all but a few countries, Schafer found that redress to the victim was a civil matter, not an issue of consideration in criminal proceedings. In advance of his time, Schafer proposed a system where reparation is an integral part of criminal justice. He justified this position on the grounds that along with the state's right to punish breaches of the law, there should be an obligation to ensure injuries are repaired.

Schafer's advocacy was based on his knowledge of history, reparation being a central feature in the resolution of disputes in primitive cultures. As an alternative to the blood feud, characterized by retaliation and revenge, a victim or his kin could receive from the offender material compensation for personal injury or loss. This process of negotiation and payment to the victim has been referred to as 'composition'. Under this system in King Alfred's England an offender could 'buy back the peace he had broken' by paying 'wer' payment for homicide, or 'bot' payment for injuries other than death, to the victim or his kin, according to a schedule of injury tariffs.

By the medieval era, the process of negotiation and settlement had been replaced by the increasing power of the king and his barons. The gradual shift towards centralization led to state control over the criminal law, which saw the link between reparation and punishment virtually severed. The victim's only recourse to justice was through the civil courts. However, this route was beset with limitations; apart from the expense in terms of time and money in bringing a civil action against the offender, the chances of collection were not high, since many offenders were poor, out of work, or destitute.

The interest in reparation was kept alive over the centuries by a number of philosophers and penologists, most notably Thomas More, Jeremy Bentham, and Herbert Spencer. From this century, apart from Schafer, the idea is chiefly associated with Margery Fry, a former Howard League secretary, whose awareness of the victim's unmet needs led to the setting up of criminal injury compensation boards in the United Kingdom and elsewhere. More recently, reparative projects have arisen for two principal reasons: first, our better understanding of victims' needs through surveys and the development of victim support schemes, and second, through the search for intermediate sanctions between probation and custody.

Victims – their situation and needs

The focus of the criminal justice process is primarily on the offender. When the police talk to victims and witnesses they gather such information as how the crime was committed, and what the offender looked like, that will help them in their first task, the arrest of the offender. Similarly, through all the stages from arrest to prosecution to sentence, the process gathers an enormous amount of information about the offender through the police, probation, court, and prison records, but gathers information about victims only incidentally.

Victimization surveys in the USA and the United Kingdom over the last decade have added a much needed corrective to our knowledge of the impact of crime. These studies complement the official, but incomplete, crime statistics by sampling the incidence of victimization amongst members of the public. They show that as little as 10 per cent of crime appears in the official statistics (Clarke 1981: 62). In the most recent British crime survey, it was estimated that two-thirds of incidents uncovered by the study went unreported to the police; crimes involving loss such as car theft and burglary were well reported, while low-value property crimes and minor assaults were not. Where people chose not to call in the police, this was because they judged incidents to be too trivial for police action; but, surprisingly, a minority of unreported crimes were serious in the subjective view of victims, including injury and material loss (Hough and Mayhew 1985: 51).

In terms of material loss calculated in the British crime survey, vehicle thefts were most costly, followed by burglary, thefts, and vandalism. Few burglary victims recovered their losses, although 41 per cent were compensated by insurance companies. Only a minority of burglary victims sustained financial losses over a £100 and few were seriously injured. However, as we shall see from further studies by Maguire and Shapland, the overall impact of crime on anxiety levels of victims and their neighbours is disturbing (Maguire 1980; Shapland 1982).

The statistics reveal that the risk of victimization is not evenly distributed in society. An American commentator, Hindelgang, has suggested that falling victim to a crime is quite highly correlated to the chances of being an offender (Hindelgang, Gottfredson, and Garofalo 1978: 278). His observation was particularly about the young, part of whose lifestyle includes going out in the evening and drinking in public places. This is frequently the case with young people living in low income areas with few facilities and little privacy at home. Findings by British criminologists echo the point (Hough and Mayhew 1983: 32; Mawby 1979: 98).

By contrast, both Sparks and Hindelgang reported that victimization was negatively related to age and fell off sharply for those over fifty (Sparks, Glenn, and Dodd 1977: 217, Hindelgang, Gottfriedson, and Garofalo 1978: 250). The British crime survey also indicated that the elderly were the group least likely to be victims of violent crime, although their fear of crime was disproportionately high (Hough and Mayhew 1985: 32).

There is a further level of agreement in the surveys that the highest levels of risks of burglary and violence to the person are closely associated in areas of social deprivation, particularly in inner cities and multi-racial public housing estates – as much as three times above the average (Hough and Mayhew 1985: 35). People living in these areas are also at risk of multiple victimization with homes being burgled twice or more over the year.

As Harrison in his observation of inner-city life in Hackney graphically reminds us:

'Hackney's thieves rob on their own doorsteps. Indeed, the poorer the area, the more likely are its inhabitants to become victims of crime, and repeatedly. Theft in Hackney most commonly amounts to robbing the poor to feed the poor. The victims of crime are not only individuals: the community as a whole is diminished. Every school, every public amenity, every community premise, faces a continual wearing down by major and minor theft and damage.'

(Harrison 1985: 343).

Apart from property and income loss, victims frequently rate physical and emotional suffering as their most serious problems. A number of recent victim studies in England revealed the level of victim need and the victims' reaction to the court setting when their appeals for compensation were considered.

Julie Vennard carried out a study of seventy-five victims in 1976 who were seeking redress for loss or injury in property offences or injuries. She recorded in the light of those findings that 'there does seem to be an unmet need among victims, if not always for practical help or referral, at least for advice on their legal position and a possible way to get compensation' (Vennard 1976: 378–80). Three-quarters of the victims of property offence and a third of the assault victims got compensation from the court. The assault victims were less successful in obtaining compensation than their property victim counterparts. This was partly explained by a reluctance of magistrates to make compensation orders, particularly where there is difficulty in assessing liability and amounts.

Shapland in her study of 279 victims of violent crime found a similar picture. Even though 60 per cent of the sample had their cases before the court, only 20 per cent were awarded compensation (Shapland 1982: 22).

Victims also had strong feelings of disappointment and anger about the sentencing process. This was largely because they often saw the sentence as excessively lenient and a reflection of the court's indifference to the pain and injury suffered.

Maguire also carried out a major study into the effects of burglary on 322 victims in the Thames Valley in 1977 and 1978. From evidence presented to him a few weeks after the respondents had been burgled, he concluded that there is little doubt that the experience was a significant event in many of the lives of a considerable proportion of victims. Persisting effects of unease and insecurity and a tendency to keep thinking about the burglary were described by 65 per cent of victims. The emotional impact of the burglary seemed more important to victims than financial loss (Maguire 1980: 261–73).

Maguire's study finds parallels with those of Vennard and

Shapland. The latter also set out the frustration victims feel about their lack of involvement with the criminal justice process. She suggests that there are four possible ways the victim might be able to participate more in the process: he or she could be given decision-making power, be consulted, be informed, or be helped with the effects of the offence and the system. Drawing on the results of the study, Shapland shows little evidence of pressure for decision making except when police and victim differ over whether to prosecute. Mediation between victim and offender might be preferred by some to participation in the court process. Consultation would be appreciated before charges are drafted or information given to the press. The major lack of information occurs in progress about the case, court appearance, bail, outcome, and sentence. Finally, Shapland endorses the need for help of two kinds: financial aid to cover the victim's involvement with the courts, and victim support on a short- and long-term basis (Shapland 1982: 23).

With our better knowledge of victims' needs a number of measures have been taken through crime prevention strategies in local communities (see Vivien Stern's chapter), voluntary organizations, the courts, and government, to protect, assist, and compensate crime victims. However, as Irvin Waller's draft declaration to the United Nations on the rights of victims clearly shows, current developments in the United Kingdom and elsewhere fall far short of a comprehensive policy (Waller 1985). The most noteworthy development in the United Kingdom has been the rapid growth of victim support schemes run by volunteers in over 300 cities and towns, offering short-term emotional and practical help to crime victims. The British crime survey found that the general public much valued the schemes, particularly for those who had experienced burglary, robbery, and snatch thefts (Hough and Mayhew 1985: 31).

Elsewhere, victims of personal injury through crime have the right to apply to the criminal injuries compensation scheme in the event of serious injury. To eliminate claims of minor injuries, the Home Secretary has set a lower limit to claims of £400. The Parliamentary All-Party Penal Affairs Group has pressed the Home Secretary to extend the powers of the scheme to include financial loss and damage to property, particularly to the 25 per cent of householders who are not able to afford the necessary insurance premium because of their reliance in fixed incomes, benefits, or low wages (PAPAG 1981: 20). To date the proposal has been rejected on cost grounds, though a growing crime rate with increasingly disaffected numbers of crime victims may in time lead the government responsible to reconsider priorities in this area.

Victims can also seek redress through a civil claim or compensation order made by the courts under the powers of the Criminal Courts Act 1973 and, as extended, by the 1982 Act. Either course of action is dependent upon the police (a) detecting the offender, and (b) securing his conviction and sentence in the court. The likelihood is that in the majority of instances the offender will not be apprehended and prosecuted, and therefore the victim will not make good the loss unless she or he has the means to take out adequate insurance protection. Even if the offender is sentenced, compensation as a reparative method is of limited application, as it is subject to the offender's means and the discretion of the court. Softley's evidence on the use of compensation in magistrates' courts shows that sentencers are more likely to use the order for offences of criminal damage and offences of dishonesty than offences of assault and wounding for two reasons: first, violent offenders may be considered unsuitable for a non-custodial disposal and second, because there is a lack of clear guidelines in determining compensation for personal injury (Softley 1977).

The search for an accountable measure

Alongside our growing awareness of victims' needs we have witnessed over the last two decades the twin rise of crime rates and prison populations throughout the Western world, more particularly in the United Kingdom and North America. During this time rehabilitative programmes, either run by the Probation Service in the community or by training establishments have come under attack from researchers for failing to reduce crime rates (Lipton, Martinson, and Wilks 1975; Brody 1976). The welfare approach has also come under criticism by exponents of the justice model in penology, who claim that treatment programmes have elements of oppression, particularly when those responsible for offenders, children in care, and others have unlimited discretion in determining release dates from care, prison, and institutions. The critics, whose case has been further consolidated in the 1982 Criminal Justice Act, urged determinate sentences where offenders know from the outset the penalty they have to pay.

The search for intermediate sanctions over the period has led penologists and legislators to look for measures between probation and the severity of the prison sentence with its stigma of isolation, its depersonalization, and overcrowding. By the beginning of the 1970s various government white papers extolled the virtues of containing offenders in the community rather than in warehouse-like institutions. The argument was based on two criteria: first, you pay less than institutional costs in keeping young people in the community, and second, separating such offenders from their networks and support systems can only exacerbate the problems which underlie criminal behaviour. Reparation fitted well into this philosophy because it implied that young or adult offenders could reconcile themselves with their victims or community through making some restoration to them via compensation, or symbolically through community service orders. The two forms of reparation are embodied in the Powers of the Criminal Court Act 1973 as compensation orders and community service by offenders.

The compensation order is more strictly reparative in that it clearly relates to the offence and holds the offender responsible for losses to the crime victim. Community service has been characterized as a time-limited penalty with specific requirements, whereby the offender, in symbolic terms, makes amends to the community he has wronged. As well as the British initiatives, parallel reparation measures were introduced in North America at all phases of the justice process – pre-trial, diversion, probation, prison, and parole, through federal grants to projects involving both juvenile and adult offenders (Hudson and Galaway 1975, 1977, 1978, and 1980; Harding 1982).

Crime from the reparative perspective represents a breach in the structure of society. The offender by his action has estranged himself from the community and the victim he has wronged. Restorative sanctions are designed neither to punish nor treat the offender, but to provide him with an opportunity to apologize and restore the injured party, thereby gaining a point of re-integration into the community. The development of criminal justice process has tended to exclude the victim from any part of the court proceedings except as a prosecution witness. The case is taken over by the professionals, be they solicitors, police officers, or probation officers. Nils Christie, in an important article, makes the point that the victim's conflict with the offender becomes the property of lawyers or treatment personnel (Christie 1978). There is no chance for the victim to explain his hurt, pain, and bewilderment to the offender, or indeed, for the latter to apologize, to make some form of restitution.

Christie feels that the blame expressed by the victim would be far harder for the offender to neutralize than the blame pronounced by the court through the sentencer. From the victim's perspective, the reparative approach gives high priority to the private nature of criminal acts, implying that the offender owes something to the victim as well as to the state.

Advocates of reparation claim a number of advantages for the principle, not least of which is its multi-faceted approach or versatility. From the viewpoint of punishment, reparation can be seen as making offenders aware of the repercussions of their unlawful acts by making them assume responsibility for what they have done. For the purposes of rehabilitation, reparation is said to have a number of beneficial elements: a sense of accomplishment from completing a court order, the acquisition of new skills or abilities, the redressing of self-image, and to some, a socially appropriate way of expressing atonement. Proponents of differing political and philosophical outlooks are attracted to the idea of reparation, but before advocating or explaining it to others they need to have its underlying purpose clearly in mind. We can identify four potential beneficiaries from reparative programmes – the offender, the victim, the public, and criminal justice personnel.

For offenders, the following benefits are generally claimed: Reparation is related to the amount of damage actually done, and offers a specific sanction with clear requirements in terms of completion. It allows the offender to exercise a sense of responsibility, which in turn can elicit a positive response from the victim and the public organizations. The notion of self-respect is also involved, since the offender can by his actions and accomplishments raise the level of his own self-esteem. Lastly, where a mediator arranges for a victim and offender to meet following the crime incident, the offender comes face to face with the consequences of his action, which provides him with a better understanding of the victim's position. The dangers of neutralizing criminal behaviour by claiming that it was due to the victim's carelessness or fault are significantly reduced in such a first-hand encounter. An opportunity is provided in the otherwise distancing process of criminal procedure for the offender to make amends, first by apology and explanation, and second by reaching agreement with the victim as to the manner and type of compensation – either cash or some form of direct service.

In certain situations, depending on the seriousness of the offence, it is also possible that the offender's willingness to participate in an act of reconciliation and reparation could lead the court to reduce the severity of sentence and avoid the damaging costs of imprisonment.

There remain a number of concerns about the offender's role in the reparative process. Most offenders are unemployed and in receipt of state benefits. How can they respond to a reparation without adequate means? Softley and others suggest that compensation amounts are generally modest (Softley 1977). Compensation may therefore impose hardship for the impecunious offender but it may be less onerous than the harsher penalty of imprisonment. There is also evidence from studies in England showing that victims of crime, once they have met the offender, are not as punitive or vindictive as popular sentiment might suggest (Shapland, Willmore, and Duff 1985; Dixon 1985).

201

They take into account the offender's circumstances and may, without pressure, decide to settle for less than a full compensation claim for goods damaged or stolen. In a court-based reparation project, however, any agreement between a victim and offender has to be returned to the judge or magistrate for ratification or variation. Depending on the gravity of the offence the sentencer may decide to add a further element of punishment alongside the reparative agreement. Concern has been expressed at this point in the procedure that an offender should not be placed in a position of greater jeopardy than if reparation had not been available to the court.

Critics of reparation further claim that it is an oppressive principle which punishes offenders who are both poor and powerless. The accusation is suspiciously apologetic, implying that deprivation removes accountability for one's actions. Reparation is not a weapon to fight the structural inequalities in society, but it is, through the process of mediation, a means of developing a better understanding between victims and offenders of each other's lives (and the conditions in which they live).

For crime victims, reparation is of only limited value. Most crime goes undetected and not every arrest leads to the conviction of an offender in court. In terms of safeguarding victims' interests a public compensation scheme would be far more effective than a pre-court or post-conviction reparation scheme. None the less, where the offender has been identified a number of benefits can follow. First, the victim has the possibility of receiving some form of financial redress or direct service by the offender for damages or losses incurred. As importantly, as we learn from the victim–offender reconciliation projects in Canada, the USA, and the United Kingdom, victims value the chance to ventilate their feelings about a crime before an offender: Why did you rob my home? What have I done to you to deserve this? Do you know what effect this had on my daughter? Such an opportunity often relieves frustration, reduces stereotypical notions about offenders, and helps to lower levels of anxiety to the point that the victim can come to terms with his or her experience (Zehr and Umbreit 1982: 65).

Reparative schemes also help to reduce the level of isolation the victim feels about the handling of his case through the courts. The very process of involving and consulting the victim is seen as an important indication that agencies or individuals associated with criminal justice care about the victim's interests and losses. Finally, there is the sense that society, through the reparative approach, is restoring certain values; that equity, though never completely, is restored; and a feeling of confidence renewed in criminal justice.

Public opinion surveys conducted in the USA and the UK in the last five years widely support the concept of reparation, particularly as an alternative to custody for the property offender. Shaw's national opinion poll survey in England found that of the 1,000-strong sample 66 per cent reported that reparation was a good idea for reducing the prison population (Shaw 1982). The two British crime surveys conducted in 1982 and 1984 involving substantially more respondents, similarly rate community service and compensation as the two principle means of reducing the prison population. The surveys also suggest that people are less punitive to law breakers than is usually imagined (Hough and Mayhew 1983: 76).

> 'Asked how their offenders should be treated, victims showed awareness of and support for court sentences involving community service and compensation and frequently favoured informal warnings and reparation. There may, therefore, be scope for diverting offenders from the courts to non-judicial arbitration and mediation schemes of the type now being developed in the USA.'
>
> (Hough and Mayhew 1983: 35)

Surveys of criminal justice personnel and others indicate support for reparation. Hudson, Chesney, and Mclagan found that over 80 per cent of samples of state legislators and correction administrators in the USA favoured the use of restitution for adult and juvenile offenders (Hudson, Chesney, and Mclagan 1977). A survey of victims and offenders who had participated in several American restitution projects found that 61 per cent of the offenders and 60 per cent of victims considered restitution requirements fair (Novack, Galaway, and Hudson 1980). In Britain, both Vennard and Shapland found support for reparation among crime victims, and indeed further evidence in Shapland's case that victims were little inclined to seek vengeance or even penalize impoverished offenders (Vennard 1978; Shapland, Willmore, and Duff 1985). Overall, despite reservations about the scope and general applicability of reparative measures, the evidence to date suggests that the principle is not out of step with moves towards greater offender accountability, victim satisfaction, and public confidence.

Reparation in practice

In Britain, as in the United States, reparation has developed in five separate but linked ways involving out-of-court settlements between victims and offenders and court-based programmes. Out-of-court or diversionary strategies include the use of reparation as an adjunct to the caution for juvenile offenders. Two examples may suffice. In Exeter, an inter-agency youth support team (probation, police, and social workers), after gaining the consent of offender and his or her parents, make arrangements for the victim and offender to meet. In nearly half of all settlements, the offender agrees to carry out work for the victim, who might be an individual householder, the owner of a small business, or the local authority. A similar process takes place in Northamptonshire where the purpose of the juvenile bureau is to divert offenders from the courts and to place reliance on informal networks of control, support, and care.

Further programmes, known as neighbourhood dispute/community mediation centres were first developed from federal funding initiatives in the USA during the mid 1970s (Harding 1982; Marshall 1985). They are in essence grass roots, community self-help schemes, close to centres of urban deprivation and public housing sectors. The theory is that crime and interpersonal disputes between neighbours are better contained and negotiated at the local level than through courts which are seen as conflict-ridden, adversarial, ritualistic, and out of touch with the lives of ordinary people. Paid organizers recruit local people as mediators to handle disputes and reach settlements that are acceptable to the parties in conflict. Centres do not have the capacity to handle serious crimes but can effectively divert many issues from the courtroom. In the United Kingdom two programmes have been recently developed. The Newham Conflict and Change project opened in 1984 in a racially mixed area of London, with the poor, elderly, and unemployed overrepresented in it. To date, fifty disputes have been handled by the local mediators. The second scheme in Sandwell was initiated by the West Midlands Probation Service in the same year on a large council estate in an area of industrial decline. Both projects are breaking new ground but no hard data have been published as yet.

Court-based reparation programmes in Britain are again of short duration, three of them stemming from the Home Secretary's initiative of 1984 to establish pilot projects in Wolverhampton, Leeds, and Coventry. All three schemes work on a post-conviction model where the court refers cases to the Probation Service with a view to officers or volunteers carrying out mediation between victims and offenders and returning agreements to the court for ratification. The two schemes in Coventry and Wolverhampton are much influenced by the victim–offender reconciliation programmes first pioneered by the Mennonites in Canada and Indiana, USA. Here, project staff recruit local volunteers to act as mediators between victims and offenders so that both can discuss the facts of the crime, ventilate their feelings, and, hopefully, reach agreements which are passed on to the court via a probation officer for ratification.

Before the Home Secretary's initiative, the only sustained court-based work was that which was and is still being carried out by the South Yorkshire Probation Service in Rotherham and Barnsley. A total of five probation officers have been exploring the feasibility of mediation during the preparation of a report for the court. Dixon, the project leader, in the first year's report, stated that in Barnsley 74 per cent of victims accepted an apology from the offenders or agreed to meet the offender in the presence of a probation officer. In Rotherham, fewer victims (46 per cent) followed the same process. Overall levels of satisfaction with the fairness of the proceedings for both parties were high (Dixon 1985). These findings echo the Mennonite experience in the USA where programme results indicate that 50 per cent of victims and offenders agree to meet, and of these some 80 per cent reach agreement prior to a court hearing (Zehr and Umbreit 1982).

The evidence from South Yorkshire also reveals that victims attached far less importance to compensation or some form of direct service carried out on their behalf than to the healing process of mediation itself. Dixon sets out the optional conditions for mediation.

'Victim/offender mediation, clearly, is most feasible, and is perceived by participants to be most relevant when it is offered in situations where parties have a stake in seeking some kind of resolution, whether within themselves (e.g. personal guilt, anxiety, anger) or between themselves (e.g. restoration of a trusting relationship, ability to meet socially without embarrassment). There will always be offenders who feel genuine remorse and wish to make amends, and victims who genuinely wish to be reassured, to be able to forgive, and help an offender learn from his actions.'

(Dixon 1985: 9)

While the process of mediation appears to have beneficial effects for both victims and offenders, there is little direct evidence that current initiatives have had much influence on sentencing in terms of reducing the likelihood of a custodial sentence. On the other hand, fears expressed by probation officers that involvement by an offender in a reparation/mediation programme with its focus on the impact of victimization and offending behaviour would lead to harsher sentences, appears groundless (Smith, Blagg, and Derricourt 1985: 7). It is clearly too early in the history of reparation and mediation projects to assess what overall impact the principles of restoration and reconciliation can achieve in the court, set alongside the more traditional emphasis on punishment and retribution. Much might depend on the seriousness of the offence and whether the quality of life enjoyed by others associated with the victim is substantially undermined. For example, apart from the hurt, loss, or injury sustained by a crime victim, avoidance action to reduce the risk of crime may have to be taken by immediate neighbours, such as installing extra security locks, alarm systems, and simply not going out at night. But there is the hope expressed by Ministers of State and, indeed, the respondents of the British Crime Survey that where an offender expresses remorse for his actions it is appropriate for the courts to pass a lesser sentence than it might otherwise have done, to mark the offender's effort (Mellor 1985).

Other key issues remain unresolved, stressing the need for careful monitoring of pioneer projects before further implementation is considered. As yet, we do not know which offenders stand to benefit most from reparative schemes – the young? property offenders? Nor do we know which victims have most to gain from an experience of mediation and reparation. For the Probation Service questions of priority clearly arise. Will reparation develop at the expense of current priorities or should we re-think the model of probation to take account of concerns about justice, the protection of the public, and victim support.

Thomson argues that probation is seen as a welfare agency meeting offenders' needs rather than a public service organization that looks at crime and its repercussions in a wider context. He suggests that the service has much to gain in terms of recognition and public appreciation by adopting a perspective which takes into account the offender, his needs and responsibilities, the individual victim, and the community as victim (Thomson 1984: 109). By identifying the crime itself the source of the conflict, there is an opportunity for both victims and offenders, through the process of mediation, to ventilate grievances, explore common areas of agreement, and reduce levels of fear and stereotypical thinking, in ways which are not possible in our courts today.

The revival of reparation coupled with the conciliatory practice of mediation poses a key challenge and critique to our current preoccupation in criminal justice terms with punishment measures that are often negative and unfulfilling to victim and offender alike. There are indications of public support for programmes that give greater prominence to victims' interests and concerns, always provided that they are balanced by a fair and equal consideration for the expressed needs of offenders. While views may differ as to the general applicability of reparation in terms of the actual numbers of victims and offenders who might benefit from a more widespread introduction of the principle, many commentators might agree that it at least offers a note of hope, empathy, and understanding in a criminal justice system too heavily coloured by retribution and unresolved conflict.

© *1987 John Harding*

References

Brody, S. (1976) *The Effectiveness of Sentencing*. Home Office Research Study no. 35. London: HMSO.

Christie, N. (1978) Conflicts as Property. *British Journal of Criminology* 17(1).

Clarke, R. (1981) *The Prospects of Controlling Crime*. Home Office Research Bulletin no. 12. London: HMSO.

Dixon, P. (1985) Interim report, Victim Offender Mediation Project. Unpublished paper, South Yorkshire Probation Service.

Harding, J. (1982) *Victims and Offenders, Needs and Responsibilities*. London: Bedford Square Press.

Harrison, P. (1985) *Inside the Inner City*. Harmondsworth: Penguin.

Hindelgang, M., Gottfredson, M., and Garofalo, R. (1978) *Victims of Personal Crime*. Chicago, Ill.: Ballinger.

Hough, M. and Mayhew, P. (1983) *The British Crime Survey*. Home Office Research Study no. 76. London: HMSO.

——— (1985) *Taking Account of Crime: Key Findings from the 1984 British Crime Survey*. Home Office Research Study no. 85. London: HMSO.

Hudson, J. and Galaway, B. (eds) (1975) *Considering the Victim*. Springfield, Ill.: Thomas.

——— (eds) (1977) *Restitution in Criminal Justice*. Lexington, Md.: D.C. Heath.

——— (eds) (1978) *Offender Restitution in Theory and Action*. Lexington, Md.: D.C. Heath.

——— (eds) (1980) *Victims, Offenders and Alternative Sanctions*. Lexington, Md.: D.C. Heath.

Hudson, J., Chesney, S., and Mclagan, S. (1977) *Restitution as Perceived by State Legislators and Correctional Administrators*. St Paul, Minn.: Department of Corrections.

Lipton, D., Martinson, R., and Wilks, J. (1975) *The Effectiveness of Correctional Treatment*. New York: Praeger.

Maguire, M. (1980) The Impact of Burglary on Victims. *British Journal of Criminology* 20(43).

Marshall, T. (1985) *Alternatives to Criminal Courts*. Aldershot: Gower.

Mawby, R. (1979) The Victimization of Juveniles. *Journal of Research in Crime and Delinquency* 16: 93–107.

Mellor, D. (1985) *The Times*. 16 September 1985.

Novack, S., Galaway, B., and Hudson, S. (1980) *National Assessment of Adult Restitution Programmes*, Report III. Duluth, Minn.: University of Minnesota.

Parliamentary All-Party Penal Affairs Group (1981) *Still too many prisoners*. London: National Association for the Care and Resettlement of Offenders.

Schafer, S. (1960) *Restitution to Victims of Crime*. London: Stevens.

Shapland, J. (1982) *The Victim in the Criminal Justice System*. Home Office Research Bulletin no. 14. London: HMSO.

Shapland, J., Willmore, J., and Duff, P. (1985) *Victims in the Criminal Justice System*. Aldershot: Gower.

Shaw, S. (1982) *The People's Justice*. London: National Opinion Poll and Prison Reform Trust.

Smith, D., Blagg, H., and Derricourt, N. (1985) Victim Offender Mediation Project. Unpublished paper, South Yorkshire Probation Service.

Softley, P. (1977) *Compensation Orders in Magistrates' Courts*. Home Office Research Study no. 43. London: HMSO.

Sparks, R., Glenn, H., and Dodd, D. (1977) *Surveying Victims*. Chichester: John Wiley.

Thomson, D. (1984) Prospects for Justice Model Probation. In P. McAnany, D. Thomson, and D. Fogel (eds) *Probation and Justice: Reconsideration of Mission*. Cambridge, Mass.: Odgeschleger, Gunn, and Hain.

Vennard, J. (1976) Justice and Recompense. *New Society* 35(658).

―――― (1978) Compensation by the Offender: the Victim's Perspective. *Victimology* 3(1–2): 154–60.

Waller, I. (1985) *Declaration on the Rights of Victims of Crime and Abuse of Power*. Canada: University of Ottawa. (Unpublished paper.)

Zehr, H. and Umbreit, M. (1982) Victim Offender Reconciliation: An Incarceration Substitute? *Federal Probation* XXXXVI(4).

11 Crime prevention – the inter-organizational approach

Vivien Stern

'Effective strategies against crime demand that we look to the community as a whole to contribute to the task of crime prevention in very practical ways. Those responsible for planning the environment in which we live, and the provision of services upon which we depend, are in a position to make a valuable contribution. We must ask whether more can be done in the management of our housing estates, in the organization of social services and in the provision of education for our children to reduce the opportunities for crime.'

(The Lord Elton, Home Office 1983: iii)

Introduction

The co-ordinated approach to crime prevention was given the seal of legitimacy as a major new element in British crime policy when a wide range of central and local government officials, chief constables, and representatives of industry, academia, and the voluntary sector met at the Bramshill Police College in 1982 for a seminar on crime prevention. In the early 1980s crime prevention, which had received little attention from policy makers, suddenly sprang into the centre of the debate. The essence of the shift which gave crime prevention such prominence was perhaps best expressed by the Lord Chief Justice in the House of Lords on 24 March 1982 when he said:

'Neither police nor courts nor prison can solve the problem of the rising crime rate. By the time that the criminal falls into the hands of the police, and more particularly, by the time he reaches court, it is too late. The damage has been done. The remedy, if it can be found, must be sought a great deal earlier.'

(Official Report Vol. 428, No. 62, Col. 988)

Several strands in thinking about criminal justice have come together to produce the new focus commonly described by the terms 'crime prevention' or 'crime reduction'. First is the growing recognition that controlling crime in a community is separate and distinct from the process of apprehending and dealing with individual offenders. As John Alderson, former Chief Constable of Devon and Cornwall, says in his book *Policing Freedom*:

'In a modern developed democratic society it should be possible to articulate a concept for the control of crime. The traditional idea that the key to control lies mainly with the system of criminal justice must now be seriously questioned in the light of our new and growing understanding of the nature of unreported crime, the complicated web or pattern of behaviour defined as criminal, and the probability that most people are or will be guilty of committing at least minor criminal offences.'   (Alderson 1979: 130)

Second is the search for more effectiveness and lower costs. The criminal justice process – police, courts, prisons, and probation – cost nearly £3,746m. in 1979–80 in real terms (real terms figures are the cash out-turn or plans adjusted to 1983–84 price levels by excluding the effect of general inflation). In 1986–87 it is planned to spend nearly £4,800m., an increase of 31 per cent. A comparison with another public spending programme, housing, may help to show how substantial this growth is. In 1979 spending on housing in real terms was £6,569m. In 1986–87 it is planned to be about one-third of that amount, £2,240m.

Yet it is hard to be confident about the effectiveness of the expenditure on 'law, order and protective services' as the public expenditure programme is called. Recorded crime rises more or less steadily, from 2½ m. notifiable offences in 1980 (when new counting rules were introduced which make comparisons with earlier years unsafe) to just over 3m. in 1983. The clear-up rate, that is the ratio of offences cleared up in a year to offences recorded in that year, has actually fallen slightly from 40 per cent in 1980 to 38 per cent in 1983. Such a growth in expenditure with no commensurate improvement in results has given a powerful impetus to the search for new approaches to the problem of crime.

A third contributory factor is the wide debate, given focus by the inner-city disturbances of 1981 and Lord Scarman's report, taking place throughout the police service and elsewhere about policing and the role of the community. Sir Kenneth Newman, Metropolitan Police Commissioner, writing in the *News of the World* in June 1983, summarized his approach thus:

'Many thinking people involved in criminal justice believe the answer to the problem is to lift our attitude above the rather narrow concept implied by the term "crime control". Instead we should think in terms of "social control" and "social responsibility" which means that the whole of society has a collective responsibility for maintaining law and order.'

Finally comes a re-appraisal of attitudes to criminal justice policy from radical criminologists who argue that:

'There was a schizophrenia about crime on the left where crimes against women and immigrant groups were quite rightly an object of concern but other types of crime were regarded as being of little interest or somehow excusable.'   (Lea and Young 1984: 262)

However, now is the time, Lea and Young argue, to 'take crime control seriously'. Echoing the Lord Chief Justice they suggest that:

'To deter crime before it is committed is infinitely better than to attempt to intervene by punishing the culprit after the event, with the aim of deterring his future activities and perhaps those of others. Environmental and public precautions against crime are always dismissed by left idealists and reformers as not relating to the heart of the problem. . . . On the contrary, the organization of communities in an attempt to pre-empt crime is of the utmost importance.'   (Lea and Young 1984: 266–67)

Analysing crime

It appears then that a shift towards crime prevention as a major element in criminal justice policy has a broad appeal across the political spectrum. One element of this shift is a diversion of research interest away from individual offenders and how they are dealt with toward a concern to analyse crime as a phenomenon, looking behind the aggregated and unhelpful format of the official criminal statistics to crime as experienced by individuals or communities. A substantial contribution to this work has been made by the British Crime Survey, commissioned by the Home Office. By the end of 1984 the Home Office had published four surveys, all addressing issues of relevance to those concerned with crime prevention. The major study *The British Crime Survey* (Hough and Mayhew 1983) reported on interviews with 11,000 people in England and Wales about their experiences of crime. It showed that between four and five times as much crime occurred as was reported to the police. On the basis of this information statistical calculations were made which showed that an average person aged 16 or more could expect to be robbed once every 500 years, assaulted even slightly every one hundred years, and have his or her house burgled once every forty years. Three further studies, based on the survey data, *Contacts between Police and Public, Fear of Crime in England and Wales*, and *Victims of Crime – The Dimensions of Risk* were all published in 1984 (Southgate and Ekblom, Maxfield, and Gottfredson respectively). The report on the fear of crime illuminated an important aspect of the crime problem by showing that 12 per cent of all inner-city residents (and higher proportions for elderly people and women generally) reported never going out at night because of fear of being a victim of crime. The report also showed that fear of crime was mainly an urban and inner-city problem – a reflection of the fact that crime rates are much higher in inner-city areas. *The British Crime Survey* showed that risks of burglary in the inner city are double those in other built-up areas and five times more than in rural areas (Hough and Mayhew 1983). The study *Victims of Crime* shows that victims of crime are most likely to live in urbanized areas, in rented accommodation, and in flats, and to be young, single males (Gottfredson 1984). A survey conducted on Merseyside, *Merseyside Crime Survey, First Report, November 1984*, showed that 13 per cent of those in Ainsdale, an affluent area, saw crime as a major problem compared with 66 per cent in Granby, in inner-city Liverpool. In a twelve-month period 3 per cent of those in Ainsdale had been victims of burglary or attempted burglary compared with 25 per cent in Granby (Kinsey 1984).

This type of analysis of how crime affects a particular geographical area is fundamental to a crime prevention approach. It is necessary to know what is to be prevented and where it takes place. A Home Office Working Group on Crime Prevention, set up in 1976 to study various approaches to crime prevention, recommended in *Co-ordinating Crime Prevention Efforts* (Gladstone 1980) a systematic approach to deciding how to try to prevent any particular offence. The approach, often called 'situational crime prevention', should consist of four stages. First would be an analysis of the situation, for example, supermarket, telephone kiosk, car park in which the offence in question occurs and the conditions which provide the opportunity for it. Second is the devising of measures which would make it more difficult. Third comes an assessment of how practical, effective, and costly these measures would be. The fourth stage is to select the measures which seem most likely to succeed.

Commentators on crime prevention techniques also seem agreed that some form of inter-agency and inter-organizational method of working is essential. The inter-departmental circular on crime prevention states: 'A co-ordinated response is required at all levels from members of the public, both as individuals and within agencies and by agencies working together' (Home Office 1984: para. 22). Official recognition of the need for all agencies to be involved is also shown by the amended *Probation Rules (1984)* which include a paragraph, 'Other duties', permitting the participation of probation officers in arrangements concerned with the prevention of crime. The *National Statement of Objectives and Priorities for the Probation Service*, also published in 1984, includes a section on 'other work in the community' which suggests an involvement in initiatives concerned with the prevention of crime.

However, even when armed with an understanding of the need for a local analysis of crime, an acceptance of the interdependence of local agencies in dealing with crime, and official encouragement to become involved in crime prevention initiatives, it is still very difficult to move from a theoretical discussion of the need for a crime prevention approach to taking practical action to prevent and reduce crime. A Home Office feasibility study of how to reduce vandalism in schools in Manchester showed how much work still needs to be done. In a discussion of the problems faced in the feasibility studies Tim Hope and Daniel Murphy point out that although a number of meetings were held with local authority officials, staff from the schools involved, and the police, and proposals were drawn up to combat vandalism, 'The proposals for most of the schools were never fully implemented' (Hope and Murphy 1983: 41).

It was proposed that windows should be glazed with vandal-proof glass. In the event not one vandal-proof window pane was installed. It was recommended and agreed that people living next to two of the schools should keep an eye on them, but this did not happen because no one was prepared to organize it. It was agreed to change the way the local authority recorded vandalism so as to obtain more accurate information. Instructions for a more precise system were laid down but complete information about operating the new system did not reach those who actually kept the records at local repair depots, so they continued with a mixture of the original and the new system which in the end gave information that was even less useful.

Two different approaches

Much more work needs to be done before it can be claimed that such difficulties have been overcome. Two different but complementary approaches are being developed by NACRO and it may be helpful to look at them in more detail, not because they are exemplary or remarkable in themselves, but because of the light they throw on the process of turning ideas about crime prevention into recognizable activities that can be described and evaluated.

At the centre of the NACRO work is a belief that the key to dealing with the types of crime that affect people's daily lives, for example, vandalism and burglary, lies in community involvement and participation. The two approaches to crime prevention described here exemplify different ways of securing this community involvement.

The first approach is based on local authority housing estates, selected in consultation with the local authority housing department. A pilot scheme run between 1976 and 1979 on a vandalized post-war housing estate in Widnes, Cheshire, set out to investigate whether the estate would recover if environmental improvements were carried out according to residents' wishes and with their co-operation. It was hoped that, by being consulted and involved in improvements, residents would feel encouraged to take care of their environment rather than accept or even contribute to its decline. The consultation method used was an alternative to public meetings, which are often poorly attended and dominated by an articulate minority. A random sample of residents was invited to join one of a number of small discussion groups of about ten persons. Each group met several times to discuss the problems residents were experiencing, to put forward solutions, and to engage in a constructive dialogue with officers from the steering group that was set up. After the process of consultation was completed, the residents' recommendations for estate improvements were reported to the council and other local agencies. Such recommendations as were thought practical and economic were then implemented. The project was evaluated by Social and Community Planning Research. The final report on the project concludes:

> 'There seems little doubt that the Cunningham Road Estate has changed importantly and for the better as a result of the project. . . . The original purpose of the project was to combat vandalism and crime (although its scope has widened considerably since then). We can be fairly confident that progress on this front has been made on the evidence of our sample survey, of police and resident opinion and of our own observation. However, the problems have by no means disappeared.'   (Hedges, Blaber, and Mostyn 1980: 4)

The evaluation of the Cunningham Road Improvement Scheme suggested that the method of consultation and involvement might usefully be applied more widely. Between 1979 and the end of 1984 the approach and a variant of it were tried on fifty-eight estates in most parts of England and Wales. Some examples give an indication of the range of different environments where estate projects have been set up. St Luke's Estate in London, for instance, is a high-rise inner-city estate with two large interconnected eight-storey blocks and one eighteen-storey tower block. Residents were concerned with security and extensive vandalism to the communal areas. The Safe Neighbourhoods Unit, as the team carrying out the project is called, reports that when the project started in September 1980 one-third of the tenants had applied for a transfer off the estate (Bright and Petterson 1984: 13). As a contrast, an estate on a windswept hill in Newcastle-under-Lyme, consists of 850 grey terraced houses built in the early 1950s. An open-cast mine still in use lies twenty to thirty yards away from the houses. The houses all have gardens interspersed with large open spaces covered with rubbish and grass three feet high. The shops have grilles over the windows.

The process followed on all types of estate is broadly the same and is described in more detail in *Neighbourhood Consultations* (NACRO 1982). A small staff team of three or four people starts work by circulating an introductory leaflet to the whole estate explaining the project. A questionnaire survey of a large sample of estate households takes place. Respondents are asked about the estate environment, quality of housing, street lighting, refuse collection, participation in local social and community activities, local schools, transport, the police, shops, experiences as a victim of crime and fear of crime.

Small group meetings follow, attended normally by a 10 to 20 per cent sample of tenants chosen at random to represent all streets and types of housing in the area. The small group meetings can contain from eight to thirty people and are the forum for the tenants to discuss the problems of the estate methodically and in detail. The groups usually need to meet two or three times to move from a listing of problems to a consideration of solutions. The outcome of the discussions and the results of the questionnaire survey are brought together in a draft action plan which contains a profile of the estate, a list of the problems raised and improvements recommended. The extract (below) from a fairly typical action plans illustrates the range of matters discussed.

The consultative process with the tenants is paralleled by the establishment of a steering committee on which all the agencies which have an interest in the estate are represented. A typical steering committee might include representatives of the local authority housing department, the police, the education and youth services, the social services, the Probation Service, and local elected members of a tenants' association, if it exists. The role of the steering committee is to support the project, to comment on the draft action plan, and agree a final action plan with the tenants. The committee members are then expected to press for implementation of the recommendations, in the departments or agencies from which they come.

Table 11

problems	resident recommendations	background information
Back and sides of the shops are covered in graffiti.	To remove graffiti possibly by means of painting, Snowcem, or pebbledash.	NACRO willing to remove graffiti subject to appropriate approvals.
Teenagers gather in doorways. Wire grilles are felt to be an eyesore.	Install metal roller blinds. Board over both doorways and windows.	Approximate cost per unit for roller blinds £1,300.
Access to rear of the shops too easy. Used as a gathering place for teenagers who at times prefer this to using the community centre facilities. Many teenagers congregate in the taxi office to use the space invader machines.	To restrict access to rear of the shopping block. This could be done by some means of fencing or walling.	Teenagers will still need somewhere to go. Any realistic attempt to prevent vandalism will need to cater for young people.
Off street lighting is insufficient from a security and safety point of view.	To site new lighting and to improve existing resources in the area. Paving around lampposts is unsatisfactory – it was damaged when new lights were installed.	The Council has begun to replace old lampposts and upgraded the lighting.
The area around the shops needs to be fully lit to help deter vandalism.	Spot lights around the shops.	Spot lights would themselves need to be designed to withstand vandalism.
Police are not often seen on the estate, especially at night. Use of Panda cars is too impersonal and often counter-productive.	To increase police patrols. More policemen on the beat.	The number of police officers available is not high enough to allow comprehensive foot patrolling. The police are looking into the possibility of establishing a police post on the estate.

Evaluation of the process is complex and will be touched on later. However, the projects do lead to a range of practical outcomes which can be listed. Environmental improvements, for example, have included rubbish clearance, creating gardens and parks, diverting or slowing down traffic, removal of graffiti. Increased security has come from changes in policing, better door and window locks, installation of entry phones into blocks of flats, and better lighting. Community activity has increased by establishing children's playgrounds, old people's clubs, and residents' associations. Services to the estates have improved; for example, a local authority housing department has decentralized its repairs service.

All these developments can be measured. Some outcomes, however, are less tangible. For example, commenting on a project in the Midlands the local beat policeman said:

'It is felt that there has been a much improved community spirit on the estate since NACRO's arrival. Residents seem to be working together and giving each other much more consideration and help, for example, much of the anti-social behaviour such as playing of music loudly at night is now virtually non-existent. Major crime, such as burglary and muggings rarely happens now on the estate, although this has never been a major problem. Vandalism has been one area where there has been a major reduction over the past couple of years.'

His senior officer added:

'Naturally there is still a long way to go along the road but it is felt that the community spirit on the estate has now reached the stage where, with everyone working together, including the police and other interested agencies, we could hope to see, in the none too distant future, a better working relationship and a considerable reduction in petty crime.'

A resident commented:

'Since the residents' association has been formed, our relationship with outside organizations such as housing, the police, etc., has greatly improved.'   (NACRO 1985)

A similar approach to that operated in the estate projects, but at the level of a town or city, is being used by NACRO Juvenile Crime Unit, set up in 1981. The unit is working in ten areas of the country to promote a co-ordinated local approach to juvenile crime. The approach derives in part from experience gained in the housing estate projects and also from other schemes, such as the Exeter Community

Policing Consultative Group. The Exeter scheme was set up in 1977 by the then Chief Constable, John Alderson, who called together a meeting of the main local agencies to form a consultative group to try to reduce crime in the city. An evaluation of the work of the first year of the consultative group by Ann Blaber reached the conclusion that the lessons of the first year were not about how to go about cutting crime, but about the mechanics of inter-agency co-operation (Blaber 1979). A number of points emerged: it is important to select very carefully who is to be invited to join a consultative group and who is to issue the invitation; the person invited must be properly 'briefed'; those organizing the meetings must be clear what the aims are and make these clear to those attending. The advantages of involving an outside consultant were also noted. An external consultant can be free from local pressures, can retain objectivity in the midst of group conflict, and can move between the agencies as an intermediary.

These lessons were incorporated into the process chosen by the Juvenile Crime Unit. In each of the ten areas chosen the unit has established a Juvenile Crime Consultative Group with a broad membership on the following lines: juvenile court magistrates, the clerk to the court, the police, the education authority, the social services, the Probation Service, the local university or polytechnic, solicitors, churches, ethnic minority organizations, youth workers, Members of Parliament, broadcasters and journalists, and people from local community associations.

The consultative group meets and agrees to accept the aims of trying to reduce juvenile crime, trying to reduce the number of young people coming to court, and trying to reduce the number of young people sent into custody. It agrees to undertake a review of juvenile crime in the area. The group then divides normally into three working parties to look at crime in that area under three headings. The first working party looks at crime and its prevention, the location and timing of juvenile crime, the characteristics of identified offenders, the areas and times of high risk, and perceptions of juvenile crime. The second looks at ways of keeping juveniles out of the system, for example, cautioning and diversion. The third working party looks at services for those appearing before the courts, for instance, intermediate treatment projects. The working parties collect information, carry out surveys, and make recommendations, all of which is put together in a final report.

By the end of 1984 four of these reviews had been published, each containing a number of recommendations about improving the procedures for dealing with juvenile crime. The recommendations ranged from detailed proposals about dealing with specific offences, for example, shoplifting in defined geographical areas, to broad proposals for new structures.

The four reviews available at the time of writing all considered the existing state of inter-organizational co-ordination and found that although there were a number of inter-agency groups and panels, for example, crime prevention panels, juvenile liaison panels, probation case committees, police consultative committees, there was nobody with overall responsibility for monitoring and commenting on measures to deal with juvenile crime as a whole. It was, therefore, recommended that in each area some form of co-ordinating machinery be set up. In one area, a standing committee was suggested. In another a permanent review body on juvenile crime was proposed. A third proposed a co-ordinating group on juvenile crime with the remit of reporting annually on policies, receiving statistical information on juvenile offenders and how they are dealt with, monitoring changes in practice, making recommendations for further improvements, planning and co-ordinating crime prevention initiatives, disseminating factual information about trends in juvenile crime locally, and informing the wider community of ways in which they can take greater responsibility for reducing the opportunities for crime.

These NACRO initiatives are but two in a range of projects with similar objectives being undertaken throughout the country. The Grange project in Grimsby and the Scotswood Estate project in Newcastle are two other examples of attempts to work with a particular community to deal with the problems afflicting it.

Some common issues

Inter-organizational approaches to crime prevention are very much at the experimental stage and there are many questions still to be answered; but it is already clear that certain common issues arise. The most basic is perhaps the issue of information. Any targeted crime prevention strategy is dependent on detailed information about the particular aspect of criminal behaviour that is causing concern. However, this seemingly simple prerequisite to a crime prevention strategy presents many difficulties. Information is often not available in the form required. The information collected in the official Criminal Statistics is no help; it covers too large an area (police force areas are the smallest geographical division) and the offence categories cover too wide a range of behaviour to inform any action. A good example comes from a BBC television programme on crime broadcast in 1983. Chief Superintendent Herold of the South Yorkshire Police explained the statistical problem thus:

'So I've got some figures off our computer this morning, and here we've got a total of ninety-four offences of robbery in our force area so far this year. If one looks at the values, there are three offences on there which I have highlighted, one is an offence where a licensee and his wife were bound and gagged, brutally assaulted, some £10,000 stolen; one is a cash-carrying bullion van, hijacked at shotgun point and £80,000 odd stolen; and the other one again is licensed premises, late at night, bank holiday weekend, licensee and his wife bound, gagged, seriously assaulted, and many thousands of pounds worth of stuff stolen; but of the ninety-four, forty-two of them are valued at £10 or less . . . in fact a school playground bully boy, where the values are 2p, 20p, 30p, and 40p, but nevertheless they are robberies. When the little bully boy says "Come on John if you don't give me your dinner money I'm going to bash you", and so Johnny gives up his dinner money, he goes home and complains to his Mum who reports it to the police who go along to the school, knowing the identity of the offender, very quickly detect him, he admits half a dozen others and we finish up with forty detected robberies which are really quite meaningless.'

An example of a local problem is vandalism (technically criminal damage). The local authority housing department may have information on repairs needed, which does not distinguish between deliberate, accidental, and wear and tear damage; the police may have information on incidents of criminal damage reported to them; the Probation and social services may have information on the age and social circumstances of some of those convicted of criminal damage offences. Without inter-agency co-ordination, the information necessary for devising a strategy to combat vandalism cannot be put together. But co-ordination may reveal that the information cannot be put together anyway because it is kept on different geographical and time bases; the police may collect for subdivisions, the housing department for estates, social services for area offices, and the Probation Service for court petty-sessional divisions. The police may collect for the calendar year, the local authority for the fiscal year. So inter-agency co-ordination can often require all the co-operating agencies to rethink the basis of their information collection or embark on an entirely new process of identifying the problems that are to be dealt with, rather than trying to agglomerate four or five sets of incompatible records.

Information sharing also raises questions of trust and confidentiality. Inter-agency co-operation has led to fears that information about individuals will be passed between agencies and confidentiality breached, and the sharing of more general information generates problems of another kind. Information about recorded crime in a particular area is needed for a crime prevention strategy to operate, but publication of such information may stigmatize an area and make life even more difficult for the people who live there. Details of the racial group of victims and offenders may be very necessary, for instance, to assess the level of racially motivated attacks and the need for leisure activities and special projects for young black people in an area; but it may be used publicly in a distorted way that adds to the mythology about the involvement of black people in criminal activities and does long-lasting harm.

Collecting and sharing information is a very basic part of inter-organizational co-operation. Even when this is achieved, however, there can still be problems of mistrust, territoriality, and clash of objectives. Perhaps this is best illustrated by describing an attempt to bring together just two agencies, social services and the Probation Service, to discuss the need for closer co-operation and procedural alignment between them in the preparation of reports for juvenile court and consideration of juveniles for alternatives to custody. The managements agree to set up an inter-departmental working group to devise a joint system for the area. They are aware that this is a sensitive subject for practitioners so they ask someone independent to chair the working group and they arrange for meetings to take place on neutral ground. At the meetings the probation representatives all sit together on the same side of the room opposite the social services representatives who are all sitting together. The social services representative present is very critical of the fact that some probation representatives are absent. The minutes record the potential for 'conflict between the two agencies'. The probation representatives regard the working group as an attempt by social services to control probation officers' social inquiry report recommendations and an assault on the individual probation officer's autonomy. The real issues are never brought out into the open and discussed. Social services do not trust probation officers to make non-custodial recommendations. Probation officers do not see why social services should be allowed to screen recommendations on probation clients. Because these issues are not dealt with directly other points assume a greater significance than they really deserve. When it is proposed to set up a screening panel there is lengthy disagreement about a proposal to have only two social services people on the panel and three probation people. Two-thirds of the clients are social services clients but the local structure of the Probation Service is such that having three panel members makes much more sense than two. Social services are suspicious that it is some sort of plot.

To such sensitivities must be added other barriers to collaboration.

For bureaucracies to collaborate with each other is very costly in terms of resources and trading information and power. There needs to be a clear incentive to do so and a belief that it will in some way be cost effective. For agencies to work together to combat glue-sniffing may well have social and political advantages for all those involved. To reduce vandalism on an estate can save a housing authority considerable amounts of money. Other aspects of crime prevention may not yield such obvious returns. Finally, much remains to be resolved about how the success of inter-organizational crime prevention strategies is evaluated. It might seem a simple matter – is there less crime? Unfortunately it is far from simple. Police figures on crime, which are the only figures available, give only an inadequate picture of the amount and nature of crime. Much crime is not reported to the police because the victims have reasons for not reporting it. Perhaps they are too timid or they have no faith that any good will come of reporting it. They may not have been insured, so have no particular incentive to report it. They may distrust the police, or not want to be seen by neighbours talking to the police. Thus, one outcome of successful crime prevention projects may be improved relationships between the police and the residents of an area, so that when the residents become victims of crime they are readier to go to the police and report the incident. So as a result of the crime prevention project recorded crime rates may go up.

A different approach might be to regard the problem not just as the incidence of crime itself but the effects of crime on a community, the fear it arouses in people, the way it reduces the quality of their lives by making them fearful of going out and suspicious of their neighbours, and the way it informs their view of the criminal justice system. If a crime prevention project managed to alleviate the damaging effects of crime on a community by improving the appearance of the environment, making people feel safer by paying attention to better lighting and security devices, and replacing alienation and suspicion by neighbourliness through establishing a range of communal activities (Patricia Allatt's evaluation of security improvements on a housing estate in Newcastle shows this can happen (Allatt 1984)), would such a project have achieved its aims? This question has yet to be resolved.

Conclusions

The increased importance given to measures to prevent or reduce crime can be seen as a step forward in crime policy. Recognizing the importance of preventing crime constitutes an acknowledgement of the futility of attempting to deal with crime through increasing the machinery of criminal justice. Police, courts, and prisons already consume an increasing share of public expenditure. There are no good reasons for believing that further increases in expenditure of the same kind will increase the effectiveness of these traditional methods. A different analysis is needed.

The various efforts to develop an inter-organizational approach to crime prevention described in this chapter are the beginnings of an attempt to respond to crime in another way. While it would be premature to claim any major successes the approach has the great merit of starting from an acceptance that although those convicted of crime are individuals, the roots of criminal activity came from what is happening in families, neighbourhoods, housing estates, and schools and can be affected by the policies of all the social and community agencies in an area as well as by national policies. Inherent in the approaches described in this chapter is also a welcome move towards more participation and consultation. The agencies of the criminal justice system – police, courts, social services and probation, prisons – can seem very remote from those they deal with and those they aim to protect (albeit indirectly). The police are increasingly recognizing this and the post-Scarman consultative arrangements are one way of bringing the police closer to the public. Regrettably, and with a few notable exceptions, the social services and the Probation Service have as yet to consider how to consult with local communities and how to involve them in their work with offenders. The whole machinery of the criminal law, even at its most informal in the juvenile court, is a world apart from the crime-ridden run-down housing estates from where a high proportion of both victims and offenders come.

However, the promise of the new crime prevention approaches may well shrivel and die if the debate about crime prevention stays at the level of words in policy documents, government circulars, and one or two demonstration projects. An injection of resources is essential. Crime prevention projects cannot be successful against a background of expenditure restrictions which exacerbate all the crime-producing features of urban life – neglect of repairs and maintenance, closure of community facilities, large-scale unemployment (on some housing estates as many as 70 per cent of heads of household are without work). Bureaucracies already overburdened and insecure cannot be expected to throw themselves with great enthusiasm into a range of new projects. There must be money for facilities and small-scale developments. The sums will be small in proportion to what can be saved but without some seedcorn money very little can be expected to happen.

The sums of money would not be substantial. The gains would be very great. Many factors have combined to break up communities. One of the most destructive results of the break-up of communities is the way criminal behaviour within a community attacks that community. The highest crime rates are in the poorest areas. To create community spirit and community identity must be a major objective of crime policy.

© *1987 Vivien Stern*

References

Alderson, J. (1979) *Policing Freedom*. Plymouth: Macdonald and Evans.

Allatt, P. (1984) Fear of Crime – The Effects of Improved Residential Security on a Difficult to Let Estate. *Howard Journal* 23(3).

Blaber, A. (1979) *The Exeter Community Policing Consultative Group*. London: National Association for the Care and Resettlement of Offenders.

Bright, J. and Petterson, G. (1984) *The Safe Neighbourhoods Unit*. London: National Association for the Care and Resettlement of Offenders.

Gladstone, F.J. (1980) *Co-ordinating Crime Prevention Efforts*. London: HMSO.

Gottfredson, M.R. (1984) *Victims of Crime: The Dimensions of Risk*. London: HMSO.

Hedges, A., Blaber, A., and Mostyn, B. (1980) *Community Planning Project: Cunningham Road Improvement Scheme, Final Report*. London: Social and Community Planning Research.

Home Office (1983) *Crime Prevention: A Co-ordinated Approach* (The Lord Elton). London: HMSO.

——— (1984) *Crime Prevention*. Circular no. 8. London: HMSO.

Hope, T. and Murphy, D.J.I. (1983) Problems of Implementing Crime Prevention: The Experience of a Demonstration Project. *Howard Journal* 22(1): 38–50.

Hough, M. and Mayhew, P. (1983) *The British Crime Survey*. London: HMSO.

House of Lords (1982) *Official Report*, Vol. 428, No. 62, Col. 988.

Kinsey, R. (1984) *Merseyside Crime Survey, First Report, November 1984*, Merseyside County Council.

Lea, J. and Young, J. (1984) *What Is To Be Done About Law and Order: Crisis in the 80s*. Harmondsworth: Penguin.

Maxfield, M.G. (1984) *Fear of Crime in England and Wales*. London: HMSO.

NACRO (1982) *Neighbourhood Consultations*. London: National Association for the Care and Resettlement of Offenders.
———— (1983) *Titford Review*. London: National Association for the Care and Resettlement of Offenders.
———— (1985) Report on Titford Link. Unpublished paper, National Association for the Care and Resettlement of Offenders.
Newman, Sir Kenneth (1983) In *News of the World*, June.
Southgate, P. and Ekblom, P. (1984) *Contacts between Police and Public*. London: HMSO.

12 Evaluating effectiveness

John Hill

Introduction

There has been growing interest in recent years in the Probation Service becoming more involved in community-based work, which moves away from a narrow focus on the needs of individual offenders towards a wider concern with the social basis of crime and its reduction and with the operation of the criminal justice system as a whole.

While this represents a major shift of emphasis in the work of the Service, it currently lacks a common rationale. Theoretical analysis has tended to be fragmentary and there is a danger that the 'community tag' will be applied somewhat indiscriminately to a variety of activities without due regard for what exactly is being achieved. As Raynor has pointed out, 'There is a risk of a wide range of ill-co-ordinated initiatives with no common purpose, or of community involvement becoming a marginal activity, the hobby of a few offices rather than a Service commitment' (Raynor 1984: 45).

It is difficult to discuss how the Probation Service's involvement in the community can be evaluated without first being clear about aims and objectives. This chapter begins by examining some of the reasons put forward in justification of community-based work and describes various models or approaches, using examples drawn from current practice. This is followed by a discussion on how such work can be evaluated, with the intention of developing evaluative guidelines which may be helpful in the future. One of the main contentions is that a shift of emphasis in the work of the Probation Service not only requires new operational skills but also implies changes in how effectiveness is measured and in the evaluative processes used.

The aims of community-based work

There appear to be two general themes which describe, at least in principle, what the Probation Service's involvement in community-based work is directed at achieving; that is, crime prevention and a greater involvement of the community in dealing with the consequences of crime and in the criminal justice process.

However, within these broad statements of intent there is a variety of operational practices with rationale drawn from different disciplines, and where the connection between means and ends is not always clear. Such definitional problems obviously make it difficult to evaluate such work and an important first step is clarification of purpose.

COMMUNITY INVOLVEMENT AND CRIME PREVENTION

Much recent discussion on the future of the Probation Service has concerned a new role, following the widespread questioning of the desirability and feasibility of a central emphasis on the 'treatment' of offenders. Research on the subject, culminating in Folkard's IMPACT study, appeared to show that attempts to reduce recidivism through social casework were unrealistic (Folkard, Smith, and Smith 1976). The best that could be realistically claimed for 'rehabilitation through casework' was that in certain circumstances marginal reductions in recidivism could be achieved, but these were difficult to predict and were more likely to be consequences of 'helping offenders with their own problems rather than through direct attempts to "treat" the problems society attributed to them' (Raynor 1984: 44).

The idea that the Probation Service should move into community work with a view to reducing or preventing crime was perhaps first advanced by Haxby (1978) but has since gained ground, particularly following the paper produced by Bottoms and McWilliams (1979) which identified the reduction of crime as one of the primary aims of the Probation Service. In support of this aim they called for a redirection from traditional client-centred methods towards crime prevention in the sense of more general community work.

The Home Office (1984a) in its statement of objectives and priorities has also suggested that the Probation Service should become involved in the wider community and that part of the duties of a probation officer shall be participation in arrangements concerned with the prevention of crime.

However, as Shaw has warned, 'there is a danger in some quarters of replacing the rehabilitation myth with the myth of crime prevention' (Shaw 1983: 128). What little is known about preventing crime seems to favour means like 'opportunity reduction' (for example, making it harder to steal things) and 'Neighbourhood watch' (neighbourly surveillance of other people's property). This is difficult to promote in deprived and disrupted communities except by involving local prople in a wide range of community development work, informed by their own perception of the problems of their neighbourhood. But as he goes on to say,

'Since crime and the fear of crime disproportionately affect the more disadvantaged members of society, and since community work may be expected to throw up other benefits aside from crime reduction, a shift in probation practice in this direction would be entirely consistent with the traditional ideals of the Service.'

(Shaw 1983: 129)

This has important implications for how the Service's involvement in community-based work is assessed (and the extent to which it is accepted as a legitimate use of resources). It means that the actual prevention of crime, to the extent that this can be measured, becomes one of a number of criteria on which effectiveness is judged, rather than the single criterion on which community-based work should stand or fall. Recognition is given to other benefits such as improving the physical environment, encouraging self-help on the part of the community, encouraging the development of local communities as effective social units by strengthening networks and relationships, contributing to economic and social reconstruction, and reducing the fear of crime.

This draws its rationale from recent thinking on community social work, especially the suggestions by Thomas (1983) and the views of Hadley (1982) on the neighbourhood approach to delivering social services to local communities. It involves the Probation Service in a much wider perspective on crime and the community by recognizing the inappropriateness of separating out, in discussions about crime and responses to it, the social and economic issues confronting the community.

There are few signs yet of the Probation Service developing into a community-focused service as so described but there are some examples of such work which are worthy of closer examination. While most of these schemes are in their infancy and few have been subject to rigorous evaluation, it is becoming possible to build up conceptual models from which evaluation criteria can be developed for future application.

Under the broad heading of community based work/crime prevention three main types of Probation Service involvement are identifiable, varying in their degree of directiveness but with a considerable degree of overlap between them.

1 Linking clients to community resources/developing community resources
This is the most common model which at its simplest involves probation officers linking their client to existing community resources, for example, drop-in centres, unemployment centres, housing associations, education projects, women's aid groups, youth schemes. This

would also include involving, liaising, and developing volunteer support, with the probation officer acting as a facilitator or broker between the client and the community resource.

In practice, crime prevention is secondary to the aim of 'helping' offenders although there is the assumption that the interest and support provided by such schemes reduce the likelihood of clients re-offending.

In an extension of this model, the Probation Service is actively involved in setting-up community projects, often in a catalytic role in conjunction with other statutory or voluntary agencies. Again crime prevention is intended to be achieved indirectly by helping offenders and other members of the community, but some of the larger probation-initiated schemes have wide-ranging spin-offs. For example, the 'Wheels' project in Birmingham was initiated by the West Midlands Probation Service, using Inner-City Partnership funding to provide constructive and exciting wheel-based activities (for example, BMX racing, banger racing) for clients of the Service and other young people at risk of offending in the inner city. Other benefits arising from the scheme have been urban renewal through the reclamation of derelict land, the creation of employment opportunities (for example, manufacture of BMX bikes, construction of the race tracks, management of the scheme), and the encouragement of trade to the city by holding national and international events.

2 Community organization with other social welfare agencies

This involves inter-agency planning to achieve co-ordination of service delivery to geographically defined communities, or a co-ordinated response to particular problems, such as juvenile crime. For example, Robinson has reported on Probation Service involvement in the setting-up of a Neighbourhood Advice Centre in which different agencies shared information about 'events, projects and "goings on" in the patch, as well as the procedures and practices of different departments' (Robinson 1982: 48).

Probation Service involvement in inter-agency crime prevention panels/consultancy groups which include representatives of community organizations is also becoming increasingly common. The objectives of this kind of work can range from a wish to develop inter-organizational understanding and communications to efforts at community planning.

3 Community development with neighbourhood residents

This model comes closest to the ideas of community work discussed earlier. It differs from the other two approaches in being primarily aimed at supporting or facilitating collective action involving the wider community, rather than starting from the interests and concerns of those people deemed to be the Service's prime beneficiaries (that is, clients or potential clients). Much of this work has been pioneered by the National Association for the Care and Resettlement of Offenders (NACRO) through the establishment of their Crime Prevention Units. The emphasis here is on 'involving residents on demoralized estates in planning improvements to their environment in such a way that they will feel inclined to maintain and protect them' (NACRO 1982: 1).

The model is less directive than the others as it is based essentially on consultation with residents and on assisting them to implement their own ideas for improvement. These are set out in broad terms as follows:

'To achieve an improvement in relation between resident and service providers; an improvement in the estate environment in line with the needs identified by residents through consultation and, as a result, improvements in the quality of life, *one aspect of which* [my emphasis] might be a reduction in vandalism and other minor crime.'   (NACRO 1982: 1)

Of particular interest is work along these lines undertaken in Sheffield by the South Yorkshire Probation Service's Special Projects Team (SPT), which attempted to put into practice, albeit in a modified form, some of the ideas set out in the paper by Bottoms and McWilliams (1979), a central tenet of which was crime reduction through community and neighbourhood involvement.

The work of the SPT has been evaluated by Celnick (1984) and her findings have important implications not only for deciding what is practicable but also for the evaluative criteria used and the methodology employed.

A stated aim of the SPT was 'With local residents, to identify and stimulate the development of those features of neighbourhood life which are seen by local residents as likely to be significant in inhibiting crime' (Celnick 1984: 8). This was based on the view that the roots of crime lie to a large degree in the community, and therefore reduction of the crime rate is only feasible through community action.

To achieve this aim, the SPT were informed by Bottoms' and McWilliams' (1979) observation that societies with strong cohesive bonds tend to produce less crime, and that such bonds could be created by encouraging informal networks of caring based on interpersonal, mutually beneficial relationships.

The team had an opportunity to put these ideas into practice after an approach was made by residents on a local housing estate concerning problems of vandalism. However, the attempts that were made to prevent vandalism were unsuccessful, a failure which Celnick (1984) attributes to a misinterpretation of Bottoms' and McWilliams' ideas. In essence, the SPT had assumed that they could have a direct and immediate impact on the problem by bringing together the residents and those teenagers responsible for the vandalism, by means of a youth association. Helping offenders by the organization of youth facilities was seen as a way of achieving the 'social cohesion' necessary to reduce crime.

But Bottoms and McWilliams (1979) do not see any *a priori* connection between helping offenders and preventing crime, in fact they seek to separate the two. Moreover, social cohesion as providing the necessary conditions for less crime is intended to be achieved indirectly and incrementally by the build-up of networks of relationships, and by what they call 'micro structural' change (micro structural changes would include, for example, breaking down institutional barriers between school and community – the community school/college idea), stimulating employment schemes (for example, co-operatives), and pressing for housing allocation policies which discourage the creation of 'dust-bin' estates). Clearly these are longer-term strategies which would only gradually begin to effect crime rates, although there would be other shorter-term benefits associated with improving the overall quality of life.

These observations suggest that it is perhaps a mistake to assume that the Probation Service's involvement in community-based schemes will necessarily have a direct and immediate effect on reducing crime (except in certain local and specific instances through encouraging 'secondary preventative measures' such as improving the security on houses and the protection of property). Obviously this has implications for how the Probation Service's initiatives in the community are evaluated.

Implications for evaluating effectiveness

Evidence from current practice suggests that the Probation Service's involvement in community-based work/crime prevention does not have a single aim or a single way of evaluating it, but a variety of objectives which are defined and perceived differently from different perspectives. While crime prevention is an important 'bottom line' objective it should not be seen as the sole justification for the Service's involvement in community-based work and, looking at it the other way round, the realization of such a goal is dependent on a variety of other factors beyond the Service's influence. Involvement in the community may be contributing towards its attainment but it is hard to gauge the weight of this contribution.

At the operational level there is much emphasis placed on what might be termed personal and social development objectives directed at improving the quality of life. For example, boosting people's confidence in themselves and their ability to change their immediate environment, developing links between different parts of the community and between previously alienated groups in ways which are mutually beneficial, and reducing the fear of crime. Such outcomes are less tangible and hence less easily measurable than the 'hard-edged' objective of preventing crime (although this in itself is not entirely without problems), but are nevertheless important and go some way to creating the social cohesion which, in the longer-term, would seem conducive to crime reduction.

What is important is for these other goals to be clearly identified and recognized in a way which informs operational practice and helps define measurable outcomes. Since the evaluation of such work is likely to involve people's perceptions of the extent to which they feel able to influence what happens to them, to solve problems in their immediate environment, to feel a sense of belonging to a community, and to become less fearful of crime, then the evaluative methodology is likely to be drawn from the 'anthropological' tradition, which focuses on participants' own meanings and interpretation of events.

The methods employed will need to include observational studies and open-ended interview techniques intended to draw out opinions and feelings. Such methods are inherently qualitative and produce information which is primarily descriptive and interpretative. A key factor in the development of community-based work will be the extent to which the Service is able to use such information to articulate its position.

COMMUNITY INVOLVEMENT IN THE CONSEQUENCES OF CRIME
AND THE CRIMINAL JUSTICE PROCESS

A second major aim for the Probation Service's community-based work is to involve the community in the consequences of crime and in the criminal justice process. This is included in the Home Office (1984a) statement of objectives and priorities for the Probation Service and is now incorporated in the Probation Rules 1984, which refer to the involvement of the Probation Service in diverting from the criminal justice system and in mediation, reparation, and victim support schemes (1984b, rule 37). As Raynor has noted 'all these have little directly to do with crime reduction, but much to do with

developing strategies to cope constructively with some of the consequences of crime after it has occurred' (Raynor 1984: 45).

As with the 'community development'/crime reduction initiatives
there are a variety of operational practices with rationale drawn from
different disciplines, and an important first step in determining how
effectiveness can be measured is again to clarify purpose. There
appear to be at least six interrelated benefits which are claimed to arise
from the community's involvement in the consequences of crime and
in the criminal justice process:

1) Victim and community involvement in the criminal justice process
   is seen as more obviously concerned with 'justice' because it treats
   crime as harm done by offenders to individual victims, or to
   communities, rather than to the state. Resolving disputes by actual
   or symbolic undoing of the harm between the parties most directly
   involved is thought to lead to a feeling that the damage has been
   repaired and the balance has been restored. This is seen as
   particularly useful when offenders and victims must continue to co-
   exist as members of the same community.

2) Resolving the disruption caused by crime in a more personal way
   rather than through abstract and adversarial legal procedures
   becomes more meaningful and less alienating to the participants.
   This is based on Christie's idea of 'conflicts as property'. He sees
   one of the consequences of industrial societies as being the removal
   of conflict from the people to whom it belongs, the complainant or
   victim, the offender, and their neighbourhood, to become 'other
   people's property – primarily the property of lawyers' (Christie
   1977: 8).

   Christie is concerned with the idea of conflicts as property
   because he sees conflict as valuable both to the individuals
   concerned and to society as a whole. He believes that conflicts offer
   a potential for activity by participants, particularly victims, and
   approves of the chance they give for 'norm clarification'; conflicts
   encourage discussion of 'what represents the law of the land. How
   wrong was the thief, how right was the victim' (Christie 1977: 14).
   This leads him to the idea of dealing with crime in a way which
   involves all those concerned and allows confrontation of offenders
   and victims to thrash out their conflicts.

3) There are thought to be potential psychological benefits for the
   victim in meeting the offender. This may be in the sense of a reduction of fear and feelings of insecurity through the realization that
   the offender was recognizably human after all, with sympathetic

problems and emotions. It may also give the victim a chance to feel a certain reintegration with the community. As Marshall has noted, 'there are many, especially among the more vulnerable – the aged, women, or scapegoated minorities who are cut off from fruitful interaction with others by fear of attack. Any initiatives which helps to bring them out from their isolation in a safe context may do much to enhance their lives' (Marshall 1984: 2).

4) By directly confronting the offender with the consequences of the crime he or she has committed and with the person harmed, a greater sense of responsibility may be induced and a genuine impulse to reform encouraged. This is seen as less damaging and more appropriate than imprisonment, since it brings the offender into a practical relationship with the local community in which he or she may feel isolated.

5) There are potential cost benefits. Passage through the formal criminal justice system and imprisonment are much more costly than community-based mediation and reparation schemes.

6) There is the potential for reducing crime through the increase in social cohesion created by victim/offender relationships in the ways described by Bottoms and McWilliams (1979), referred to earlier in this chapter.

A variety of practices are emerging in this field intended to embrace some or all of these features. But these need to be classified in a way which enables their key elements to be identified so that measures of effectiveness can be appropriately defined.

Marshall (1984) has attempted to produce a typology of practice based on the kinds of projects which are being established in this country at present. The following table is derived from this typology, with the aim of identifying some of the factors evaluative exercises will need to consider.

Implications for evaluating effectiveness
As with community-based work/crime prevention, it is important that the various objectives of the community's involvement in the consequences of crime and in the criminal justice process are clearly identified in a way which informs operational practice and helps to measure success.

The six potential benefits suggested earlier, related to the operational framework, provide a basis for developing evaluative criteria. Again, most of the objectives of this work involve changes in participants' feelings, attitudes, and behaviour, which do not easily lend themselves to quantitative techniques. In order to determine the extent to which fear of crime is reduced or the extent to which victims are satisfied and feel a greater sense of justice, it will be necessary to use methods which can elicit qualitative information of this sort. Similarly, the extent to which the offender feels a greater responsibility to the community or to the victim by being confronted with the consequences of his/her action require evaluative techniques sensitive to this type of information.

It will also be necessary to follow up the interviews and observations made during or immediately following the mediation/reparation process in order to determine the longer-term effects. For example, are victims or potential victims of crime in a particular neighbourhood likely to be more involved in the community and less fearful of crime following their involvement in mediation/reparation schemes? Are offenders involved in these schemes less likely to re-offend and do the instances of, say, vandalism and burglary in a neighbourhood reduce as a consequence?

Certain objectives are, however, more amenable to quantitative measures. For example, the diversionary effects of the schemes either from the criminal justice system or from other court disposals can be measured by recording the number and characteristics of offenders involved. Pre-court mediation may reduce the number of offenders appearing before the court, whereas reparation used in conjunction with another disposal as, say, an alternative to custody should reduce the number of custodial sentences. This can be measured indirectly by recording the offence, previous convictions, and previous disposals of offenders involved, or directly by comparing court sentencing practices over time. In the same way the unit cost of mediation/reparation could be calculated in a manner which allows comparison with other procedures or disposals.

Summary

Within the Probation Service there has been a developing interest in community-based work with a shift in emphasis away from the 'treatment' of the individual offender to the social basis of crime and its reduction, and to a concern with the operation of the criminal justice system as a whole. A variety of practices has begun to emerge but with no common rationale and with an often ill-defined theoretical basis, yet clarification of objectives informed by theory is necessary to evaluate effectiveness.

Two broad statements of intent are identifiable, that is, community-based work leading to the reduction of crime, and the

Table 12   Typology of mediation/reparation schemes (derived in part from Marshall 1984: 5–8)

type of scheme	point of intervention	organizational structure	focus
Community mediation projects	Pre-court, mainly dealing with non-criminal neighbourhood disputes	Strong local base using volunteers in the settlement of neighbourhood disputes or more basic social conflicts (e.g. racial attitudes)	Main focus on 'conflicts as property' and 'social cohesion'
Mediation and diversion from the criminal justice system	Pre-court, mainly dealing with minor offences	Local base with similar structure to above but in cases where parties are usually known to each other but in cases where a minor criminal offence has been committed	Focus as above but also concerned with diversion from formal criminal justice system on basis that 'offence has arisen from interpersonal conflict which does not at present necessitate social condemnation but which could escalate into more serious offences in absence of resolution through mediation process' (Marshall 1984: 5)
Mediation in 'encounter groups'	Post-court	Groups composed of persons convicted of a particular offence and victims of similar offences convened to discuss features of such offending	Intended to be 'therapeutic for the victims (allowing them to express their feelings and convert a negative experience into something more positive) and rehabilitative for offenders (who can also put their point of view and come to understand the effects of what they have done)' (Marshall 1984: 7)

Reparation and diversion from the criminal justice system	Pre-court, mainly dealing with juvenile offenders. Point of intervention at police decision whether to caution or prosecute	Reparation agreements made on a voluntary basis by the offender alongside a decision to caution rather than prosecute	Induces greater sense of responsibility from offender and meets victim's need for the 'wrong' to have been acknowledged and 'righted', at least symbolically. Principle that keeping juvenile out of formal court process lessens the risk of delinquent labelling and hence further offending
Reparation as an alternative court disposal	Post-court. Intervention can occur at different stages in the court process: – adjournment; – deferment of sentence; – as part of another court order such as probation; – community service	Can involve 'direct' reparation from offender to victim or 'indirect' from offender to victims of crime generally. Probation Service (or representatives) negotiate agreement between victim(s)/offender which is presented to court for consideration when making their sentencing decision	As above but more of a direct focus on reparation as an alternative, usually to a more punitive disposal

involvement of the community in the consequences of crime and in the criminal justice process. Within these broad statements there is a variety of objectives, defined and perceived differently. In particular, much of the Probation Service's current involvement in community-based work is to do with helping offenders and improving the overall quality of life, rather than being directly concerned with crime reduction: the danger of confusing the two should be recognized. However, the process of helping offenders and improving the quality of life within communities may be instrumental in creating the conditions necessary for reducing crime. The Probation Service needs to be able to justify its operation in these terms as being a legitimate and appropriate use of its resources.

The community's involvement in the consequences of crime and in the criminal justice process is aimed at resolving the disruption caused by crime in a way that is more meaningful and less alienating to the participants. Again a variety of objectives can be distinguished, including reducing the fear of crime, helping victims and offenders to reconcile their differences, providing the offender with an opportunity to make amends, minimizing the pain and resentment felt by the victim, and reducing the cost of the criminal justice process.

The evaluation of such work will necessitate techniques which draw their methodology from the anthropological tradition, focusing on participants' own meanings and the interpretations they give to events. This is likely to involve an emphasis on observational studies and open-ended interviews sensitive to the assessment of attitudes, opinions, and feelings. In some cases, quantifiable measures will be appropriate, for example, in assessing the diversionary effects of various schemes.

A key factor in the establishment of community-based work as a legitimate activity for the Probation Service will be the extent to which it can develop the theory, practice, and evaluative techniques necessary to articulate its position in the political arena.

© *1987 John Hill*

References

Bottoms, A.E. and McWilliams, W. (1979) A Non-Treatment Paradigm for Probation Practice. *British Journal of Social Work* 9(2): 159–202.

Celnick, A. (1984) Hallam Project Evaluation Report. Research report, no. 4, South Yorkshire Probation Service Research Unit.

Christie, N. (1977) Conflicts as Property. *British Journal of Criminology* 17(1): 1–19.

Folkard, M.S., Smith, D.E., and Smith, D.D. (1976) *Impact Intensive Matched Probation and After-Care Treatment, Vol. 2: The Results of the Experiment*. Home Office Research Study no. 36. London: HMSO.

Hadley, R., Brown, P., and White, K.J. (1982) A Case for Neighbourhood Social Work and Social Services. In P. Barclay (ed.) *Social Workers: Their Role and Tasks*. Appendix A. London: Bedford Square Press.

Haxby, D. (1978) *Probation: A Changing Service*. London: Constable.

Home Office (1984a) *Probation Service in England and Wales, Statement of National Objectives and Priorities*. London: HMSO.

———— (1984b) *The Probation Rules 1984*. Statutory Instrument no. 647. London: HMSO.

Marshall, T. (1984) *Reparation, Conciliation and Mediation*. Home Office Research and Planning Unit Paper no. 27. London: HMSO.

NACRO Crime Prevention Unit (1982) *Neighbourhood Consultations: A Practical Guide*. London: National Association for the Care and Resettlement of Offenders.

Raynor, P. (1984) National Purpose and Objectives: A Comment. *Probation Journal* 31(2): 43–7.

Robinson, S. (1982) Setting up a Neighbourhood Advice Centre in Central Harrow. *Probation Journal* 29(2): 47–50.

Shaw, S. (1983) Crime Prevention and the Future of the Probation Service. *Probation Journal* 30(4): 127–29.

Thomas, D.N. (1983) *The Making of Community Work*. London: George Allen and Unwin.

Name index

Note: Names of reports and institutions can be found in the *Subject index*.

Adair, H.S. 75
Alderson, John 210
Allatt, Patricia 222
Allen, G.F. 103, 115
Angwin, P. 12
Arnold, Sir John 45
Austin, J. 109

Bailey, H. 163
Bailey, R. 37, 188
Banks, C. 3
Barclay, P. 10
Bean, P. 43
Beaumont, B. 44
Becker, H.S. 108
Benn, Tony 31
Blaber, Ann 214, 218
Blagg, H. 205
Bottoms, A.E. 43, 48, 51, 227, 230–31
Boyle, Lord 11
Brake, M. 188
Braverman, H. 111
Brewer, C. 166
Bright, J. 215
Brittan, Leon 27, 40, 81, 92; working
    paper on Criminal Justice 4, 5–6; on
    reparation 204
Brody, S. 199
Brown, A. 66
Brown, E.J. 103
Bryant, M. 48
Burchell, A. 158, 159

Carlen, P. 45
Cartwright, A.K.J. 159
Casburn, M. 45
Catchpole, Roy 87, 88–9
Celnick, A. 230–31
Chesney, S. 203
Christie, Nils 112, 200, 233
Clark, G.A. 107
Clark, Kenneth 8

Clarke, D. 106
Clarke, R. 195
Cohen, S. 88
Corden, J. 89, 93
Crolley, T. 37
Crook, B. 95
Crow, I. 139, 140–41
Cullen, F. 103, 107

Davies, Edmund 26
Davies, Martin 83, 89, 93
Davis, G. 45
Derricourt, N. 205
Dinsmore, J. 114
Ditton, J. 167
Dixon, P. 201, 205
Dodd, D. 196
Donnan, S. 155
Downes, D. 96
Duff, P. 201, 203
Duffee, D.E. 112, 115
Dunbar, I. 96

Ekblom, P. 212
Elton, Lord 209
Empey, L.T. 105
Evans, T. 55

Fairhead, Susan 3, 158, 164
Falkingham, P. 12
Farrington, D. 89
Finley, Revd James B. 92
Fisher, A. 43
Fitzharris, T.C. 118
Fitzmaurice, C. 92
Flanagan, T.J. 103
Fogel, D. 101, 102, 105, 107
Folkard, M.S. 227
Fry, Margery 195

Galaway, B. 76, 200, 203
Garofalo, R. 196
Gendreau, P. 103

Gibson, Sir Ralph 50
Gladstone, F.J. 212
Glenn, H. 196
Goffman, E. 85, 86, 88, 89
Goodman, P. 163, 164
Goodstein, L. 114
Gordon, A.M. 172
Gottfredson, M.R. 196, 212
Grimes, J. 172
Guest, C.L. 181

Hadley, R. 228
Hagan, J. 120
Halmos, P. 36, 44, 47
Hamson, C. 164
Harding, J. 200, 204
Harlow, N. 113, 114, 115, 118, 121
Harman, J. 54
Harrison, P. 196
Hashimi, L. 165
Haskey, J. 155
Hawkins, G. 94
Haxby, D. 64, 227
Haynes, P. 115, 116
Headlee, S. 103, 106
Heather, N. 156, 163
Hedges, A. 214
Heidensohn, F. 90
Helber, N.L. 108
Hermann, Hanus 84–5, 86, 89
Herold, Chief Superintendent 219–20
Hill, J. 134, 139
Hindelang, M. 196
Holmes, Thomas 35, 40, 43
Holtermann, S. 158, 159
Hope, Tim 213
Hough, M. 3, 158, 196, 203, 211, 212
Hudson, J. 200, 203
Hugman, B. 12
Humphries, D. 106
Husband, C. 182

James, A.L. 41, 44, 46
Jarvis, F.V. 35, 36, 38, 40
Jeffs, D. 157
Jenkins, Roy 1
Johnson, T. 40, 41
Jones, Bill 133
Jones, H. 42
Joshua, H. 182

Kessel, N. 165
Kidder, J. 113
King, J.S. 43

King, R. 94
Kinsey, R. 212
Knapman, E. 157
Kramer, J.H. 114
Kuipers, J. 89, 93

Lacey, M. 50
Larsen, C.R. 115, 116
Lea, J. 211
Leibrich, J. 76
Lewis, P. 12, 54, 55, 60, 64
Lipson, A.J. 111
Lipton, D. 102, 103, 199
Lloyd, C. 5

McAnany, P. 105, 107, 111, 113, 115
Mclagan, S. 203
Mcleod, M. 103
McWilliams, B. 72, 78
McWilliams, W. 36, 38, 41–2, 43, 48, 51, 227, 230–31
McGuire, J. 95
Maguire, M. 196, 197–98
Marshall, T. 204, 234
Martin, J.P. 9, 164
Martinson, R. 102–03, 199
Mathieson, D.A. 42, 50, 187
Matthews, J. 95
Maull, G. 78
Mawby, R. 196
Maxfield, M.G. 212
Mayhew, P. 3, 158, 196, 203, 211, 212
Mellor, D. 206
Meyer, J.W. 120, 121
Millard, D.A. 41, 43, 54–5
Morgan, R. 94
Morris, N. 114
Morris, P. 89
Morris, R. 157
Mostyn, B. 214
Mott, J. 172
Murch, M. 45
Murphy, Daniel 213
Murphy, E. 157

Nelson, E.K. 114, 115, 118, 121
Newman, Sir Kenneth 210
Novack, S. 203
Nuss, L. 114

O'Connor, J.F. 103
Olsen, M. 55
Orford, J. 174
Othen, M. 84
Otto, S. 165

Parker, H. 45, 46, 51
Parker, T. 84, 86, 87, 88, 91
Parnas, R. 115
Parsloe, P. 44
Pashukanis, E. 103
Paterson, Sir Alexander 94
Pease, K. 76, 78, 79, 92
Perry, F.G. 43
Petersilia, J. 115–16, 118
Peterson, M.A. 111
Petterson, G. 215
Phelan, B. 96
Phillips, C. 167
Pinker, R. 10
Plant, M. 171
Powell, M. 45
Priestley, P. 83, 95
Prins, H. 152, 172
Purser, R. 163

Ragona, A.J. 117
Raynor, P. 226, 227, 232–33
Read, G. 55
Reiman, J.H. 103, 106
Rex, J. 182, 188
Richards, N. 78
Roberts, C. 47
Roberts, J. 47, 49, 149
Robertson, I. 156, 163
Robinson, S. 229
Ross, R.R. 103
Rowan, B. 120
Rutherford, A. 6

Sapsford, R.J. 90–1
Saunders, W. 157
Scarman, Lord 210
Schafer, S. 194
Scott, D. 12
Scott, J. 163
Scott, W.R. 110, 114, 121
Sechrest, L. 103
Segal, L. 115
Seymour, B. 59, 80
Shapland, J. 196, 197, 201, 203
Shaw, S.J. 159, 165, 203, 227–28
Simpson, P. 12
Smith, D. 205, 227
Softley, P. 201
Solomos, J. 182
Southgate, P. 212
Sparks, R. 196

Spratley, T.A. 159
Stanley, A. 59
Stanton, A. 134
Stevens, P. 140
Stewart, A. 164
Stone, N. 12

Taylor, D. 158
Taylor, T. 88
Taylor, W. 181
Tether, P. 168
Thomas, D.N. 228
Thomas, H.A. 92
Thomas, J.E. 84
Thomson, D. 101, 105, 107, 111, 113, 115, 117, 206
Tomlinson, S. 182, 188
Tonnies, F. 112
Turnbull, D. 45
Turner, M. 9

Umbriet, M. 202, 205
Underhill, Y. 76

van den Haag, E. 102
Varah, M. 77
Vennard, J. 197–98, 203
Vickery, A. 55
von Hirsch, A. 102, 111

Walker, D. 12
Walker, H. 44
Wallace, T. 182
Waller, Irwin 198
Ward, Ken 9
Webster, D. 9
West, J. 76
Weston, W.R. 48
White, S.O. 103
Whitelaw, Lord 26, 92
Wilks, J. 102, 103, 199
Willis, A. 47
Willmore, J. 201, 203
Wilson, A. 89, 93
Wilson, J. 102
Wilson, K. 44, 46
Windlesham, Lord 91
Worrall, A. 89
Wozniak, T. 103, 107

Young, J. 211

Zehr, H. 202, 205

Subject index

ABA *see* American Bar Associates
ACA *see* American Corrections
  Association
ACOP *see* Association of Chief Officers
  of Probation
Action on Alcohol Abuse (1984) 168,
  170
Advisory Council on the Misuse of
  Drugs, report (1982) 174
Advisory Council on the Penal System
  (1970) 68
Advisory Council on the Treatment of
  Offenders (1963) 38, 83
AFSC *see* American Friends Service
  Committee
'after-care' services 38, 40, 83
alcohol 127–28; Advisory Service 163;
  Council on 163; costs of 158–59; and
  criminal behaviour 5, 153–54, 157–
  58; disease model 155–56; education
  on 59, 163–67; laws relating to 152–
  53; prevention policies 167–75;
  problems of 160–63
Alcohol Concern 163, 168, 170
Alcohol – Our Favourite Drug (1986) 155
Alcohol Policies (1982) 168
Alcoholics Anonymous 166
American Bar Associates (ABA) 101
American Corrections Association
  (ACA) 101
American Friends Service Committee
  (AFSC) 102
American Probation and Parole
  Association (APPA) 101
ancillary staff 70–1
APEX 141, 143
APPA *see* American Probation and
  Parole Association
Aquarius, Birmingham 167
Assistant Chief Probation Officers 63, 66
Assistant Principal Officers 40
Association of Chief Officers of

Probation (ACOP) 33, 144, 168
Association of Chief Police Officers 165
Aston University 180

Bail Act (1976) 136
bail hostels 136
BASW *see* British Association of Social
  Workers
Birmingham 128; adventure park in 7,
  229; Magistrates Court 30; 'wet
  shelter' 137
Birmingham Post 30
'blacks', research on 181–94; term
  defined 180
Blennerhassett (Committee) 159, 164
Bramshill Police College 209
Bridging the Gap (1981) 146
Bristol, disturbances in (1980) 182
British Association of Social Workers
  (BASW) 95
British Crime Surveys 3–6, 158,
  195–96, 203, 206, 211

California 111, 116; probation in 118
Calouste Gulbenkian Foundation (1970)
  11
Campaign for the Single Homeless
  People (CHAR) 165
casework 42-81-3, 131
Central Council of Probation and After-
  Care Committees 33, 50, 165, 168
CEP 143
Certificate of Qualification in Social
  Work (CQSW) 184
CHAR *see* Campaign for the Single
  Homeless People
children 37–8, 46–7, 92, 113; *see also*
  juveniles
class conflict, in USA 103
Clerk to the Justices 41
clients 40–1, 131; and alcohol 156, 157–
  78, 160–67; and community service
  78, 80; effect of 'teamwork' on 58–9,

61–2, 66; 'hard-risk' 54; services for 55; unemployed 143–44; in USA 103; *see also* offenders
communities, attitudes of 54; clarification 9–10; development 56, 64, 226, 233; involvement 12–13, 227–28, 239; local 6; and prisons 94, 95; resources 54; in USA 112–14, 117
Community Programme (CP) 143, 145
Community Service 1, 11, 31, 39, 68; fine defaulters 76; national seminars on 79–80; organization 70–1; and probation service 77–8; schemes 11, 25, 28; wide variety of 72–3
Community Service Orders 7, 141–42
Community Service by Offenders (Scotland) Act (1978) 68
conciliation 45, 47
Conference of Chief Probation Officers (1982) 145
consultation, with government 25
Contacts between Police and Public (1984) 212
conviction and re-conviction, and community service 76–7; and prison 85; rates of 6–8, 149; social consequences 8–9
Co-ordinating Crime Prevention Efforts (1980) 212
Corby project (1983) 164
court missionaries *see* police courts 35–6, 50, 61, 63; civil 37, 38, 44–5, 46, 47; and community service 79; criminal 36, 38, 44, 47; and housing 135–36; juvenile 39, 45, 105, 113, 187; magistrates 29, 37, 157; personnel 11, 41, 51; power of 37, 74; and reparation 204–05; requirements of 48
CP *see* Community Programme
CQSW *see* Certificate of Qualification in Social Work
crime 27, 50, 91, 127, 129; and alcohol 156–60; impact of 13; politics 21; prevention 1, 10, 209–24, 227, 228–29, 235; and racism 182; and reparation 202; rise in 44, 199; surveys of 3–6, 195–96, 203, 206, 211; types 2–3; and unemployment 140; in USA 116–17
criminals, in USA 102–05, 116
Criminal Justice Acts (1925) 40; (1948)

35; (1967) 84; (1972) 39, 68, 76, 136; (1973) 1, 199; (1977) 1; (1982) 1, 2, 23, 27, 39, 74, 84, 199
criminal justice system 21, 24, 29, 34, 187, 232
Cunningham Road improvement scheme 214
custody 5, 8, 26, 85, 181; alternatives to 50, 83, 93, 131, 132, 136, 140–42, 149

Daily Telegraph 30
Dance Centre, Accra University 30
Danish probation service 9
day centres 1, 11, 39, 49, 59, 142, 148, 165
Department of Environment 135
determinate sentencing 104, 111, 114
Devon and Cornwall, police experiment 169
DHSS 8, 138, 143, 165, 168, 170
disadvantaged areas 140
Discharged Prisoners' Aid Societies 83
Divorce Court Welfare Service 45
drink drivers 164
Drinking in England and Wales (1980) 155, 158
Drinking Sensibly (1982) 168
drugs, Antabuse 166, criminal behaviour 5, 172–74; problems 159–71; youth 171–72

education 6, 88, 131–32, 142, 228; alcohol abuse 163–64; for offenders 144–48
Emergency Provisions Act (1974) 31
Exeter 204; Community Policing Consultative Group 217–18

Fear of Crime in England and Wales (1984) 212
Federal Probation Quarterly 101
females, and alcohol 157–59; and drugs 171; housing 134; offenders 74; in prison 89–90
finance and resources 210; of community service 71, 74, 77–8; detoxification centres 165; for drug abuse 174; drunkenness 158–59; education 147; housing 135; for information sharing 222; of judiciary 22–3; prisons 92–3; probation service 1–2, 10–11, 23, 27–8, 95; in USA 116, 117–18

general election (1979) 23
Ghana 30
government 26; alcohol forum 168; and crime 21, 199–200; finance 27; and housing 138; law and order 49; local reorganization 22; policies 24–5; reports 26, 223
Government Economic Service Working Paper (1981) 158–59
Grange project, Grimsby 219

Habitual Drunken Offender (1971) 164
Hackney 196–97
Handsworth 188; alternative scheme 30, 181, 190–92; cultural centre 30, 181, 190–92
Health Advisory Service 174
Health Education Council 155
Holloway prison 90
Home Affairs Committee (1981) 92
Home Office 43; circulars and reports 38–40, 42, 83, 88, 164; development programme 12; and fine defaulters 76; policy statements 23, 33–4; Research Unit 164–65, 169; survey of south east prisons 5, 132, 158; Working Group on Crime Prevention 212; working paper (1984) 4, 50, 92, 227, 232
Home Secretary 26; *see also* Leon Brittan and Lord Whitelaw *under Name index*
House of Lords Committee on Unemployment 139
housing and accommodation 49, 127, 131, 132; for offenders 133–38, 148; in prison 88; for single persons 165–66; and unemployment 5; vandalism of 214–15, 231
Housing Act (1974) 135
Housing Corporation 135
Housing (Homeless Persons) Act (1977) 134, 165
Howard League for Penal Reform (1979) 92, 195
Humberside Probation Service 158

IMPACT study (1976) 227
Index to Probation Projects (1982–83) 132
industrial action 24
information sharing 222
Inner-City Partnership Scheme 189, 229

Inner London demonstration unit 6
Inner London Probation Service, research by 6
Institute of Health Studies, Hull University 158, 168
Interdepartmental Committee on the Business of Criminal Courts (1961) 39
Intermittent Custody, Green Paper on 27
inter-organizational approach 13, 219–24

judicial system 22, 25, 32, 37–8
justice model, in USA 104, 106–07, 114; proposals 111–12; reactions to 108–09
Juvenile Crime Unit 217, 218
juveniles, as 'black' offenders 180–81; and community service 75–6; and drugs 171–72; as offenders 39, 217; in Washington State 111; *see also* children

law and order 29, 44; defiance of 31; and general election (1979) 23; politics of 3, 49
Leeds Detoxification Centre 137
Local Authorities 1; and community service 79; labour controlled 27
London Police Court Mission 35
Low Moss Prison, Glasgow 167

magistrates, in Birmingham 30; case-committees 36; courts 29, 37, 157; fears of 22–3; and probation officers 39, 46, 50, 62
Manpower Services Commission 5, 7, 131; schemes 73; unemployment 141; work creation 143; Voluntary Projects programme 146
Marxist theory 106, 182
matrimonial work 46
Maxwell Report (1953) 83
May Committee (1979) 92
Mayer Report (1979) 88
media interest in USA 115–16
mediation 205; centres 204
Mennonites 204, 205
Merseyside Crime Survey (1984) 212
miners' strike 29
Minnesota Sentencing Guidelines Commission 111

NACCJSG *see* National Advisory Commission on Criminal Justice Standards
NACRO *see* National Association for the Care and Resettlement of Offenders
NAPE *see* National Association of Probation Executives
NAPO *see* National Association of Probation Officers
National Academy of Sciences 103
National Activity Recording Survey 41
National Advisory Committee on Criminal Justice Standards and Goals (NACCJSG) 100, 101
National Association for the Care and Resettlement of Offenders (NACRO) 96, 128–29, 138, 139, 141, 143, 190; crime prevention 213–14, 217, 230; and employment schemes 145–46
National Association of Probation Executives (NAPE) 101
National Association of Probation Officers (NAPO) 24, 33, 69, 96, 165; AGM (1975) 31–2; and prison policy 84
National Association of Victim Support Schemes 81
National Conference of Commissions on Uniform State Laws (NCCUSL) 101
National Institute of Corrections (NIC) 101, 107, 118
National Statement of Objectives and Priorities for the Probation Service 23, 213
NCCUSL *see* National Conference of Commissions on Uniform State Laws
Neighbourhood Consultations (1982) 215
neighbourhood, advice centre 229; watch 227; work 10–11
neo-classicism in USA 102, 104; *see also* justice model
Newham Conflict and Change Project (1984) 204
News of the World 210
NIC *see* National Institute of Corrections
Northamptonshire 204; case study (1982) 5, 159
Northern Ireland 32; conspiracy laws 31
Nottingham prison 91
Nottinghamshire Probation Service 169

offenders, and alcohol 152, 157, 164–65; community service 69, 72, 78–9, 141–42; education 144–48; 'hard-end' 54; housing 133–36; increase of 70; integration 188–89; needs of 48; prison 89; Probation Service 28, 36–7, 39, 42, 51, 59; reconviction 7–8, 76–7; reparation 199–207, 233–34; 'at risk' 4–5; studies of 5–6, 46, 195; supervision of 18, 44; types of 1, 9, 49; unemployment 138–41, 201; in USA 102, 104, 113; *see also* clients
'Out of Court' 165

parole 93, 105; introduction of (1967) 38, 84
patch-based work 56, 58
Penal Affairs Group, Parliamentary All-Party 198
penal system, in UK 91–2; in USA 102
Pentonville prison 158
Perspectives newsletter 101
police 1, 2, 23, 36, 63; and alcohol offenders 165; court missionaries 35, 37, 38, 40; and crime prevention 222–23; hostility to 31
Policing Freedom (1979) 210
politics, concerns of 21, 44; influence 28; and probation service 17, 32–3, 108, 114
Portsmouth 7
Powers of the Criminal Courts Act (1973) 49, 200
Principal Probation Officers' Conference (1968) 42
Prison Officers' Association 84
prisoners 83, 141; adaptation of 88; humiliation of 86; isolation 93; life 90–1; release 89; visits to 87
prisons 11, 23, 96; alternatives to 68; buildings 2, 26, 92; characteristics of 85; education in 146–47; officers 2, 92; population of 1–3, 18, 92, 199; responsibilities of 94–5; survey of 5; 'teamwork' 62; in USA 115
Probation Act (1907) 4, 49
Probation and After-Care Statistics 41
probation officers 6, 8, 9, 24–6, 33, 51, 221; and community service 80–1; and the courts 35–8, 41, 45–6; duties of 48–9, 95; expansion 40–1, 55; influence of 39–40; liaison officers 137; morale of 78–9; recruitment 56, 183–84; religious beliefs of 36, 37; training 184–85

Probation Rules 10, 213, 232; Rule 37 (1984) 128; in USA 111
Probation Service, buildings for 55, 58; changes 17–18, 42, 43, 54, 84; and community service 77–8, 81, 226, 228; in court 51; history of 83–4; and neo-classicism 105; objectives 4, 8, 11–13, 31, 34, 93; and politics 21, 24–5; in USA 106–10, 114, 115–16, 117, 119
punishment 69, 200, 206; in USA 104, 107, 109, 112, 113

racism 5, 29–30, 128, 188–94; case studies 186; and crime 140, 182, 187; and education 185; and housing 134; in prison 90; in USA 116–17
Reagan administration 118
rehabilitation 69, 84; and integration 188–89; and reparation 201; in USA 103, 105, 106, 113, 114
religion 36, 46
reparation 69, 128; benefits of 200–03; critics of 202; history of 194–95; in practice 203–07; schemes 236–38
research 211; on alcohol-related offending 159; in USA 100, 115; in West Midlands 180–94
Royal College of Psychiatrists 15, 167
Royal Medical Colleges 168

St Basil's Court workers 30
St Luke's Estate, London 214
Sandwell project 204
Scotswood Estate project, Newcastle 219
secretaries, and effect of 'teamwork' on 59–60, 62
Sentenced to Social Work (1978) 48
Shangri-La effect 89
Shelter 165
Social and Community Planning Research, report 214
social inquiry reports 1, 5, 27, 39–40, 44, 47, 56; custody 93; importance of 50; incompetence of 43; and racism 182–83
social services 10, 39; and Probation Service 22, 63, 221; and racism 187–88; in USA 118
Social Work in Prisons schemes 95
social workers 45
South Yorkshire Probation Service 205
Southampton 7
Special Projects Team (SPT) 230

Statement of National Aims and Objectives of the Probation Service (1983) 78
Statement of National Objectives and Priorities (1984) 93

teamwork 54; and the community 57–8, 64–5; effect on clients 59–62; personnel 58–9, 62, 63; reviews of 65–6; shared resources 55, 60–1; specialization 55–7
Thames Valley study 197
through-care 83, 93
trade unions 22, 24, 32, 33, 34
training, day centres 39, 59; for officers 60; in prison 88
treatment model 42–5, 84; decline of 47–8; in USA 106

unemployment 3, 5, 49, 127, 132, 228; and offenders 138–41, 144
United States of America, probation service in 12, 19, 35, 100–21; public services in 25; reparation 200, 203–05; victims in 196
University of Illinois, Chicago 107
University of Southern California 118
Urban Aid 6, 27

vandalism 213, 220
victims, redress for 198–99; reparation 202–07, 233–34; surveys of 195–98
Victims of Crime – The Dimensions of Risk (1984) 212

Wakefield prison 166
welfare officers 37–8, 46, 47, 83; and racism 188; reports 44, 45; rights 143
WEP 143
West Midlands, Probation Service 7, 30, 75, 229; research in 180–92
Wheels, adventure park 7, 119
Winson Green prison 134
Wolverhampton, juveniles in 181
Wootton Report 25
work creation schemes 143

The Yellow Book 23
YOP see Youth Opportunities Programme
youth custody orders 75
Youth Training Scheme (YTS) 6, 143
Youth Opportunities Programme (YOP) 143
YTS see Youth Training Scheme

Probation and the Community